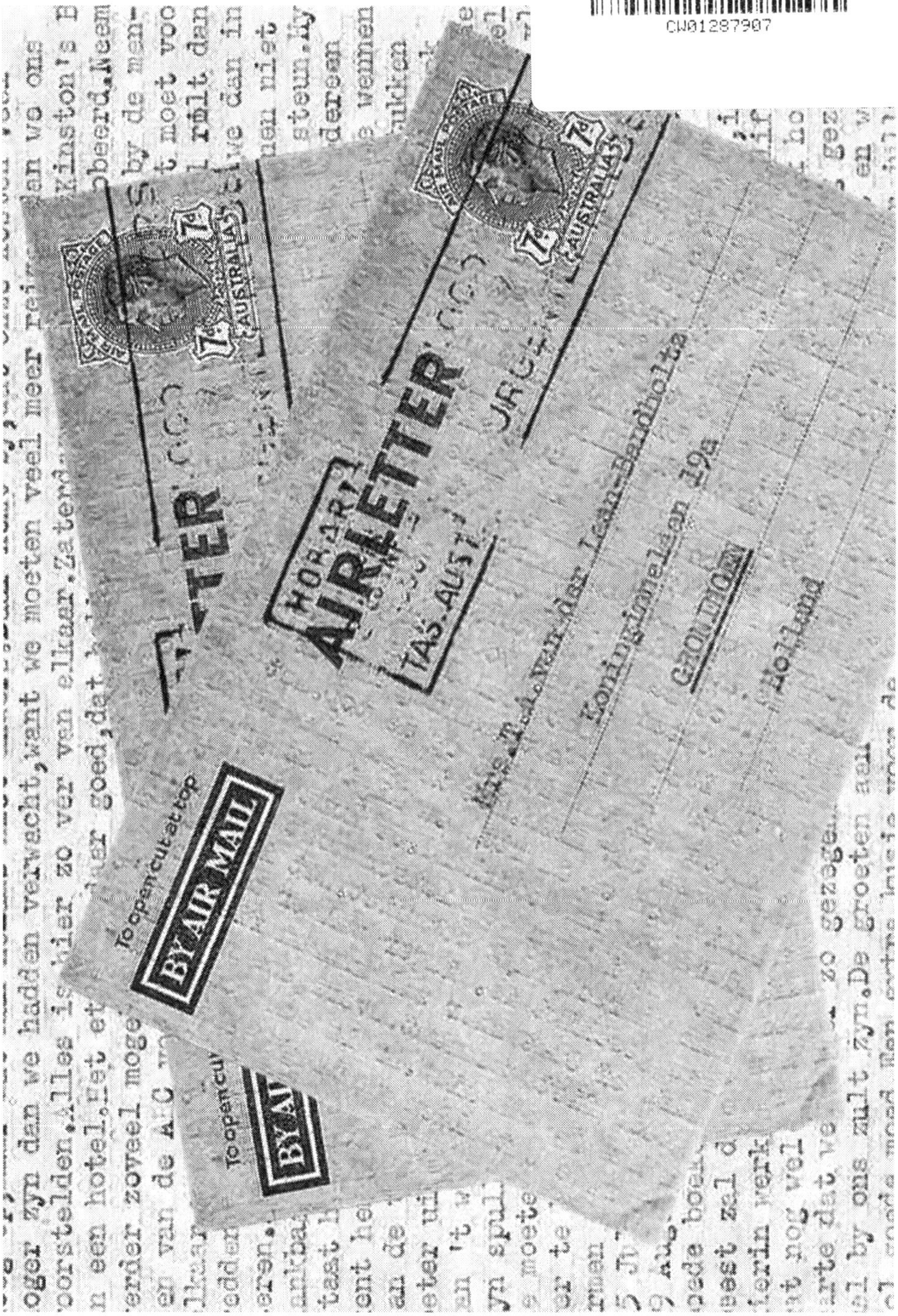
BY AIR MAIL
To open cut at top
AIR LETTER
AUSTRALIA
Holland

AuthorHouse™ UK
1663 Liberty Drive
Bloomington, IN 47403 USA
www.authorhouse.co.uk
Phone: 0800.197.4150

© 2015 Kusha Bolt. All rights reserved

No part of this book may be reproduced, stored in a retrieval system, or transmitted by any means without the written permission of the author.

Published by AuthorHouse   22/05/2015

ISBN: 978-1-5049-3701-6 (sc)
ISBN: 978-1-5049-3702-3 (e)

Print information available on the last page.

This book is printed on acid-free paper.

Because of the dynamic nature of the internet, any web addresses or links contained in this book may have changed since publication and may no longer be valid. The views expressed in this work are solely those of the author and do not necessarily reflect the views of the publisher, and the publisher hereby disclaims any responsibility for them.

Front and Back Cover
Photo of Kingston Beach courtesy Lee Weller
Stamp images courtesy the Tasmanian Philatelic Society

Disclaimer

The author has made every effort to ensure that the information in this book was correct at press time and has tried to recreate events, locales and conversations from recorded or repeated memories of them and made every attempt to correctly cite sources of information and to credit contributors accordingly. If names of individuals and places are incorrect the author hereby disclaims any liability to any party for any loss, damage, or disruption caused by errors or omissions, whether such errors or omissions result from negligence, accident, or any other cause. The readers agree to indemnify the author from any errors or omissions and/or from any misunderstandings or misinterpretations arising from the information contained herein and the author invites any reader to notify any such error or omission. Some names and identifying details have been changed to protect the privacy of individuals.

Letters from Tasmania

the resistance
the search for freedom
a secret

Kusha Bolt

Acknowledgements

First of all my very special thanks go to my husband Dirk who spurred me on and who spent hours slogging through tomes and websites to come up with relevant facts. Next, I mention my lovely children who all in their own ways encouraged and assisted me in getting the work done.

I am indebted to my brother Wicky, his wife April and my sister Nicky, who contributed valuable material. Sita de Haan née Folkerts; Aafje Mol née De Vries; Sietske MacDonald née Pinkster; Freddie Steen and Klaas Laning, all descendants of members of the group, supplied me with papers and photos. Piet Laning's booklet, 'Memoirs of Neuengamme Concentration Camp', shed light on his plight, and that of fellow members of the resistance. Kees Wierenga helped in many ways and photographer Lee Weller took some pictures especially for the book. Both Ray Brownell and my friend Henk Sikkema sadly have missed the final version but made valuable comments and contributions. To all, my heartfelt thanks.

To those strangers who have helped and have not been mentioned also a big Thank You. Last but not least, a warm thank you to John Longden for helping to edit the story.

There have been so many contributors towards the book that I like to compare it to the platypus that lives in the Brown's River in Kingston, Tasmania, that strange animal that was designed by a committee.

Kusha Bolt née Van der Laan
Scotland, November 2014

A note on names

A friend of my mother decided that my name Auguste was such a mouthful it should be shortened to 'Guusje'. Perfectly alright for a Dutch name, but has it given me headaches in English speaking countries where no one could pronounce it! I changed it to Kusha and that's worked. In Australia my brother, Wieger, is called Wicky and my sister, Antonia, Nicky.

Where there is no city context Groningen refers to the Province. With the exception of the jail, *Huis van Bewaring*, original places names have been retained. The jail is called the House of Detention.

Just a quick comment on an often asked question. What is the difference between the Netherlands, Holland and Dutch? The Netherlands is the proper name of the country. Holland is in popular use as its name but actually refers to the two western provinces, North and South Holland. Just as the Dutch convention of calling the whole of the UK 'England' does not go down well with Scots, the Welsh and the Irish, so the name 'Holland' for the Netherlands does not always match the perception of those from the North. Such sentiments did not bother my father. He used both names almost without distinction in his letters. To be from the Netherlands or from Holland is to be Dutch.

To

the descendants of the group from Groningen,

and the generation of 2045

*'...this young tree, that one day
will be the mighty tree Australia.'*

Eric van der Laan

The book is the story of a group migration from Groningen to Tasmania. I was inspired to write this book by the letters my father wrote when he and Ep Pinkster were sent to Tasmania to scout it out for the group of intending migrants from Groningen. The letters are an almost daily account of their experiences in setting about starting life in a new country. The letters describe how they meet people, start the business, tackle obstacles, and, later on, how they settle in as New Australians.

When I read the letters, it made me wonder why we actually migrated. To find the answer I started to gather facts. Every effort has been made to check that the information is correct. I found the wartime information about the role of the members of the group in the 2183 *Systeemkaarten* archives of the OVCG, Oorlog en Verzets Centrum Groningen, in Groningen. In Edinburgh, the British National Collection of Aerial Photography was an eye-opener, although what I was interested in was not available at the time. The National Archives in London supplied valuable material, but some of it is classified and will remain secret until 2045.

The group of Groningers

In 1950, a group of citizens migrated from the northernmost province in the Netherlands to the most southern state of Australia. They carried legacies with them to their new homeland. These were the images of the city they hailed from, and the nature of the people who formed its history. There were the silent stark memories of their fight for freedom, and the bonds of trust that had formed between them. Fearlessly, they started on their economic and social venture with a bold plan.

The men from left are Bob Houwen, Geert de Haan, Bart Folkerts, Frank Haan, Tom Steen, Ep Pinkster, Gerrit Zuidland, Eric van der Laan and Jan de Vries.
The ladies in the middle row from the left are Annie Houwen, Tinie de Vries, Tjits Haan, Klara Pinkster, Toni van der Laan and Dineke Laning.
In the front row from the left are Douwien Folkerts, Els Steen, Piet Laning, Ellie Zuidland and Kusha van der Laan.

Contents
Part One - Groningen

1 June 1945	11
The heritage of the Groningers	12
Eerke Jacob van der Laan	18
War in Groningen	20
Resistance	25
In the Resistance	30
Jan Thomas Steen	31
Reinder Paul Houwen	33
Egbert Pinkster	34
Gerrit Zuidland	35
Frank Haan	36
Jan de Vries	38
Pieter Laning	40
Barteld Jan Folkerts	42
Capture	55
KZ-Neuengamme, Germany	60
Friday 13 April 1945	62
The start of the Cold War	64
The fight for the Baltic	67
The years after the war	75
Starting a new life	85
Geert de Haan	88

Part Two - Little Groningen

En route to Tasmania	103
Sydney, 3 June 1950	103
Letters from Tasmania	116
Hobart 14 June 1950	116
17 June 1950	121
18 June 1950	126
19 June 1950	128
19 June 1950	129
Thursday, 22 June 1950	130
27 June 1950	138
5 July 1950	143
14 July 1950	149
Meanwhile in Holland	*153*
18 July - 23 August 1950	*156*
Letters from Tasmania	160
20 July 1950	160
24 July 1950	163
2 August 1950	164
3 August 1950	171
3 August 1950	174
7 August 1950	177
14 August 1950	180
16 August 1950	187
19 August 1950	190
25 August 1950	194
4 September 1950	197
18 September 1950	200
25 September 1950	204
From emigrant to immigrant	224
New Australians in Little Groningen	233
Thursday 9 April 1959	239
The last letter from Tasmania	240
References	246
Appendix - The Deed of Contract	250

Part One

Groningen

1 June 1945

World War II in Europe ended early in May 1945. In the northern Netherlands, the people of the city of Groningen had endured five years of occupation, days of house to house fighting and finally the heady drama of their liberation. The people of the city were exhausted.

At home my mother, my younger brother Wicky and I were asleep when, in the dead of night, there was the shrill sound of the doorbell. Sleep drunk we stumbled out of bed. There was a man at the door. His head was shaven. He did not look well. He was skinny, yet his stomach was as swollen as that of a pregnant woman. That man was father. We had not seen him since 14 November 1944, nearly seven months before. All his beautiful, wavy hair had gone. Wicky did not recognise him and asked, 'Mother, who's that strange man?'

He was wearing an odd outfit. The jacket and trousers didn't match. Underneath he was wearing dark blue pyjamas. Father said the clothes came from the German navy. He had been in a German navy hospital that the British had requisitioned. He was taken there after he survived the sinking of a ship he was on in the Baltic.

Father had a flag with him, a maritime signal flag with three vertical bars in red, white and blue. A swastika and other markings were printed on the white inside edge. If you turned it horizontally, it looked like the Dutch flag. He said this had helped him when over the past four days as he was trying to get food and lifts from Allied soldiers and to pass control points to get back home after being discharged from hospital.

Father also had cutlery with him: a spoon and a silver fork. The spoon was dented and without any identification, but on the back of the fork was a German eagle above a circle with a swastika in it. Underneath the circle was the capital letter 'M' for *Marine*, Navy. Above the eagle were two small silver hallmarks. Father explained that he had been able to eat with it. I did not understand why he was so proud of this. I did not yet know of the conditions he had lived under since his capture. We were just so pleased to see him home again.

Years later I found the fork in a drawer. It was heavy and had gone black with age. For a moment, I did not know where I had first seen it... then I remembered that I saw it after the war when father had brought it home from Germany. The fork was in the same drawer as a book with copies of letters that father had written to the group in Groningen when he first came to Tasmania.

11

The heritage of the Groningers

Groningen, the northernmost province of the Netherlands, shares its eastern border and the Dollard Bay with its German neighbours. To the north lie the mud flats and the sandy islands of the shallow Wadden Sea. The sparsely populated provinces of Drenthe to the south and Friesland to the west ensured that the north developed largely in isolation from the rest of the Netherlands. With little influence from the central government, the capital, Groningen, acted as a city state controlling the surrounding countryside.

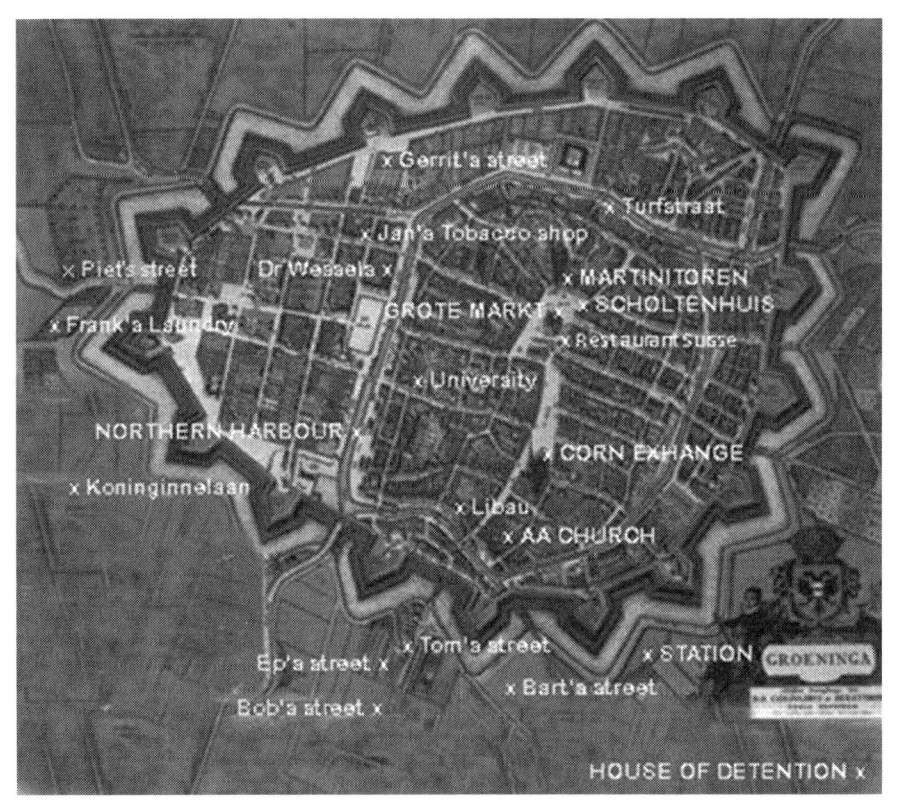

Old map of Groningen superimposed with the locations of a resistance hub during WW2

For over a thousand years the city of Groningen has been the commercial, industrial, agricultural and cultural centre of the north. Seven rivers and canals radiate from the city into the rich agriculture countryside. Like a jewel in a crown, the city centre, with its maze of narrow streets, was originally protected by a star shaped moat with 17 bulwarks. It was only after 1900 that the city started to expand beyond this defensive ring. By 1940 the population of the city had grown to approximately 125,000.

The city is dominated by its tower, the *Martinitoren*, on the central market square, the *Grote Markt*. The 13th century Martini church is the oldest church in Groningen. The tower, built in the 15th century, was Europe's tallest building at the time. A series of turrets reaching 97 metres in height offered a rewarding view over Groningen and the surrounding countryside; in winter, a blanket of white, in spring, swatches of green and in late summer the patchwork of fields glimmered with golden grain. At the top is a carillon with over 60 bells that ring every quarter of an hour, with a longer ring on the half hour and a booming peal that floats over the city centre on the hour. Special tunes played on the carillon herald the beginning of important events.

Celebrations on the Grote Markt

Groningen became a city of the Hanseatic League in the 14th century. At the southern end of the harbour, the gables of the warehouses fronting the river Aa form a beautiful curve by the medieval Aa church. The church was dedicated to Saint Nicolas, who amongst his patronages offers sailors and ships safe voyage and protection from storms. Long ago fragrances of faraway places floated in the air, like that of cinnamon and nutmeg. It was here that men pulled boats ashore and stacked bales along the water's edge. The warehouses stored herbs and spices from the tropics. There was coffee and tea. One of the waterfront gables is that of the Libau warehouse, named after a port in Latvia on the Baltic. Originally, people lived on

The frozen River Aa dominated by the Aa church

Bicycles in the snow at the Korenbeurs

13

the ground floor of the Libau and used the upper floors for storing goods. In 1882, when imports from America increased, most of the premises were converted for storing grain. It was also used as a brewery and much of the grain was used to brew large quantities of beer. Just around the corner, at the end of the fish market square is the *Korenbeurs*, where traditionally traders traded and distributed grain in jute bags.

17th century Goudkantoor

In the early 17th century an office, bearing the coat of arms of the city above the door, was built for the tax collector of Groningen on the Grote Markt. As the economy of the north strengthened, gold and silver coins were hallmarked here to prove they were real. The building is called the *Goudkantoor*.

In some respects the people hailing from the north are remarkable. Centuries of toil and perseverance created a determined and proudly liberal population. In independently minded Groningen, tolerance and respect formed the framework of opinion. This tradition manifested itself in a number of ways. Not only were the Catholics a bit less Roman, but those on the left were a bit more right and those on the right a bit more left than elsewhere in Holland. In time, Groningen developed as a cradle of original thought and through the centuries produced many philosophical and political thinkers. Groningers are open to new ideas and typically they speak their minds.

In Groningen mutual actions to achieve common goals are frequently evident. Throughout the province dairy farms and milk factories are operated cooperatively. The Dutch polder model, whereby people of all classes and persuasions in society worked together, was a classic example of this cooperation. From the 12th century onwards the people of Groningen worked hand in hand, step by step, dike by dike, to form polders. The age-old tradition of cooperation created vast fields of rich farmland. Large areas of sea and bog were enclosed by dikes and drained to create new arable land. The polders gained from the Wadden Sea north of Groningen and Friesland added substantially to those areas below sea level that fringe these provinces. New towns emerged in newly created polders on what once was the *Zuiderzee*, upon which boats used to sail to take butter, cheese and grain from the rich agricultural eastern provinces to Amsterdam and cities in the west.

An Italian traveller, Edmondo de Amicis, visited the grain rich northern parts of the Netherlands and in 1870 wrote a book, *l'Olanda*, in which he described what he came across. A unique system of land rights for farmers ensured that land could be leased from its owner for a fixed sum for an indefinite period. The farmer could pass this right on through inheritance or through sale of the lease. He couldn't subdivide the land without the owner's permission and renegotiation of the lease. This ensured that the land was not cut up into small parcels and that the large parcels of land could be used efficiently. In practice the system represented a form of cheap credit to farmers. Capital could be invested and land was improved with modern agricultural machines and methods.

De Amicis was amazed at the social and economic effects of the system. He described how, early in the morning, well dressed farmers and their wives came to the weekly market in Groningen in trains and gaily painted wagons, sometimes pulled by as many as five black horses. Boats laden with country produce came into the city via the canals. Within a few hours the city was full of noise and people.

Market day on the Grote Markt, before the war.

Hundreds of stalls each with their own speciality occupied the city's market squares. There were colourful flower stalls with beautiful bouquets. Wheels of strongly smelling cheese were piled high at the cheese sellers. The most popular cheese was cumin seed cheese and the Frisian speciality, clove cheese. At the cut meat stalls, smoked and cured sausages hung from the awning supports. At the bakers' stalls loaves of all shapes and sizes, from sugar bread to moist black Gronings rye bread, were laid out on the bench. There were stalls that sold muffins, apple flapjacks and *oliebollen* that were baked on the spot while customers waited. Cries of the stall keepers competed with the mechanical tones of street organs. Two organs, the Arab and the Jewel, entertained. The organ grinder turned the wheel to make the music and earned his living by rattling his shiny brass collection tin for people to put a coin or two in.

Farmers' wives shopped with the air of people who knew they would be welcome. Shop attendants hastened to sell them expensive merchandise from the top shelves. People visited the museums, art galleries and restaurants where the tables would be set with bottles of claret and Rhine wine or they went to cafés to negotiate business, read the latest newspapers and sip, a *borreltje*, a shot of Dutch genever gin. This surprised de Amicis because in all the countries he had visited until then farmers were poor, without schooling and chained to an existence at the bottom of society. He wrote that a stranger on arriving in Groningen might believe that he'd come to a country where a great revolution had taken place.

Typical street organ

Alas, the import of cheap wheat from the United States undermined agricultural prosperity and by 1880 the system had collapsed. By 1890, farm workers were so badly off that the centre of gravity of dissatisfaction and social unrest had shifted from the industrialised west to the agricultural north. Socially responsible thinking became an integral part of life in the north. Today, there is evidence of this on the outside wall of a café next to the Corn Exchange where once upon a time wealthy grain merchants would raise their glasses to celebrate their latest deals. The black commemorative stone on the wall of the café is inscribed:

> In 1885, the Social Democratic League was founded on these
> premises. 'Considering, that the emancipation of the working classes
> must be the work of the working classes themselves ...' K. Marx.

A number of socialistic leaders had northern roots. In time, conflicts with the rebel leanings of the movement developed and tensions between orthodoxy and the new radicalism increased. Not all socialists were extremists. Some were very concerned about extremism in all its forms. By 1918 however, there were warnings about the direction communism was taking. After 1930 National Socialism and Fascism threatened. For the many who believed in freedom of thought and the right to a Christian education, this was worrying.

Political, economic, social and educational institutions in Holland were organized according to religious or political beliefs. For most people, the natural course of one's life, from birth to death, was decided by the inclination of the parents. Reformed children went to Reformed schools and youth clubs, friends and partners would be Reformed. There were also

Catholic, Jewish, socialist, communist and liberal pillars. This pillarization was an ingrained feature of Dutch society.

In Groningen, of those with religious affiliations, about half of the population was Protestant. About one tenth of the population was Roman Catholic and there were a few thousand Jews who worshipped at the synagogue. Of the Protestants, about one-third were Reformed. Many of them were members of the Anti Revolutionary party. The AR party had been formed in 1879 by Reformed Protestants who were alarmed by the growth of socialism. The party sought the revival of the three values that had made the Netherlands great before the French Revolution: God, the country and the monarchy, the House of Orange. The AR party believed in democracy. The anti-revolutionists rejected hierarchical religious structures and believed that the church was an assembly of free citizens who participated in democratic governance: every man responsible to God alone.

Groningen was and still is a city where people know how to enjoy themselves and how to celebrate important events. The most important regional holiday is 28 August, when the city celebrates its liberation from siege by the German Bishop of Münster. Some of the cannon balls with which the Bishop's army bombarded the city are still embedded in the facades of houses to the south. One of the balls is marked with the year: 1.6.7.2. Each year the Grote Markt was cleared and made ready for the annual horse show and the celebrations afterwards. Wooden scaffolding was erected for the fireworks display to be held in the evening in front of the *Scholtenhuis*, a grand mansion built by Mr Scholten, a rich and important businessman. The burgomaster and other notables stood on the balcony of the town hall opposite and ordinary folk packed into the crowded square. Excitement filled the air as the bells of the Martinitoren rang. Everybody sang verse after verse of *Wilhelmus*, the oldest national anthem in the world, the rebel song from Holland's struggle for independence from Spain, and then the crowd cheered in awe as the coloured stars exploded high in the night sky.

Eric
Eerke Jacob van der Laan
1903

My father was born in Groningen into a Reformed family. His mother was from Friesland, his father from Wildervank in Groningen. From a young age he lived in the Turfstraat in the shadow of the Martinitoren, the landmark that Groningers affectionately call 'the Old Grey One'. When he was about ten the Van der Laan family moved to a house in the Melkweg across the city near the river Aa.

Eerke's first job was with a tea trader. He attended evening classes at the school of commerce and was awarded a diploma in German commercial correspondence, issued by the Federation of Commercial and Office Workers Societies. Three years later he gained a similar diploma in English. With these diplomas he changed jobs and was taken on by the North Netherlands Sack Company, the NNZ, to do book keeping and general administration. He was accurate and skilled in administration, which he enjoyed. He relished reading and immersed himself in theological and political matters, following debates and affairs of the church and the State closely. This led to his membership of the AR party.

Eerke enjoyed sport and infused fellow team members with enthusiasm. He represented the sports club in a range of events, but he refused to participate in contests held on a Sunday. Even an invitation to represent the Netherlands in high jump at the 1924 Olympic Games didn't change his mind.

It was 28 August 1927 and hundreds of Groningers were on the Grote Markt celebrating. As Eerke followed the explosions his eyes fell on a young woman. She and her friends were obviously enjoying the show. Her light-hearted laugh was infectious.

The young woman was my mother, Toni Auguste Bandholz. She was born in a leap year, on 29 February 1904, in Schönkirchen, in Schleswich Holstein in Germany, just south of the border with Denmark. She came from a Lutheran family. She had three sisters and a brother. It was a musical family and they loved singing. Mother inherited an instinctive musical talent and had the voice of a nightingale. She always sang.

After WWI conditions in a defeated Germany were extremely difficult and Toni, in her early twenties, decided to go to Groningen to find a job. It did not take her long to find work as a domestic help with the Roders family. She loved her work and the two small Roders boys and soon felt at home. Mrs Roders treated her like a daughter and helped her with her Dutch. She never quite lost her German accent. The most difficult sound for her was 'sch'. Mother never managed that one, but it added to her charm.

Eerke and Toni met on that Groningen fireworks night and fell in love. The courtship lasted two years. They married on 14 November 1929. On that day mother gained Dutch nationality. Whereas father was tall, mother was small. Together they were known as penny ha'penny.

I was born in 1930 and was christened Auguste Marie Christine, after my mother's mother. My brother was born three years later and was named Wieger Eerke after father's father. The Dutch tradition of name giving was upheld. We were a perfect pigeon pair family.

From the time I was a baby until the war broke out we visited mother's parents in Germany each year. We loved going there, but our last visit in the summer of 1939 was laden with political tension. In the sports arena next to my grandfather's house there were Hitler youth demonstrations. Young people, all in uniform, paraded with swastika flags and sang patriotic songs. When it was dark torches were lit by a big bonfire. The enthusiastic torch waving and loud rhythmic songs of the gatherings were quite scary.

A week after we arrived back in Groningen, Germany invaded Poland and war broke out.

War in Groningen

I was nine years old when the war started and my brother, Wicky, six. We had a happy childhood in a happy home. I cannot say that we lived happily forever after because when Nazi Germany attacked the Netherlands it upset the household for many years to come.

Throughout history, the Netherlands had been a haven of civil rights, reason and tolerance but all this came to an abrupt end in May 1940 when the Germans invaded Holland. When the Dutch military resistance was much tougher than anticipated by the Germans, they carpet bombed Rotterdam. This was the first time that the *Luftwaffe*, the German air force, used this horrific aerial warfare technique in World War II. The German command said that unless the Netherlands capitulated Amsterdam would be their next target. Six days after the bombing the Dutch government and the Royal family left to find refuge in London and the Nazi victors became the occupiers.

Parade on the Grote Markt 1940, in front of the Scholtenhuis.

When the German army entered Groningen they headed straight for the *Scholtenhuis*, the largest house on the Grote Markt. They commandeered it and installed their regional headquarters there. The Nazi special police force, the *Schutzstaffel* or defence squadron, better known as the SS, ripped down our red, white and blue national flag. The orange flag of the royal family and the provincial flag were banned. No flags flew from the town hall. No flags adorned the shop fronts. Flag holders are fixed next to a window or above a door on the facades of all Dutch buildings and houses, so everyone can fly a flag. They were empty. The only flags to be seen were hung on the front of the Scholtenhuis, the huge red flag with the swastika and the black and white double sigrune, the emblem of the SS.

When the Germans invaded Holland, the efficiency of the Dutch registration system made it easy for the Germans to control the population. Towards the end of 1939 the neutral Dutch government had introduced a system of ration cards and coupons to ensure that food, household goods and clothing would be distributed fairly and evenly amongst the population. This coincided with the first sugar rationing. All registered persons were entitled to receive a ration card and coupons. Mother kept ours in a delft blue pot. The coupons were numbered. Each week the local newspaper printed the numbers of the coupons that could be redeemed that week and the ration redeemed was then marked off the card.

Within a year of the invasion curfew was introduced. Taxation on wages started. Milk, potatoes and jam were added to the ration list of cigarettes, tea and coffee, cakes, eggs, flour, bread, cheese and soap. The hours that electricity and gas could be used were restricted. Then the Germans set up collection points. Radios had to be handed in, so that people would not be able to listen to foreign stations any more. Many radios were hidden. Valuables were also to be handed over. This was a tall order. Instead of complying with the order, many people hid their valuables in attics, wall cavities and chimneystacks. Weapons were concealed. Many people had to redecorate their homes to cover up the work that was done to hide things. Vehicles were taken to the countryside and hidden in barns under hay. Although most of the people in Groningen resented German control, they adjusted themselves and lived with the consequences of being occupied.

Things changed gradually. At the beginning of the war life on the surface went on as normal. Mother went about her housework singing as if nothing extraordinary was going on. On weekdays we went to school as usual. On Saturdays father took us to the playing fields and we took turns perched high on his shoulders for a bird's eye view of the soccer games. Father was a member of a sports association that still exists, and is now more than a hundred years old. Sometimes he took us with him to the gymnasium where he took to the parallel bars, spinning round and round. Then with new found energy he would swing from the rings and hang with his arms stretched out, suspended in mid-air. Sundays we went to church. We had our Sunday dinner with a thin slice of pork, boiled potatoes and lessening amounts of apple sauce and in the afternoon there were the usual visits with my parents' friends.

Wicky's and my friends often came to play and we had our birthday parties just as before. But we missed the traditional celebrations, like the birthdays of the members of the royal family, when we would have the day off school. Summer times before the war, we cycled from village to village chasing funfairs with turning gondolas, racing car stands, pigeon shooting and crazy roller coasters: but there were no longer funfairs. The sideshows, floats decorated with flowers and parades of sports clubs, with impressive banner waving in perfect time to the bands, had all disappeared. Street organs taken right through the city visiting each neighbourhood used to be heard even with the sound of music all around. The organ grinder, who turned the wheel to make the music, stopped the organ at a town square or crossing where many people could hear the music. But then came the time that even the street organs were banned from the street corners.

The age-old tradition of market days, held every Tuesday and Saturday, were memorable. That was before the rationing of eggs, flour and sugar. Candy and sweets were soon added to the ration list. No longer were there traditional stalls with peppermint sticks, sweet and salt liquorice in all sorts, candyfloss and magic sweet balls that changed colour as you sucked them. The greatest Dutch delicacy of all became impossible to get. Raw herrings heralded the start of summer. They were sometimes offered with a borreltje and were traditionally eaten at fishmongers'. One clutched the tail with two fingers, held one's head back and with mouth open wide, the brined fish filet slithered down the throat. As rationing hit harder, the stalls disappeared one by one, and the city squares became dull empty spaces.

When it was summer, we amused ourselves along the river Aa fishing, happy to catch small fish that we took home for mother to fry. Just as father had done as a boy, we roamed the Northern Harbour to admire the boats. Father told us the stories that the old sailors told him, tales from the 14th century about trading with the foreign countries around the Baltic. The sailors had described their own sailings from Groningen's seaport Delfzijl to the North Sea, round Denmark and through the narrow strait to the Baltic. They told him that they could be understood in all the ports, if they spoke the Gronings dialect.

After his job with the tea merchant, father traded jute bags. Talking about tea, father must have done well in his first job because within a short time he was promoted to tea taster. No wonder he always loved a good cup of tea! Before the war, Father worked at the Libau warehouse. Summer and winter, there was a lively commerce in new, used and repaired bags. Then the NNZ moved to new premises on the canal that linked Groningen to the sea. Father took us there. We fished, father counted boats as they passed by. After the first few years of war Wicky and I spent most of the summer holidays on a farm in the sparsely populated polder area to the north of Groningen. To us, city children, life on the farm was strange, and the stink! There was the constant smell of cows from the stalls that were a part of the farmhouse. After a while we adjusted, found ways to amuse ourselves and it was fun.

In winter, the canals and ponds in the parks froze over and it would be time to get the skates out. There used to be stalls on the ice selling soft round cakes filled with almond paste and beakers with hot aniseed milk, a delicacy. The stalls had gone, but we attached our wooden skates to our shoes with long laces (there were no Norwegian skates in those days) and we skated like everyone else round and round the pond in the same direction, until it got dark. Beginners, with stretched legs and splayed feet, pushed a kitchen chair in an effort to stay upright on the slippery surface. Having outskated the pond fun we took to the canals, where the boats were frozen in the ice, and we skated from village to village without a break. Wooden sledges were used on the snowed-under grass slopes in the parks, but as Groningen was flat there were not many places to sledge, so we pulled each other on sledges through the streets instead.

Our friends loved coming to our place. They were always welcome. Mother was cheerful and made them feel at home. Despite the shortages, there was always a cup of tea and some kind of war biscuit from the biscuit tin every time they came.

Koninginnelaan 19A, Groningen

Our home was considered a large apartment. It was a modern flat over two floors. On the first floor facing the street were the dining and sitting rooms, separated by double sliding doors. At the back we had a large kitchen, with a dining table and a potbelly stove. The kitchen opened on to a balcony where coal and potatoes were kept, and the washing was dried. For some time we even kept rabbits there to fatten the pot, but father could never bring himself to eat them. In the winter during the war we used the kitchen as a sitting room in order to save coal. The main bedroom was off the hallway and the bathroom was at the end of it. Stairs, next to the kitchen, led up to the second floor where there were two large rooms facing the street and two smaller rooms at the back, overlooking a courtyard below. Our front door was at the bottom of a flight of stairs facing the street. It was painted typical Gronings green, which is a very dark green.

After our *oma* died, *opa* Van der Laan came to live with us. He occupied the two front rooms at the top of the stairs to the second floor. He was a travelling salesman, so was often away from home. He adored his daughter-in-law and she him. He would spoil her. If there was something mother would very much like to have opa would buy it for her. When dinner was finished, opa would read from the Bible. He usually read a whole chapter. We knew which the shortest chapters were! When the reading went on too long and we could not sit still any longer, mother would say, 'Now, now Pa, it's been long enough.' To our great relief, opa would put the Bible down and say, 'Amen.'

If time allowed, Wicky and I played draughts against father or he let us win at chess. He was good at chess and liked solving problems. Father read a lot and he contributed articles to different newssheets. We teased him when, through lack of material, he wrote letters to the editor of the newssheets that he was the editor of!

Resistance

The Scholtenhuis was the regional centre for the *Sicherheitsdienst*, the SD, the German Intelligence Service. The SD was the information organisation of the SS, the fanatical security arm of the Nazi party. For anybody opposed to the Nazis, the SS and SD were very bad news.

The SD started as a reporting service on objectors to German National Socialism. As this service grew, it worked closely with the German criminal police and the secret service police, the *Gestapo*. From the start of the war the SD had thousands of agents who reported on the political views of individuals and on resistance outside Germany. There was a special Dutch section dealing with resistance from the defiant, largely Protestant political groupings which leant towards the conservative side of the Dutch political spectrum.

In June 1941 the Nazis banned all political parties except the newly founded Dutch Nazi party, the NSB, and ordered their activities to cease. The Dutch were shocked. The imposed political ban, and Nazification of Dutch institutions, was fiercely opposed in many quarters.

The Communists were the first group to organize active opposition to the Germans. Their initial actions influenced other groups and the course of events. Religious and humanitarian groups soon followed. Prominent Nazis and members of the NSB were attacked. Official seals and ID cards were falsified. Those who had to go into hiding were found safe houses and assisted with food. Personal data was stolen in order to make it impossible to find people.

Opposition to the Nazi occupation grew, and drew from all segments of society, attracting adults of all ages and social backgrounds. Many ordinary citizens felt compelled to adopt a secret existence in which they resisted the enemy that threatened their freedom. For some, it was a political belief. The Dutch political right, the socialists and the communists all rejected the Nazi platform and Hitler's totalitarian dictatorship. For some, it was a religious matter. The Catholic and the Protestant churches both saw their power being diminished by growing Nazi authority and used the pulpit as a platform for resistance. For others, it was a humanitarian matter and an obligation to protect their fellow Dutchmen from the Nazi occupiers. There were those motivated purely by resentment of the German presence. The spirit of defiance developed into a complex arrangement of groups of people. These groups later became linked in chains that were spread throughout the Netherlands. Unintentionally, fighting men and women became comrades-in-arms of the Dutch resistance forces, which under the command of Prince Bernard became a formal and formidable part of the Allied war effort.

At the time, father was secretary of the Groningen branch of the AR party. Despite the ban, the AR study circle, named after its founder, Dr A Kuyper, decided to continue to meet. When Eerke started his illegal career, he adopted the codename Eric, the name that he used throughout the war and that stayed with him thereafter. The Kuyper group was split into small units, called cells. In these cells the measures taken by the Germans to subjugate and control the population were discussed. The cells determined the 'red lines' beyond which compliance with the demands of the occupation would not go. Eric was put in charge of the cell that was made responsible for active resistance to German directives. Other AR cells continued with important work in education and in the preparation and distribution of illegal guidelines and other literature. The cells sourced food coupons, money and documents, delivering them where needed. They found hiding places for goods and safe houses for people, and over time contributed to a wide variety of resistance activities.

Resistance revealed the heart of the people, and true to their character as Groningers, determination was as strong as steel. By the end of 1942, tolerance of German directives had diminished and significant civil opposition to the Germans had emerged along lines that reflected Dutch pillarization. Apart from illegal underground presses run by the various political and religious cells there were in the main three resistance categories that emerged: the KP, the OD and the LO.

The KP, the *Knokploeg*, was an ill-defined collection of independent cells collectively forming assault groups known as Knockout Squads. The KP squads were often named after their leaders, as for instance KP Heidema. Their members were brave, mostly young men, many of them without military training. The KP was the armed branch of the underground movement. It was led by career officers and had a paramilitary approach. The major role of the KP was to obtain supplies that were needed by other resistance factions to support their activities. The KP cells were active in raiding printing establishments and storage facilities for coupons and ration books. They destroyed records. They sabotaged facilities like bridges, railway and telephone lines. They stole German vehicles, weaponry and uniforms and sometimes had to carry out liquidations. The clearing of incriminating materials and removal of furniture from houses of those hunted by the Germans was done by specialist groups. They moved and hid cars, equipment and anything that might be useful to the Nazis. As the war progressed, KP groups were heavily involved in retrieving and hiding arms, ammunition and communication equipment that were dropped by the Allies. The KP cells were small, tight knit cells with only a few people involved. The various groups had to adjust continuously to changes. Members were lost, new people joined. The success of a group relied on absolute trust in each other. Good planning was essential. Resourcefulness, the ability to improvise, to think quickly and act immediately played a large role in the outcome of assignments. Not all missions succeeded. Sometimes people were caught and often lives were lost.

The OD, *Ordedienst* or Law and Order Service, was formed from army and ex-army personnel. Armed and military in nature, the role of the OD was to prepare for the return of the exiled Dutch government and to organize the administration of the country after its liberation. The task of the OD was to ensure that the country would not descend into chaos in the absence of police and other authorities after the war.

The war lasted longer than expected and, after the arrests of leading figures in 1943, the role of the OD changed, to concentrate on collecting military intelligence. The OD had its own intelligence groups that reported on the German military and forwarded information to the Dutch government in exile.

The LO, *Landelijke Organizatie* or National Organisation, was an unarmed organization that provided civil support to the Resistance and to members of the allied forces. The LO would help anyone who was against the oppressor, no matter his or her religion or political belief. Men and women of all ages and from all walks of life contributed to the varied activities of the LO. For those who had to disappear, the LO provided false identity papers, money, food coupons, ration books and safe accommodation.

Everywhere in the province, the LO made lists of matters that were of local strategic significance. Locations of the all important keys that were needed to raise or lower the many bridges were known to the LO. In all neighbourhoods buildings were identified that at the time of the liberation could become command headquarters for the provincial sectors. In the city, schools and similar buildings were catalogued. Lists were made of the names of boats passing along the canal connecting the city and the port. These were laden with confiscated goods such as radios, copper, brass and bronze ornaments - even church bells - and other resources, and were destined for onward transport to Germany. Names of people who gave information to the Gestapo as well as the names of traitors living in the neighbourhoods were recorded. The LO recorded the telephone numbers of German authorities and the locations of trenches and tank traps. Surveys were made of military installations in Delfzijl. This information was passed on to the intelligence service.

Eric came into contact with Evert Drenth, who was the leader of the underground AR party. Drenth travelled around the provinces speaking to Christian men's groups explaining the consequences of the new German directives and encouraging them to join the Resistance. In 1942, Drenth was arrested at Eric's cousin's house, where he was hiding. He had been delivering food coupons. The SD stormed into the house. 'Ah, there we have Drenth!' He had been betrayed. He and his hosts were tortured and sent to a concentration camp. Drenth's enthusiastic arguments and spirit of resistance were a great influence on the Dr Kuyper group. After his arrest, he continued to inspire Eric and other members of the cells. They were determined to continue Drenth's work.

Both sons of Eric's employer were heavily involved in various resistance activities. Through his work, Eric was put in touch with the leadership of the LO organization and it was not long before he was involved in a good deal of resistance activity. He coordinated with many LO, OD and KP units. His position on the Board of Directors of Dijkstra's printing establishment in Groningen became very important. The fact that he knew his way around the printing business was invaluable. Well printed false documents would save countless lives.

By 1942 all telephone subscribers had to be registered and approved. Tobacco and candy were added to the ration list. The ration of potatoes, the Dutch staple food, was again reduced. Anti Jewish orders had followed one upon the other since the German occupation, and now further restrictions limited their freedom. All Jews were forced to wear a badge, a yellow Star of David. I remember the Jewish man who drove his horse and cart to school each morning with his children in the back. Each afternoon he returned to collect them to make sure they were safe. Then Jews were forbidden access to public parks, swimming pools and sports grounds. Certain professions could not be practiced, Jews were dismissed and jobs were lost. Jews were banned from teaching. Jewish children were taken out of schools. There were reshuffles of school teachers and headmasters, and lecturers at the University of Groningen, one of the oldest and most prestigious universities of the Netherlands.

Jewish people had been living in Groningen in small numbers since the 17th century. By 1800 the Israelite Dutchmen had gained the same rights as all other citizens in Groningen. In July 1942 the lights went out for the Jewish people. Some 600 Jewish men were rounded up and deported to Westerbork, not far from where we lived. It was only after the war that we learned Westerbork was a transit camp and that from there many were sent to Auschwitz and other death camps. In September, another hundred followed. I remember that my mother had Jewish friends, who lived just around the corner. They visited each other regularly and chatted over morning coffee. One night in a major *razzia, or* raid, the Nazis arrested another 650 Jewish people. By that time, there were few Jewish men left so most of those arrested were women and children. My mother's friends were amongst them. Mother was distraught. She never heard of them again, and we never saw the Jewish children who had been at our school again. From Groningen 2,550 Jews were deported.

Students protested. The Germans issued an order that students sign a declaration agreeing not to engage in activities against the occupier, or be sent to Germany to work. Most refused to sign and went into hiding. The university fell apart, but academics and students organized themselves and joined the Resistance.

By the end of 1942 the Folkingestraat, where the synagogue is and where many of the Jewish community had lived, was empty. Some succeeded in finding a place to hide, but in many cases this was only temporary. Living in hiding became part of everyday existence for many. Hiding or sheltering enemies of the Nazis was a risky activity, but, along with numerous other families, our family became involved when Dutch Jews were compelled to sew the hated yellow badge on their clothes. The humiliation of fellow Dutchmen drove increasing numbers of ordinary people to resist.

Unfortunately, individual cells within the KP, OD and LO, were often in conflict with each other. Nor did the various pillars work together. For the Resistance to be efficient and effective, a system was needed to coordinate the complex network of resistance cells that had emerged. Cooperation was the key.

Late in December 1942, a mission from Holland was sent to Groningen to organize the existing resistance groups into a provincial organization. The province of Groningen was divided into seven sections. Each section had its own KP, OD and LO commander or leader. It was the responsibility of these group leaders to coordinate the cell networks and to liaise with each other. A hierarchy of cell layers organized on a geographical basis was built up. All streets, buildings and apartments in the area were identified by coding. Aliases were used to safeguard identities. Communication was through radio messages and illegal newssheets such as Trouw, Parool, Vrij Nederland and others that were published by the different pillars and distributed via a labyrinth of courier networks.

In the Resistance

Our home became a hub of illegal activities. Mother had taken an active part in the Resistance right from the beginning and as she was always home, it was an ideal place for people to drop off messages, ration cards, false papers and so on. Despite this, the stigma of my mother having been born in Germany was always there. My brother and I were affected by it at school.

Members of the Resistance often met at our house. The meetings were held in the adjoining front rooms. Sometimes the meetings lasted long into the night. Because there was a curfew people slept over and then it was quite crowded. In the mornings we collected the cigarette butts. As tobacco was rationed the precious butts were cleaned and with some dried linden leaves rolled into new cigarettes.

When the arrests of Jews started in 1942 a Jewish couple, Uncle and Aunt as we had to call them, came to live at our place. They stayed for more than a year and a half. This was really too long for their, and our, safety. The rule was that the more they were after you, the more often you had to change your place of hiding. Uncle and Aunt lived upstairs in the front room that was opa's sitting room. When there were people in the house Uncle and Aunt could not use the bathroom that was on the first floor. They had to stay on their chairs so that the floor did not creak. They only came downstairs when they had to and only if one of us was in the house. If neighbours downstairs heard noises, like the flushing of the toilet, and knew we were out, they might have become suspicious. They also had their meals upstairs, which meant a lot of work for my mother. Finally they left in all secrecy to go to a different address. I do not know what happened to them after that. We never heard whether they managed to stay alive.

In the spring of 1943 the Germans issued compulsory employment orders for Dutch men to work in Germany. All men between the ages of 18 and 45 were obliged to work in the German factories. Government employees, whose names were readily available from the registry offices, were amongst the first to be conscripted. In May Dutch soldiers were ordered to report, to be interned in military prison camps. Pressure on resources increased when they went underground. This worsened when Dutch men who had been forced to work in Germany later returned on leave. Rather than going back to Germany many more men went into hiding. Thousands of young men disappeared. Throughout the province there was a desperate shortage of safe houses. An overwhelming need developed not only for safe accommodation but also for food, money and permits.

Shortly after the Jewish couple left we hid a young Jewess. We had been asked to take her in by the ladies Goedhart and Van Buren who lived just round the corner from us. They devoted themselves entirely to the unending task' of finding safe houses for Jews. The young woman was as negligent as 'our' Uncle and Aunt had been strict about keeping to the safety rules, and she gave cause for concern. She had a room at the back of our house. The window to that room could be seen from Misses Goedhart and Van Buren's apartment. They saw her standing, against all the rules, at the window. Miss Goedhart warned my parents immediately with the result that another less sensitive hiding place was found.

Except for the ladies Goedhart and Van Buren nobody ever knew what was going on. Nobody, not even our friends in the Resistance, knew that Jewish fugitives lived in our home. It was impressed on us children never ever to speak of it. We took it to heart and have never done so... until now.

When the Germans came to our house at the beginning of the new school year in 1943, it was an anxious moment. But it was only to tell my parents that Wicky and I had to attend the German school. The German authorities confiscated a school building just round the corner from where we lived and established a German school there. The newly founded school had to have pupils. Anyone with a German parent, or parents, was supposed to register and attend the school. As my parents had not registered us the Germans came to our house to find out why. Father spoke with them, of what I don't know, and they left. We all breathed a sigh of relief.

'Not over my dead body,' father declared after they had gone, and that was the end of that.

Tom
Jan Thomas Steen
1912

It was no secret that Jan Steen, like many, was embittered towards the German occupiers. He strongly opposed the indignities of the Nazis. For him, there was no question that Holland belonged to the Dutch and not the Germans. Jan and his wife Els lived in the city of Groningen. Originally from Assen in Drenthe, the province south of Groningen, Jan worked for the Groningen Municipal Council at the Births and Deaths registration office. He was familiar with the registration system and his position gave him access to personal records. His knowledge of bureaucratic procedures and his relations with officials in Groningen and outside the province were very useful. Many were prepared to cooperate with him. Like many resistance fighters he was not only astute, but practical and good at getting things done. Contacts outside the province of Groningen stood him in good stead. His nom de guerre, Tom, stuck with him for the rest of his life.

The control the Germans had of registered citizens made it necessary, and challenging, to hide people involved in illegal activities and supply them with what they needed to survive. As German directives intensified there was an urgency to destroy municipal records. Tom was approached after the order that all Dutch military personnel were to report to the Germans. He was asked to make a list of men in the city of Groningen who in May 1940 were serving in the armed forces. A plan was formed to contact all these people and to encourage them not to report.

Tom and three others made four hundred cards, each with individual particulars of the men, including the address. They allocated the cards to four geographic areas of the city and each took the cards that had been allocated to their quarter. Next, they found reliable people amongst their friends who could be placed in charge of the neighbourhoods that they knew well. With the help of the cards the ex-soldiers were contacted, except those who for whatever reason could not be relied upon, such as those who had become members of the Dutch fascist party.

Tom worked on preparations for raids on various council offices, and it was not long before his active involvement with the KP came into being. The purpose of these raids was to destroy the registry records so that the information they contained would not be available to the Nazis for identifying and tracing those who were in hiding. Tom was involved with various KP groups within the province of Groningen and in the surrounding provinces, mostly raiding distribution offices for coupons and rubber stamps that were needed by the LO.

A plan was devised to raid the municipal council office in Groningen and destroy the documents. Tom had obtained the necessary explosives and fuses needed for the raid through a butcher in The Hague. The raid, on 19 May 1943, was planned for the lunch hour because normally at that time only two people would be in the office. However, for some reason there was an unforeseen development. The registrar himself was there. He was a giant of a man and strong as an ox. Tom was strong and fit but had great difficulty in wrestling the registrar to the ground. Tom and his comrades were still only amateurs and it became apparent that the plan had failed. The registrar, who was sympathetic to the German cause, recognised Tom and yelled out of a window to the guard below that Steen was participating in the raid. The situation was very dangerous. The raiders managed to escape from the premises and ran for their lives. Tom was now on the wanted list and his identity was known. He had to flee the city and the province to go into hiding. He cycled to Meppel, 86 kilometres south of Groningen, and temporarily joined another resistance group. Just two days after the failed attempt in Groningen, Tom was invited to participate in a raid on a transport of rationing cards. The officers and policemen escorting the transport were disarmed, the cards were confiscated and delivered to the Resistance. This time, the raid was a success. It was the first raid on ration cards in the Netherlands.

Tom travelled all over the country throughout the summer of 1943. A series of raids were undertaken. There were shootouts. People on both sides died. The results varied. An attempt to blow up an employment office, where the records of people who would be forced to work in Germany were kept, failed because of a mechanical hitch.

Three months after Tom had gone underground he heard that one of the KP assault groups in the city of Groningen had run into trouble. They had lost four of the eight group members in a raid. Tom went back to Groningen. On 8 August 1943 the group, under his leadership, raided the regional distribution office. They succeeded in capturing rationing cards and food coupons. The haul was delivered to another group and then hidden at a farm. Within a month there was a similar raid on another regional office, which also succeeded.

Bob
Reinder Paul Houwen
1913

As a non-commissioned officer in the Dutch army, Bob Houwen sought support for the military anti-reporting campaign and encouraged ex-servicemen to join in. He refused to report to the Germans. Instead he contacted Tom and they started to plan anti-reporting action in Groningen.

Bob was married to Annie. He was a director of the firm Bruynzeel, a manufacturer of wood based products. He was a dynamic character with a wide range of contacts. A Groninger, he was a member of the Reformed Church, belonged to the AR party and joined the resistance using the alias Bob. Bob started by hiding Jews, sourcing food coupons and finding safe houses. He was in close contact with Eric and the leadership of the LO. Bob helped to plan and coordinate raids, acts of sabotage and eliminations and was actively involved in many of these KP activities.

In May 1944 an important raid took place in the centre of the city. Bob was involved. Two KP groups were charged with breaking into the Hoitsema printing premises. Hoitsema was a company responsible for printing food coupons and ration cards. The raid took place in broad daylight. Postmen's uniforms were borrowed and, with a policeman who supported the cause, the group of nine successfully raided the printers.

The Hoitsema haul was enormous. The raid was to be the most successful single coup of the war, delivering 133,450 coupons to the LO. This huge yield was divided into small quantities and hidden in different places. It was in an unrelated incident the SD raided a farmhouse, where the participants involved in the raid happened to be. They were arrested. When Bob found out, he had to go into hiding. It was during this time that he became involved in the organisation of the OD. As the war progressed, Bob became an OD section commander. He concentrated on collecting intelligence and subsequently became responsible for military intelligence in the three northern provinces: Groningen, Friesland and Drenthe.

By the end of 1943, resistance throughout the northern provinces had expanded. Groups that straddled the borders of the neighbouring provinces, Drenthe and Friesland, worked with the Resistance in Groningen. Independent groups continued to plan their own operations but supported the LO, the OD and the KP when needed by swapping goods and services.

Financial support for OD and KP actions came from the LO. The LO had become the largest and most structured group in the Resistance. Funding was initially collected from friends, businesses and churches. Later most of the money for the Resistance was received from the Dutch National

Support Fund, the NSF. This organization, supported by the exiled Dutch government, set up large scale financial scams involving the National Bank and the tax department. The Dutch Resistance was not short of money.

In early 1944 Eric became responsible for the collection of funds. He had been introduced to the new leaders of the LO by Leendert Boot, his employer's son, and assigned to the financial section of the pivotal Zero group. His network of contacts expanded rapidly. He was in touch with the KP and the OD. By spring Eric was Head of Housing. Shortly thereafter, he lost the support of his neighbours, the ladies Goedhart and Van Buren. The SD had detained them for hiding illegals.

By July 1944, news on all fronts was not good. It seemed that things were going well for the Germans. They had entered Rome, and the fear of death from the sky gripped Londoners as rockets rained down on them. In Groningen information filtered through to the resistance that a female collaborator had betrayed leaders of groups in the city and the province. The SD targeted leaders of the OD, forcing those with whom they worked into hiding. When the Zero group lost an important member, Eric was appointed to the vital post of Head of Information, responsible for gathering intelligence. With the escalating arrests and groups reshuffling responsibilities, there was an urgency to find reliable contacts. Towards the end of the month Ep Pinkster, commander of an OD section, asked Eric to take on the administration of his section of the OD. Eric got on well with Ep, and agreed.

Ep
Egbert Pinkster
(Blonde Ep, Van Delden, Van Dellen, Otto van Duyn) 1910

Ep was born in Veendam, a small town in the northeast of the province of Groningen, not far from the German border. A Lutheran, he married Klara Jager on 28 December 1934. They lived in the southern part of the city of Groningen with their two young daughters, Ina and Sietske, both traditionally named after an oma. Fluent in German and English, Ep had an administrative background and was employed as an accountant at a fertilizer factory in Groningen.

When Tom joined the KP, he asked Ep to replace him in the anti-reporting campaign. Ep, who had been a captain in the army, had become more and more frustrated with the German occupation. In 1943 when 300,000 Dutch ex-soldiers were required to report to the Germans, Ep decided it was time for action. The new reporting order led to a great deal of opposition and ultimately a strike in May. In the following mayhem, the occupiers executed 80 men, and arrested 900 and sent them to meet their fate in concentration camps. These brutalities and injustices only served to cement Ep's commitment to the Resistance.

As the demands of resistance intensified and duties and pressure on those involved increased, reorganization was necessary. To organize activities and maintain order the Club of Five, forerunner of the OD, was formed. Ep was a member. He was by nature methodical, adaptable and reliable. His first assignment was administration. He had contacts with the LO and coordinated with various KP groups. During the summer of 1944 there were numerous arrests of OD leaders and many executions. Following a wave of arrests in July, Ep took on the duties of chief of staff of the OD for the city of Groningen. With his extended military contacts throughout the north, Ep then concentrated on collecting, collating and passing on military information. He had many codenames, Van Delden, Van Dellen, Otto van Duyn and, probably because of his hair: Blonde Ep.

Jurrien, Ep's younger brother, also joined the Resistance. He became the OD section commander for the district of Veendam, where he lived. Every now and again, Ep would go into hiding there.

Gerrit
Gerrit Zuidland
(Gerrit de Graaf) 1915

Gerrit and his wife Ellie were good friends of Ep and Klara.

Gerrit, from Delfzijl, was 24 years old when the war started. At the time, he was deputy director of a wood supply and kitchen furniture company. Gerrit belonged to the Reformed Church and supported the AR party.

Gerrit had served in the Dutch army. He refused to report to the Germans and met Bob and Tom through the anti-reporting campaign. He became extremely active in it. Gerrit was a member of the LO and initially he concentrated on hiding Dutch military men, preventing them from being arrested. After he joined the Club of Five, Gerrit worked with Ep and Bob helping to structure and build up the OD organisation.

Eric, now drawn into OD activities, multiplied his contacts and soon he was deeply involved. As demand for false identity papers and money grew, there was significant competition for the limited resources that the LO had access to. The LO turned to the De Groot group, an independent humanitarian organisation operating in the city. The De Groot group, whose members believed that resistance should take place without the use of force, helped the LO with false documents, safe houses and a steady stream of ration cards and food coupons.

It was clear, by the end of August, that the SD had shifted their focus to the LO. Leading figures, including Eric's friend and contact Frank Haan, had been forced to leave the city and go into hiding.

Frank
Frank Haan
(007) 1903

Born and bred a Groninger, Frank was a master of the Gronings dialect, which he enjoyed using to entertain. He was a member of the Reformed Church and belonged to the Kuyper group of the AR party. He knew my father well, long before the war.

Frank owned a large laundry in the city. When he started working with the LO, his knowledge of chemistry was put to good use in removing ink from documents. In early 1944, after the leader of the LO group in the city of Groningen was betrayed and arrested it was decided to restructure the city group and split it into small units. The leader of each section had a codename starting with 0. The group became known as the Zero group. Their initial meeting place was in the Turfstraat, in the centre of town not far from the Scholtenhuis.

Frank joined the Zero group and was soon appointed head of the department that falsified documents issued by the Germans. He adopted the codename 007, after the name of the section he headed. Frank maintained an important link with the leader of the student resistance in Groningen, as well as with the KP leader of the three northern provinces.

The laundry was used as a point of contact and provided a hiding place for some of the leading members of the Resistance. Following a short time as head of the Zero group, Frank became chairman of the LO Council in July 1944. Within a month Frank discovered he had been betrayed by his courier. Her duplicity would have devastating effects on the Resistance in Groningen. Frank broke all contact with the various resistance sections and he was not seen again until the end of the war.

Frank's departure left the LO in disarray. The Zero group collapsed. The leadership and the organization's structure were in chaos. Nevertheless the remaining members of the group tried to continue its activities. By now there was serious tension between Eric's increasing need to go into hiding and the ever-growing workload of the Resistance. With the losses to Zero group and the virtual elimination of a parallel independent group, it was necessary to reorganize. A new Provincial Committee was formed. Eric and three others were appointed as its members. A key objective of the new team was to create a sense of unity amongst the many different groups of the Resistance operating in the city and around the province.

It was around this time that Tom had a meeting with three other KP members to plan a new action. Just as they were seated the doorbell sounded. The host of the meeting opened the door and was immediately shot down by the SD. Tom and his friends bolted and were able to escape through the back door. Tom ran in one direction, his two friends stormed out in the other. Tom made his way to a hideout, where he stayed for a few days. A friend supplied him with new identity papers and a bicycle so he could move on. Taking back roads he cycled to the safe house, where his pregnant wife Els and their young son were hiding. Later Tom heard about the terrible outcome of the meeting. There had been a shoot-out. The SD had arrested the host and his wife. The host was so badly tortured that he died from his wounds the next day. His last words were: 'I had to do this for my country.'

Tom would never again see his friends. They had trusted each other completely, and he had been able to rely on their courage and support under the most testing of circumstances. They were heroes, their deaths a part of the toll extracted for the success of the KP in Groningen.

Tom found that not all Germans were Nazis. He got on well with a commander in Delfzijl. This man was secretly a communist and wanted nothing to do with the Nazis. To help the Resistance undermine the position of the Nazis in Holland he gave Tom all kinds of useful information and supplied him with technical drawings and other documents. It was one of the many anomalies of the war that, later, the German commander was sent to the eastern front to fight against the communist regime in Russia.

On 4 September 1944, the day I turned 14, the Allies conquered Antwerp in Belgium. It was expected that they would advance on the Netherlands any day. Mad Tuesday is the name for Tuesday 5 September 1944. On this day rumours spread that the occupied Netherlands would soon be liberated. People left their offices and workplaces to wait in anticipation of the Allies' arrival. Many Dutch people prepared to receive and cheer the Allies with coloured bunting and flags. German occupation forces, Dutch fascist party members and collaborators panicked. Documents were destroyed and many thousands fled the Netherlands for Germany. But the Allied advance did not continue. They had over-extended themselves and come to a halt in the south of the Netherlands.

In the north, the Resistance in Groningen continued to be depleted by arrests. The situation worsened after Mad Tuesday when a new Dutch team from the SD in Amsterdam was sent to the Scholtenhuis to support Robert Lehnhoff. Lehnhoff was the German officer who headed the SD in the north. He was known as the Executioner of Groningen. He was an excellent interrogator, but his mood swings made him an unpredictable and cruel tyrant. Lehnhoff's torture chamber was Room 15 at the Scholtenhuis; his trademark method was a blow to the stomach with a knotted length of rubber.

With the arrival of this team of ten highly qualified and experienced investigators interrogation methods intensified. Each officer had his own special way of questioning and cross-examination. Information on the Resistance improved.

The arrests started again. One of Eric's colleagues in the newly formed Provincial Committee was arrested at his office for avoiding work orders. Within two weeks he was found shot dead. He had provided a postal address, hiding places, transport and falsifications. His contact, Jan, whose shop in the centre of town was also used as a postal address and meeting point, had valuable connections. He was asked to join the leadership of the Provincial Committee.

Jan
Jan de Vries
1910

Jan de Vries was a tobacconist and had a popular, well stocked tobacco and cigarette shop. He lived above the shop with his family. He took his first, passive steps in the Resistance at the beginning of the war when, like many others, he resisted German orders to hand over radios, bikes and articles made of gold or silver. As time passed, he watched with anguish as more and more people in Groningen were arrested: friends, acquaintances, neighbours and Jews.

In 1942 Jan became active distributing illegal newssheets and pamphlets encouraging resistance. Then he started helping those in hiding with accommodation and transport. He became heavily involved in LO resistance activities and his shop became a convenient postal address for communication between members of the Resistance.

Within a month of the May strike in 1943, new orders were issued for all men aged 16 to 35 to report to the Germans. Jan, aged 33, did not report. He was suddenly very busy.

During the war anyone sixteen years or older had to have an identification card which matched the registry documents. Falsifying these required great skill. Jan worked with Frank to meet the ever increasing need for false documents and papers for those who had to have new identities. Jan maintained quiet, unassuming contact with a small group of professional photographers, printers, typographers and stamp makers who specialized in counterfeiting documents. The falsifications section was so well equipped that it had over 200 fake stamps.

Within a fortnight of joining the LO leadership in September Jan heard that his main contact for falsifications had been betrayed, arrested and taken for interrogation. Jan had to go into hiding. He could not be seen on the street. With roadblocks and curfew, it was difficult for members of the group to meet. Even so, Jan had to continue supplying false papers to those who needed them, and he had to keep in touch with Eric. His tobacco shop was no longer safe. He had to leave his wife Tinie, son Koos and toddler daughter Aafje and he had to disappear.

That's how Jan came to stay at our house. He lived on the second floor in the small bedroom at the back of the house. It was not a secure place, but if he was to remain in contact with my father there was no other option.

Father too had to stay at home for his own safety. German soldiers frequently blocked roads and stopped people on the streets to check their identity and other papers. Father had no permit to exempt him from the latest work orders and so was supposed to report to the Nazis. It was not until after he obtained new false papers that he could venture outside. In the meantime, he had his ear glued to the radio every night. He had to follow the news from England on the BBC and he had to follow the Dutch broadcasts of Radio Orange.

Listening to these radio stations carried the death penalty. Father maintained contact with the Resistance through couriers.

False ID card

They were mostly women. The Germans checked them less frequently than men. Often mother had to go out. She was roped in to transporting coupons. When there was a shortage of couriers, older children, like me, were asked to help and told what to do.

It was a frantic time. Sometimes dangerous members of the SD, traitors and collaborators had to be killed in order to avoid further arrests of members of the Resistance. Tom took part in sabotage missions and other high risk activities, sometimes as far away as Amsterdam and The Hague. By now it was no longer safe for him or his family to live in Groningen. Tom, Els and their two children, son Thomas and baby daughter Frederika found refuge in the south of the country.

As Allied missions flying over the Netherlands increased, crash landings put a huge strain on the Resistance. Allied aircraft were picked off by much faster German jets, or crashed when pushed beyond their limits in their effort to escape. Pilots hit or with damaged planes had instructions to try to reach Holland to land. Downed reconnaissance and fighter pilots needed escort. Escaped prisoners needed escort. The LO provided shelter and escape routes, delivering the men to Sweden or Spain so that they could return to Britain and get back into service.

Tom continued his service providing escort to English and French pilots, who landed near the Lemelerberg, a lone hill some 100 kilometres south of Groningen. Travelling at night to reach the south of Holland, Tom delivered them to crossings where they could link up with Allied forces.

In the north, Leendert Boot was busy rescuing pilots and coordinating weapons and agent drops that followed on the request for reinforcement from the Heidema and Packard KP groups in Groningen to Dutch intelligence. Some of the agents were *Engelandvaarders*. These Dutch men and women had managed to escape from occupied Holland to England. Many of them joined the armed forces in Britain. Some were trained as

Special Operations Executive agents, SOE, whose mission was to sabotage the German war machine and assist resistance groups in enemy occupied territory. Others were MI6 agents tasked to collect information on the military situation.

The Heidema group, named after its leader, was a large group that worked on intelligence gathering, raids and sabotage. Piet Laning, an active member, acted as a contact between the Heidema and the Packard groups.

Piet
Pieter Laning
1914

Pieter was a bachelor when the war started. He had an infectious sense of humour and you could have a good laugh with him. However, when it came to resisting the Nazi occupation he was very serious. A baker by trade, he was well acquainted with many people in the hospitality trade in and around the city. A number of these became vital points of contact.

Pieter was born in Groningen. He lived above the bakery, which was on a main road leading out of town. He belonged to the Reformed Church and was a member of the AR party. His alias was Piet.

Like most young men Piet had been conscripted into the army and served his time. Bob Houwen approached Piet to help with the anti-reporting campaign. It took little convincing. Piet was given a hundred cards and put in charge of his district. This led to membership of the central LO group and coupon distribution. Piet became a member of the OD and his role changed after meeting with a group who worked with the British. His soccer friend, Bart Folkerts, taught him the art of intelligence gathering and Piet became a section commander attached to the national intelligence service. Tasks varied. He set up cells to monitor the German 'protectors' and collected military information. He cleared the houses of those who had been caught and arrested, or had been forced to leave their homes. He provided escort for escaped prisoners and downed pilots. He helped to bring in and hide British agents, transmission equipment and weapons that were parachuted into the north of the country. It was dangerous work.

On a bright sunny Sunday morning, 17 September 1944, Operation Market Garden started. The objective was to capture the bridges over the rivers and canals between Eindhoven, Nijmegen and Arnhem, thus opening a corridor through Nazi held Holland giving access to the industrial heartland of Germany. British, American and Polish paratroopers landed in the eastern Netherlands. They were reinforced by ground troops following tree lined roads through flat sandy polder land. Just before midnight the night before, the Dutch government in exile had broadcast a message on the Dutch language radio station, Radio Orange.

'The children of Versteegh have to go to bed.'

This was the signal from London that the employees of the Netherlands Railways were to go on strike. The general railway strike was to make it very difficult for the German command to move their men, arms and supporting material by rail to fight the Allied paratroopers in Arnhem. This action had been requested by the commander of the Allied troops in Europe, General Eisenhower.

Information from the Dutch intelligence to the Allies that the German troops were well entrenched was disregarded. Favorable weather, which was needed to ensure the success of the plan, had been forecast. Over a three day period Allied troops were parachuted in. The weather changed for the worst, the Germans had superior air power and their forces surrounded the Allies on three sides threatening to encircle and destroy them. The Allies were short of stores and suffered high casualties. After a week the remaining Allied troops were evacuated, exhausted, and Operation Market Garden was over. The plan to cross the Rhine and end the war by the end of the year had failed. In response to the Dutch strike, the Germans stopped all civilian transport. Hopes for a quick liberation were smashed.

From the moment that the Radio Orange message had come through father faced an enormous problem. 30,000 railway workers needed housing. This peak in demand coincided with further German working orders. All men between the ages of 17 and 50 were required to report to the Germans for digging trenches and for labour in Germany. Many refused to do so and had to go into hiding. How could he possibly meet the need to find safe accommodation quickly? Even after the LO had found safe accommodation, money, food coupons and ration cards were needed. Although the government in exile provided part of the money, collection and distribution had to be resolved. The sheer volume of so many banknotes, coupons and ration cards alone meant that the risks the LO people had to take were substantial.

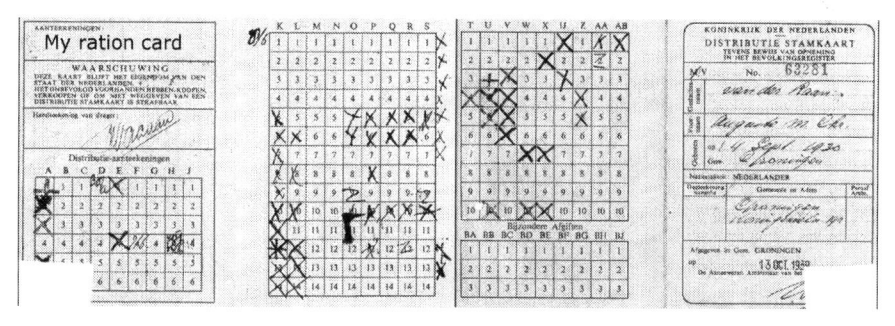

My ration card

I will never forget the day mother had to take a suitcase full of ration cards to an address in the other side of the city. She went by bike with the suitcase strapped to the carrier on the back. The rubber tyres on the bike had worn out and had been replaced with tyres made from bent wood. It was hard going over the cobblestones. She completed her mission successfully and returned just before curfew. We were very relieved when she arrived home safely. You never knew what might happen.

It was around this time that my best friend's father, a section leader in the OD, was arrested. Some days later as I walked into the kitchen, I overheard father say, 'Shot by Faber.' He studied me over the top of his round glasses. His blue eyes begged. 'Not a word,' he said.

Although father was able to find people who were willing to help shoulder his responsibilities, more and more supporters were being arrested and tortured in the usual Nazi manner, in many cases never to be heard of again.

The Market Garden period was a tense time for the resistance fighters. Besides the problems of housing, ID papers, coupon distribution and fund raising, there were Allied agents and arms drops urgently needing to be coordinated.

Towards the end of September, the head of the air defence section of the OD was arrested and the SD discovered a list of pseudonyms in his satchel. Ep's name was amongst them. Bob had run into Ep, Klara and their girls at a local café. Carrying suitcases, they were escaping to yet another unknown destination. The SD had raided Ep's house the previous night. Although he was in hiding, the city was clearly no longer safe. Ep was now in search of a safe house for himself and his family. Ep asked if Bob could attend a meeting on his behalf at the house of Jakob Nieuwenhuis. Bob agreed.

Jakob Nieuwenhuis, the son of the fiery pioneer of Dutch socialism, was a solicitor and preacher. Some hours before Bob arrived at the address, the SD raided the house and shot and killed Jakob. They were now waiting for victims to turn up. Bob was greeted at the door by the SD agent Bouman. He turned to run, but was grabbed from behind. They grappled, and Bob fumbled for his pistol, which he dropped. As Bob raced into the street, Bouman snatched up the pistol and fired. Bouman's colleague was wounded through the thumb, but Bob was shot in the calf and back. He fell to the ground, seriously wounded. The shooter wanted to kill him. 'So now I have you and I'll put a bullet through your brain!' Kindel, one of the officers, stepped in. They took Bob to hospital.

Bart
Barteld Jan Folkerts
(Willem de Ridder) 1911

Bart Folkerts was Bob Houwen's right hand man. Together with Ep, Gerrit and a fifth member they formed the Club of Five.

Bart had a busy painting and decorating business. He was married to Douwien and they had two young children, Henk and Sita, by the time the war started. Another daughter, Tineke, was born in the summer of 1941. Towards the end of the summer of 1944, Bart and Douwien had a third daughter whom they named after her aunt, Jeltje. In the 17th century, this old Frisian name was translated into Latin to Juliana. The Princess of Orange was called Juliana and she had two young daughters, Beatrix and Irene. Jeltje's second name was Irene. It was often the case that children born during the war years were given names relating to the Dutch royal family. Interestingly, Beatrix and Irene were also the names of two wireless transmitters that were parachuted into Holland for the use of the Resistance in Groningen.

The Folkerts lived in the same neighbourhood as the Steens, the Houwens and the Pinksters. Bart joined the Resistance in 1943 as part of the military anti-reporting campaign. Bart's demeanour was modest, but he was systematic and determined by nature and like so many others strongly resisted the German occupation. He started by finding financial support for ex-servicemen who were in hiding. This initial involvement brought him into contact with the LO and Eric. Through his good connections with civil servants dealing with the food distribution authorities he was able to supply ex-servicemen with food coupons and ration cards. Bart came in contact with a resistance group in Amsterdam working on a new numbering system for coupons and cards. This new system enabled the Resistance to accumulate reserves of food coupons and ration cards.

By the summer of 1944, Bart had delegated a large part of his humanitarian work to others, enabling him and his section leader, Bob, to focus on the dangerous and strenuous work of intelligence gathering. Bart was in contact with Ep who coordinated military information. Bart's connections with the Dutch Post, Telephone and Telegraph organization, PTT, became useful when the PTT developed a separate telephone network that the Germans were unaware of. This network played an important role maintaining contacts and enabled the Packard group to establish direct contact with Prince Bernhard and Colonel Somers, the head of Dutch intelligence at Eisenhower's headquarters in Britain.

The Packard group was started towards the end of 1942. Its role was to supply the Dutch intelligence service in Britain with information. Agents from Section 6 of Military Intelligence, MI6, the agency that supplied the British with foreign intelligence, were sent to Holland to help. A plan was made for the Netherlands to stay in touch with London and after a difficult start the Packard group established four secret radio transmission channels. These four channels supposedly recorded and transmitted meteorological information, but in reality passed on military intelligence.

Bart was one of Packard's vital links to the Heidema group. Each intelligence group had its own specialization. The Packard group worked on collecting data about airfields, war industries and the nationwide import and export of war related materials. The Heidema group collected information on the location, strength and movements of German troops. The information was passed on at meetings in a Groningen restaurant, Restaurant Suisse. Piet, who was Bart's Heidema contact, worked closely with the Irene transmission group, while Bart worked closely with the Beatrix transmission group. The coded messages that came in from the provinces were passed to the national information centre in Groningen and relayed on from there. Assignments were risky and led to huge losses. Quite a number of the Resistance with whom Bart and Piet worked were captured. In many cases nothing was heard of them again...

Bob was in possession of a telegram. A meeting had been arranged with an officer from England who would present himself to the Resistance. The MI6 agent, an Engelandvaarder codenamed Lighthouse, had been dropped into Holland in August 1944. His codename, *Vuurtoren* in Dutch, is the nickname for someone with red hair; we might say 'Bluey'. Lighthouse's mission was to check the security of the Packard intelligence group. He was to ensure that there was no infiltration by the enemy and that the information from Packard was reliable. Once there was confirmation that the various communication connections were safe, Lighthouse's task was to establish new lines of communication between Packard and the Allies. Piet, on his way to the meeting place, learned that the man he had previously seen lying in the street was Bob. He diverted to Bart's house.

As soon as Bart heard of Bob's capture he arranged to have the wireless transmitter that Bob knew about moved to a new location. As planned, he went to the rendezvous. Bob's situation was discussed. One member of the group had to go in hiding. New arrangements were made to accommodate Lighthouse and it was agreed to meet a few days later at Restaurant Suisse. Bart's sister would be courier.

Piet and Bart plotted Bob's rescue. His comrades attempted to get him out of the hospital but it was too late; he had already been transferred to the criminal section of the Groningen jail, the infamous House of Detention.

Bart's doorbell rang. A young man, claiming to be a guard from the House of Detention, spoke haltingly and carefully, and said, 'I have a message from Bob.'

Bart did not know this man. Bart looked puzzled and said, 'What do you mean?' Times were treacherous and unless you knew somebody really well it was essential not to trust anyone.

'Bob asked me to ask you to remove some papers from their hiding place.'

'Me?' Bart asked. 'Sure, I know him. I heard he'd been arrested, but strange that you'd come to me with that request. Maybe people do things like that, but I wouldn't have the pluck to even think of it.'

'Then why did he send me to you?' the guard asked.

'Of course he would,' Bart replied. 'The people he worked with would be in hiding and now he'd look for somebody else, but really, I wouldn't dare to. Just imagine that I'd get caught.'

'Well, that's what he said.' The man left.

Bart knew that Bob's identity papers were hidden at his mother's place under her mattress. The house had by now been sealed off by the SD. It was decided that they would have to break in. This was not without danger as a home guard, a German collaborator, lived next door, and a member of the pro-Nazi Dutch fascist party lived on the other side of the street. That night a friend picked the lock and stood on guard while Bart and Piet fumbled in the dark to find and retrieve the papers.

Bob faced certain death. Another attempt to rescue him was called off when a suspicious looking person was seen dallying by the entrance to the prison. The difficulties were stacking up. The number of guards had been increased. Some argued that it would not be possible to get Bob out of the House of Detention.

After much discussion the leader of the Heidema group evolved a plan to rescue him. Bart was put in charge of the job. It was going to be risky but they had no choice. Before a prisoner could be released from the House of Detention the SD in the Scholtenhuis had to authorize the release by phone. As Bart had good contacts with the telephone company he arranged with the PTT technicians to help with these telephone calls. Piet arranged for an apartment to be converted to a makeshift office, complete with typewriters and noisy staff. The manager of Restaurant Suisse, Mr Jagt, who was fluent in German, had agreed to impersonate Knorr, head of the Gestapo at the Scholtenhuis.

A new date had been set. The guard who worked with the Resistance supplied Bob with a set of clothes and warned him something was about to happen. It was Wednesday morning, 4 October. Everyone was at Piet's mock-up office.

The telephonist dialled the number of the House of Detention. The phone rang.

'Knorr here,' Jagt said. 'How are Houwen and his cellmate, Westen?'

'Sir, Westen is fine. Houwen is *sehr krank*, Sir,' the SD officer replied.

'They are to be brought to the Scholtenhuis immediately,' Jagt ordered.

'Sir?' Prisoners who were ill were not to be moved.

'They are to be brought to the Scholtenhuis, immediately,' Jagt repeated sharply. In the background the sound of typewriters and chat swelled.

'Be quiet!' Jagt barked to his staff. The noise stopped. He continued to the SD officer, 'Prepare the prisoners for transport. They will be collected by police officers. Make sure you check that all the papers are properly in order!'

He hung up.

Bart went outside and signalled to the three Resistance men, dressed as police officers, who were sitting waiting in a van. They had been briefed. As they drove off to the House of Detention, Bart cycled to a strategic position from where he could watch the entrance to the prison. By the time he got there the van was already parked in front of the building. As time passed, tension rose. Bart watched, motionless. The risk was considerable. If things went wrong, the three police officers would surely lose their lives.

In the House of Detention the Scholtenhuis telephone number was dialled. Jagt watched the telephonist. The PTT technicians followed the numbers carefully... 2, 5, 2, 4. The next number was 1... the telephonist flicked the call switch, and in a cool voice answered the call in the normal way, and then diverted the caller at the jail to Jagt's phone.

'Knorr,' Jagt said. He listened. 'Yes, yes, correct. I realise Houwen is ill and shouldn't be transported, nevertheless, both men are to be brought to the Scholtenhuis, immediately.'

After some time, one of the heavy doors to the House of Detention opened. Two policemen came out, followed by the two prisoners. Bob could barely walk. The third policeman appeared. The prisoners were put in the back of the van. The three policemen sat in front. The van left. Bart took a deep breath. He raced back to the apartment from where Jagt had made his call to tell them that all had gone according to plan. The room was already being stripped clean and most of the participants had disappeared.

Bart continued on to the rendezvous farm. The van carrying Bob and Westen had already arrived and had been hidden in a barn. The police officers were changing back into civilian clothes. Two of them went to a safe house that had been reserved for them and the driver went home. The ex-prisoners had been separated and moved to addresses where they could be attended to and cared for. Bart cycled back to Groningen to give Bob's wife the good news that he had escaped.

Within an hour of returning home, Bart's doorbell rang. It was the guard from the House of Detention. Douwien let him in.

'Bob's just been transferred,' he told Bart. 'Very strange,' he added. 'Bob and his cellmate Westen were picked up earlier this afternoon to be taken to Scholtenhuis.'

'Oh, how awful! That must be terrible for the poor men,' Douwien commiserated.

'Mmm, but there's some funny business going on,' the guard said shaking his head. 'They didn't arrive at the Scholtenhuis. They were kidnapped.'

'Impossible. I've never heard of anyone being taken to the Scholtenhuis and not arriving.'

'Well, that's what happened,' the guard maintained.

Bart then moved closer to the guard, dropped his voice and said to him, 'For people to be kidnapped like that seems impossible to me. If you can find out for sure that is what happened, I'd like to know more. Any chance of that?' The guard said he would let him know and left.

Things had come very close to disaster. The PTT technicians who switched the telephone lines thought that the Scholtenhuis only had three lines. In fact, there were five. They had been extremely lucky with their phone switching. After the abduction however, something did go very wrong. One of the guards at the House of Detention had noted the registration number of the van. Before the day was over the driver who owned the van was arrested at his home. The fugitives were all moved again, as the owner knew where the safe house for the other police officers was and he knew who had taken Bob and Westen from the barn. The information might be forcibly extracted from him. Bart re-sheltered Westen with an old school friend of his. Wounded Bob was dressed again, as well as circumstances allowed, and Bart took him on the back of his bicycle to another temporary refuge. They were welcomed and taken care of but neither host family was told anything about the abduction.

The following morning, Bob was taken to a makeshift hospital. In reality this was the home of a general practitioner who normally held his surgery there. The doctor had gone to the south of the country and was unable to return because of the advancing frontline. His house could be used by the Resistance. They had equipped the house to care for wounded resistance fighters under the supervision of a nurse and a number of cooperating doctors. The nursing helped Bob's recovery and there was good reason to believe that he would soon be his old self again.

When Bob was well enough he had to move again, this time to the cellar of a safe house. After he descended the steep steps into the cellar, the hatch above Bob was closed and hidden under a load of potatoes. The two policemen who had kidnapped Bob were there, together with three others and, as Bob soon found out, a family of rats. In the side wall of the cellar there was an opening that gave access to the subfloor space of the house next door. In case of emergency it was possible to crawl from there to a hollow in the sandy soil below the footing of the house, and so to exit under bushes into the neighbour's garden.

It was not long after Bob was billeted in his new quarters that the SD turned up to search the house. Bob had just returned after having his leg dressed. Down in the cellar the fugitives heard heavy boots on the floor above their heads. Amazingly, the SD didn't discover the hatch below the potatoes, but they were suspicious. As a Nazi sympathiser lived nearby, this house was clearly not safe.

After dark the next day the six men crawled, one after the other, through the hole under the footing. They met again at a farm at the edge of the city where friends were waiting for them with bicycles. Bidding farewell, they dispersed to the neighbouring province. Bob couldn't cycle that far. He was first taken to one of the doctor's friends to recuperate before he was reunited, in a village in Friesland, with his wife and their two children.

The Houwens' happiness lasted six weeks. Towards the end of November there was a razzia in the village. The whole village was searched by scores of German troops who systematically combed through every house. Bob and twenty others who were in hiding were caught and taken to a classroom in the local school.

There was an armed guard in the corridor and another at the front pacing the length of the building. The detainees could hear vehicles in the distance. The guard in the corridor went out to speak to the guard at the front. Bob eased open the door... and seeing the corridor empty, shot across to the door on the other side without thinking twice. He knew there was a back door there because he had been brought in that way, through the store and utility space. Behind him somebody silently shut the classroom door. Unbolting the back door, Bob headed straight for the drainage ditch full of water, stumbled across it, clambered over a fence and crawled through a garden. Wet through, he was now in the backyard of the headmistress, whose house had just been searched. She hid him... Bob had escaped again.

It was not until 4 October that father received his new false papers and after six weeks in hiding was able to go back to work. It was a good thing he did. That afternoon, our house was raided and searched by the SD.

We had just had our midday meal. I was doing my homework. Jan was in his room. Father had left for the office and Mother had gone to the laundry in town, not having a laundry at home. My brother Wicky was not at home either. The doorbell rang. From the hall of our apartment on the first floor, the street door was opened by pulling a rope that released the door lock. I pulled the rope to open the front door... two men dressed in black uniforms, with a German shepherd dog in tow, rushed inside and stormed up the stairs. The German Secret Police, the Gestapo! What was I to do? I tried to keep the men talking by admiring the dog, speaking loudly so that Jan could hear us and prepare for whatever was to come. I knew he should be able to hear us because his door was always ajar just in case... and now it was happening. Jan had all kinds of false documents and other papers in his room. Because of the delay he had a chance to throw them out of the window. They landed in the garden of the ground floor apartment below us. Jan managed to close the window quietly, just before the Gestapo got to his room.

The doorbell rang again. What now? There was an arrangement that if, after the door had been opened, we called from the head of the stairs: 'Yes, come in,' the caller knew that it was safe to go upstairs. If there was no answer they were not to come in as something would be going on... trouble!

I pulled the door open but said nothing. My brother Wicky came in and started to come up the stairs... he had not noticed that I had not given the all clear signal! I had to do something.

'Wicky is not at home!' I yelled. He stopped and looked up at me, not understanding... upstairs I heard one of the men come to the top of the stairs. I called again, 'Wicky is not at home!' and that did it... Wicky flew out of the door, just as I was asked who was there. I told the man that the caller was a friend of my brother's, but he had gone again.

Wicky knew that something was wrong. He was only ten years old but smart enough to take to his legs and to run to father's office. He ran through the park and the narrow streets past the print setter's office and Jan's tobacco shop to the other side of the city. He got there just in time to warn father not to come home. After that, father did not come home again. Now it was his turn to go underground.

The Gestapo took Jan away. I never heard what happened to the papers that he threw out of the window. The elderly neighbours downstairs were friendly but timid people. Perhaps they just disposed of the documents. For the first time in years, there were now no illegal residents in the house. Only mother, opa, Wicky and I were left.

Bart under the codename Willem de Ridder briefed Lighthouse on operations in the northern provinces. Lighthouse made few changes. He was pleased with the set up and was impressed by the spirit of camaraderie amongst the resistance fighters.

To support the Resistance in the north, four Engelandvaarders had been parachuted into Friesland and Drenthe. They were dropped with radio equipment, weapons and ammunition. The mission to extend the network started badly. At the moonlight drop in Drenthe the Germans were waiting. The agents escaped, but one was wounded. It was arranged that the other, Beacon, would meet Lighthouse in Groningen on the Grote Markt. When he arrived he found Lighthouse reading a map, looking like a tourist. Beacon knew the city well having been a student at the University there and was nervous that someone might recognise him. The safe house was a large apartment and as it turned out was opposite where the German commander lived. Together they set up the transmitter. Lighthouse told Beacon about the torture methods of the SD and he was curious about the transmission codes Beacon used. Before he left, Lighthouse gave Beacon ID documents. They were damaged. Beacon was annoyed. He knew he would not be able to leave the house with these papers.

The two wireless operators who parachuted in near Dokkum in Friesland were separated. One was hidden by the Resistance and waited for further orders. The other, Breadbin, cycled from Friesland to Groningen with Lighthouse. Breadbin was anxious, dreading the thought of being caught. The transmitter that had broken in the landing was strapped to the back of Lighthouse's bike and he had the code book in his saddle bag. Finally reaching Groningen, Breadbin was billeted with the head of the PTT. This important contact of Bart's was involved in a multitude of KP actions: he tapped phones, supplied Bart with false papers, was heavily involved in weapons drops, rescued parachutists and hid them.

A-MkIII suitcase receiver transmitter typically used by SOE and MI6 agents

Following Jan's arrest, it was clear that the remaining LO leaders were in danger. They all left the city. Eric could no longer conduct his many resistance activities from our home. He had to find a new place to hold meetings, and he had to find a place to stay. He found refuge in Haren, five kilometres south of Groningen, and continued his work from there. But things got progressively worse.

Many LO members were being arrested. The cells in the House of Detention were continually being emptied and refilled. After interrogation in the Scholtenhuis, Jan was transferred to the House of Detention and subsequently transported to Helgoland, a prison camp on Alderney, ten miles from the shores of France. Alderney was the most northerly of the British Channel Islands that were occupied by the Germans during the Second World War. There were four camps on Alderney: Lager Borkum,

Lager Helgoland, Lager Sylt and Lager Norderney, each named after a German North Sea island. All were dependencies of the concentration camp Neuengamme, near Hamburg in northern Germany. The Germans used the prisoners to build fortifications, air-raid shelters and sea defence structures to protect the French coast and the Channel Islands from an Allied invasion.

By mid October liberation was expected, soon. Eric had scheduled a meeting of heads of the LO, KP and NSF groups to discuss how the different groups would coordinate after the liberation. But on 17 October 1944, the day before the meeting, the SD raided the headquarters of Trouw magazine. Trouw had produced over 10,000 newssheets, distributing them throughout Groningen and was instrumental in maintaining vital contact twice a week with the Resistance in Holland. This disruption to the line of communications was a great blow. That night the SD raided the intended meeting place, arresting the home owner, his wife and a resistance fighter who was hiding there.

The SD occupied the house. As usual they waited for new victims to turn up. Both the KP leader of Groningen, who was in charge of sabotage and the district head of the NSF, who was responsible for the distribution of funds were greeted at the door by the SD. The courier tried to shout a warning to those arriving but did not succeed. The SD shot the NSF leader as he escaped on his bicycle. He managed to cycle to a shop and dump incriminating papers before the SD caught up with him. One of Eric's most trusted couriers, Truus, the daughter of his good friend Van der Munnick, delivered a message to the house. She was arrested. They were all taken to the Scholtenhuis and badly beaten during interrogation; the men until they were unconscious. Substantial ransom offers were made to no avail. The couriers were sent to Borkum and the men were sent to a transit camp, but were shot dead en route.

That same day the SD arrested Truus' father in his optician's shop. It was a busy street where, in the shop, Resistance members had been able to meet casually without raising suspicion. It had been the latest daily meeting place of the LO, KP, OD and other resistance groups. Not only had the events deprived the Resistance of key individuals and safe communication. It also caused Eric great personal losses.

Some days later, 23 October 1944, a week before my father's birthday, was a sad day. Our opa died. He had been ill for some time and mother nursed him all the while. Every day there had been a lot extra washing to be done. As we did not have a washing machine in those days, it had to be done by hand. Water needed to be heated, gas was only available for a few hours in the morning, and there was a scarcity of soap. For security reasons, we could not have any help in the house. It was a most difficult time. I have no idea how mother managed to send a message to father with the sad news. She did not know where he was hiding. She begged him not to come to the funeral. It was too dangerous. The funeral was arranged to take place a few days later. Clattering over the cobblestones, a black horse drew the hearse. Mother, Wicky and I followed in a horse drawn carriage. At the graveyard father was standing a long way off in the background. He didn't acknowledge us, but he was watching us as opa was laid to rest in the same grave as oma. Before the funeral was finished father had disappeared on his bike.

It was 8 November. The SD, following a lead, searched the office of a fertiliser factory in Groningen. The factory owner was the leader of a KP group. He had been a great help to Eric, first hiding Jews then distributing NSF funds and providing safe housing for many group leaders, including the head of NSF. The SD found weapons and transmission equipment and, hidden in the garden of the factory office, a list of names with coded addresses. They shadowed the factory owner's wife. Unknowingly, she led them to a farm where weapons had been dropped and where her husband was hiding. He was arrested and taken to the Scholtenhuis where he was interrogated and badly beaten. Using the factory list, another wave of arrests started the next day. More than twenty were arrested in the city. The list found during the factory raid resulted in Lehnhoff being able to make numerous arrests and collecting more information on resistance activities over the next days and weeks. Resistance groups dispersed and members disappeared.

9 November was the last day of the school holidays. Piet had just returned from a nine day mission in the provinces. Bart was at Hotel Suisse, waiting for Lighthouse. The meeting was to arrange new accommodation for Breadbin. Whilst waiting there, Bart was given the message that the SD had raided the street nearby. He left immediately, furious. The Beatrix transmitter was kept in this area, and the red haired agent was billeted with the operator. Bart bumped into Lighthouse in the street. By nightfall it was confirmed. Beatrix had been discovered. The wireless operator had been busy behind the transmitter when the SD charged into the house. The transmitter was confiscated. The host and the operator were arrested and taken to the Scholtenhuis. Arrangements were immediately made to change Lighthouse's accommodation. Bart was no longer sure that the addresses in his book were safe.

10 November, Piet was arrested in a street control. He had two false work exemptions in his satchel. He was taken to the Scholtenhuis, interrogated by Lehnhoff and Knorr, handcuffed and stood against the wall of the attic with forty others. That evening, the SD burst in on the head of the PTT. They found weapons and by coincidence had another good catch: a policeman was in hiding there, Breadbin was repairing the broken transmitter and Lighthouse was visiting. Everyone was arrested and taken to the Scholtenhuis.

Tensions in the Scholtenhuis were high. The owner of the fertilizer factory had just died from the beatings he received and the host of the Beatrix transmitter, fearing he might reveal valuable information in a second round of torture, had committed suicide by jumping from a window.

At the Scholtenhuis Lighthouse told Knorr everything he knew about the leader of and the brains behind the Heidema group, who had masterminded Bob Houwen's escape. He revealed the whereabouts of Beacon's transmitter, told Knorr about Bart and about Packard's dependency on the De Groot group.

Knorr had been in pursuit of the De Groot group for a long time, but Heidema was far more important. His group was instrumental in intelligence gathering and had supplied the Packard group with valuable information. A week before, Knorr had scribbled Heidema's name on the blotting paper on his desk. Knorr and Lighthouse made a deal.

Two more radio operators were captured that night and two escaped. The following morning, 11 November 1944, the SD raided the house where Lighthouse had installed the transmitter with Beacon. After removing the transmitter from under the bed, the SD shot the house owner dead and occupied the house. Beacon remained undetected. He had managed to take cover in a walk-in cupboard. Whilst there, Beacon thought about his last transmission that he had cut short because he suspected interference on the line. He wondered why Lighthouse had been so keen to know the frequencies he used and he pondered Lighthouse's discussion on the torture methods of the SD. After 18 hours, Beacon managed to escape. He was able to warn others that the frequencies were no longer safe, and that they had been betrayed, but the warning came too late for many.

Raids were never on a Sunday but in the absence of Lehnhoff, Knorr decided to act immediately. In the early hours of Sunday 12 November 1944, there was a sweeping roundup of members of the Heidema group. Sixty or so were caught. Heidema, his courier and her two children were arrested. Jagt, the manager of Restaurant Suisse, was also arrested. They were taken to the Scholtenhuis. The Heidema catch was an enormous blow to the Resistance. The setbacks for the resistance fighters were mounting.

That same morning, Lighthouse escaped from the Scholtenhuis. He was accommodated by a member of the De Groot group and the next day moved on. The SD arrived soon after Lighthouse had left. His host was arrested and badly tortured. More members of the Beatrix transmitter group were captured that Monday and the SD were looking for Bart. They searched his house. Neither Bart nor Douwien was at home, but his mother, brother, sister and the housekeeper were in the house. They were taken to the Scholtenhuis. Bart's brother and the housekeeper were released after 17 days, but his sister and mother were kept in detention.

For six days, handcuffed Piet watched as people came and went and returned to the icy silence of the attic of the Scholtenhuis, bloodied and beaten. Unable to link him to criminal activity, Piet was charged with being in possession of a false work permit. He was sent to prison. Four days later he arrived in Borkum to work on bunker construction.

On Tuesday 14 November 1944, the SD raided our home in the Koninginnelaan again. It was going to be a special day as my father and mother had been married for fifteen years. We would have a secret get-together to celebrate the occasion. There would be a small party at the home of a distant aunt, on the other side of the city. Mother was going there on her bicycle, Wicky and I would walk. Although father had gone underground he was determined to be there. After we arrived we were given a glass of surrogate orange squash and a piece of war cake, well... wasn't that a real treat! We spent a few hours enjoying each other's company, then it was time to go back home. Father went back to his address. Nobody knew and nobody asked where that was, not even mother. She cycled back home, while Wicky and I walked.

When we arrived home and rang the doorbell there was something that was not right. As the door opened, we saw that mother's bicycle was at the foot of the stairs, so she was home. But at the top of the stairs were two men. One of them told us to come up. There was something wrong... where was mother?

'Oh yes,' the tall one said, 'she'll be back in a minute.' But she did not come back. Instead, the SD occupied the house.

They asked us lots of questions. Of course, we knew nothing. We had been drilled into answering, 'No' or 'I don't know.' They spoke Dutch, so we knew that the men were from the SD. They said that they had found a clandestine radio, but no, we didn't know that it had been hidden under the stairs to the second floor. Of course we knew. The stairs had a runner that was held in place by polished brass rods. To be able to listen to the BBC, the rods were removed every evening and the carpet runner rolled up. This gave access to the risers. Part of a riser was removable and the radio was hidden behind it. To listen to the BBC news father lay on his stomach with his ear to the opening. Wicky and I were sent outside to play noisy games in the street at the front door so that the crackle of the radio could not be heard.

I can't recall whether or not we ate that night but I remember that when it was time to go to bed I was terribly afraid of these men and really did not dare to go to bed alone in my room. I told Wicky to go to my room, which he did without protesting. The men thought this was strange but I said that my brother suffered from nightmares and as mother was away he should sleep in my room. That night we didn't sleep much at all. We heard lots of noises. There were opening and shutting of drawers and knocking on walls, obviously in search of concealed spaces.

The next morning I wanted to make sure that our security measures were in place. This meant that I should close all the net curtains to the street windows on the first floor to warn the resistance people, who knew this signal meant 'stay away'. When I came downstairs I saw that the net curtains to the two rooms at the front of house were open. I thought, 'If I do the dusting of the window sills, I can close the net curtains.'

I had almost succeeded when the shorter of the two SD men came into the room with a revolver in his hand. He said he had found it in the house. I was scared to death. The man then sent me out of the room, before it had been possible to close all the curtains. The SD now waited for victims to turn up.

Wicky and I were told to go to the kitchen at the back of the house. It was cold, so I relit the potbellied stove. We soon had our first visitor. He was questioned in the interconnecting rooms at the front of the house. It was a cousin of my father's, also named Eerke. He distributed Trouw, the smeary illegal news sheet that was printed on stencil machines. Because he was a relative his visit was not particularly suspicious - wasn't he just dropping in for a cup of coffee and a chat? Fortunately he did not have any incriminating papers on him and after some questioning he was allowed to go. Once outside, he warned as many people as he could. As visitors arrived they were told to wait in the kitchen until called to the room to be questioned. I knew that some of the visitors carried illegal documents, such as false identity papers or extra food coupons. We managed to put these in the fire before the visitors were summoned into the front room. All of those who sat in the kitchen were sad to see such valuable material go up in flames... but, thank goodness, nobody was arrested.

It was not long before the whole street knew that the SD was at our place. After a second sleepless night Wicky and I were put out on the street, as we were clearly no longer useful. Moreover, by putting a tail on us the SD hoped to be able to find out where father was hiding. There we stood in the street. We didn't know what to do. We decided to ring the doorbell of our neighbours in the house to the left and told them that we didn't know where to go and could we please stay for the night. They took us in for a few days but they were scared. They said they didn't know what kind of risks they ran by accommodating us. In the meantime it had become known that mother had been arrested. After a couple of days we moved to stay with friends of our parents and their four children on a farm on the outskirts of Groningen. But they could only help us for a few days. Each time I left their house to bike to school, I was shadowed. I told our hostess.

Eric was one of Lehnhoff's prime targets. He abandoned his temporary shelter in Haren as that was no longer safe. Indeed, shortly after he moved from there the SD arrived. He returned to Groningen, found a new place to hide and a new meeting place for the various resistance groups in the centre of the city at Dr Wessels' surgery.

Mother, who had contributed so much to the work of the LO, especially in the hectic days that followed the railway strike, was taken to the infamous Scholtenhuis for questioning. She was taken to the top floor of the southern wing, where the women and children were kept together in an attic room. The top floor was notorious for interrogations and the women were often kept for weeks on end.

We, like many others, held the Scholtenhuis under constant observation. Crossing the Grote Markt could always be justified as schooling was haphazard. After the German soldiers occupied our school as barracks, the school board found other buildings throughout the centre of Groningen and split the lessons into either morning or afternoon sessions. Taking care to avoid attracting attention, we combed our fingers through our hair, hoping that mother might be able to come to a window overlooking the square and, in case she should see us, to let her know that we were OK. Sometimes the bells of the Martinitoren rang. Unbeknown to the Germans, songs popular amongst the resistance fighters were played to support those detained and to give them strength.

It was time for Wicky and I to move again. In the dark of a cold afternoon, we were spirited out of the house where we were staying and taken on the back of bicycles to Leendert Boot and his wife Fie, who had also disappeared from the scene. They were hiding in a cottage that belonged to the parents of my school friend, Dirk. The cottage was on the outskirts of a small village on the Groningen-Drenthe border. Many of the village inhabitants were NSB followers. The cottage was timber-clad and quite quaint, surrounded by natural parkland, meadows and a creek. I'd been there before during the summer holidays when I was staying nearby at

Dirk's cousin's. She'd introduced me to him. We were 13 at the time and just about to start high school. I knew the Bolt family from these visits. Of course, this time, the Bolts did not know of my whereabouts and it was not the idea that they should know. As long as school continued Wicky and I were not allowed outside in case someone might see us, and we were not allowed to make any noise. Most days we sat upstairs quietly playing cards. By the time the school holidays started Leendert had arranged for Dirk's brother, Jelmer, to come and stay at the cottage. After all the Germans might be looking for two children, but not three. When it was time for Jelmer to go back to the city Leendert pressed upon him not to say a word of having seen Wicky and me. He promised. But, when he arrived home he whistled the tune that I always whistled. Dirk recognised the melody and knew where I was!

After five weeks, just before Christmas, mother was released probably so that, by following her, the Germans would be able to catch father. She couldn't go home. One day the Nazis had arrived at our house in the Koninginnelaan with a removal van bearing a sign 'Gifts of Love from Holland' and taken furniture, bedding, pots and pans, tea towels, clothes, carpets and the potbellied stove. The Nazis allocated the house to someone else.

With the help of the Resistance, mother managed to disappear from sight. We didn't know where she was. We couldn't contact her. Sometime in the New Year, a small summer cottage was found for her in Zeegse, a settlement of a few farms about 2 kilometres further into Drenthe from where we were staying. The cottage was near the moors, which were popular hunting grounds, surrounded by birch trees. It was here, after more than two months, that Wicky and I saw mother again. The cottage was called Regina Cottage. Now mother was also in hiding and her new name was Mrs Regina.

The biggest problem in hiding was that life was boring, so when the Germans were out duck shooting Wicky and I crept on our stomachs through the moors, quacking, pretending to be ducks. One day we decided to make birch wine. We thought we could collect the sap and get drunk. Cutting the tree trunk carefully we hung little glass bottles underneath to collect the sap. It was totally unsuccessful. Not a drop of sap was collected.

Leendert was our sole visitor. One afternoon when we came home from the moors we found mother and Leendert sitting at the small table in the kitchen. Mother's eyes were as red as the bloodied shirt that lay in front of them. The shirt belonged to Marinus, Leendert's brother.

Capture

Although the Allies had liberated the south of the country, there was still no end to the occupation of the Netherlands north of the rivers Meuse and Rhine. The Market Garden invasion had failed and the battle at Arnhem was lost. Germany strengthened its troops in the west and, close to The Hague, installed launching sites for its V2 rockets. These rockets, aimed at Britain, travelled at supersonic speed and arrived without warning. The explosion came afterwards. Those who heard it had survived.

Although the movement of German troops was made more difficult by the railway strike, there were unforeseen consequences. The only viable means of transporting food from the production areas was by rail. Food supplies to the western Netherlands stopped. Tragically, this worsened the already existing famine and the misery of the cold winter that followed. Thousands died of hunger before the long delayed liberation of the country.

During September, the LO evacuated and re-housed tens of hundreds of striking railway workers and their families along with their belongings, so that the Germans would not be able to trace and arrest them. The influx of railway strikers from other provinces into Groningen swelled the population by twenty percent and caused an acute shortage of housing. Most LO members were kept busy looking after people needing a place to stay. As the war continued, the task of finding refuge for thousands of people became exhausting and ultimately almost impossible to fulfill. Although the LO was the largest, best organised group in the Resistance and the best at outwitting the Nazis, the increasing attentions of Lehnhoff and the SD led to fewer and fewer leaders in the province being able to support Eric. Whole sections of the Resistance had been rounded up or effectively crippled. The gaps were growing and Eric stood almost alone in executing the numerous tasks that needed to be done.

It was not until December that Eric was able to re-established contact with the KP groups. He had managed to maintain contact with the national central LO committee in the west of Holland through his Trouw connections and regular meetings now took place at Dr Wessels' surgery. As many leaders had been arrested or disappeared, it was decided to regroup. Eric was charged to assume the leadership of the LO in the province of Groningen. Arie van der Kaaden of Trouw joined the group and Dr Harry Diemer, a university academic, took over the responsibility for housing. Harry joined the student resistance after he lost his job at the university when he refused to agree with the politics of his department. Arie, a student, had been instrumental in re-establishing contact between the LO and KP after the Trouw raid and the arrests of 17 October. Sister Faber, a nurse, became a new courier. She kept contact with the De Groot group.

Early in 1945, the SD uncovered the De Groot group. The Germans rounded them up. A heavy price was paid for the social work they had carried out. The leaders were tortured, ten members were shot dead and double that number would later die in concentration camps.

In Borkum, Piet and a friend planned to escape by boat. But, while waiting for a compass to arrive, Piet was suddenly returned to Groningen. He sensed something was wrong. He had been uncovered, was interrogated, beaten and returned handcuffed to the attic of the Scholtenhuis. It continued for days. The favourite subjects were Bob and especially Bart. When his interrogator asked what he thought would happen to him Piet said, 'I'll be shot.'

'No, boy, you'll be hanged because we don't shoot spies.' He was moved to the House of Detention and put in cell 35. Two Heidema friends were there. Piet had transformed the flat of one of them into the office used in Bob's rescue. On Boxing Day, Piet had a visit from his father and courier sister. With the guard out of earshot, she told him he wouldn't be shot.

The single cells were overcrowded, some with up to six prisoners. In cell 35 the three friends talked and talked, and decided that they would be shot. The weeks passed. A priest joined the cell. The days were filled with uncertainty. Some prisoners wrote letters to their loved ones. The early morning noise of steel cell doors clanging open and shut and names being called became a familiar part of the nerve wracking routine.

One day the names of Piet's friends were called. Piet was disappointed that his name was not on the list. He was saddened at being separated from his friends and the rest of the Heidema group. After embraces and heartbreaking goodbyes, the cell door slammed shut behind them. By now a large number of cells were empty. Another rail transport left Groningen and Lehnhoff doggedly continued his campaign against the resistance fighters.

24 January 1945 was a freezing cold day. Eric, now hiding at Dr Wessels', went downstairs to the surgery waiting room to prepare for a meeting. During previous meetings, the first statutes of the Foundation 1940-1945 had been formulated. Groundwork for the Foundation had already started in Amsterdam in October 1944 and the preliminary discussions helped to establish the type of support that would be needed, and available, after the war had ended for the families of the resistance fighters. At 10.30 in the morning the SD burst into the room. 'Well, well, look who we have here!'

There was no escape. Eric was handcuffed and pushed onto a stool. The house was searched. The three Wessel girls had gone to school. Dr Wessels and his wife were arrested and taken away. While the SD waited for new victims to turn up, they picked through the papers in Eric's briefcase. His captors questioned him. He refused to answer. They kicked his shins, stood on his toes, and hit him over the head. He remained silent. An hour later, Harry Diemer arrived. There had been no chance to warn him. The detainees were kept seated on small stools for hours and the entertainment continued until about four in the afternoon. Then they were taken with two others, who had turned up, to the House of Detention.

After being made to stand facing a wall for several hours Eric was moved to cell 30. There were four others in the cell. Nobody spoke. It was still dark when he was taken for interrogation. There were eight to ten interrogators, some in uniform. He was placed facing a fierce spotlight. After some preliminaries, he was told to give the names and addresses of the people he worked with, whose pseudonyms they had found in his satchel. He refused.

Eric was ordered to take off his glasses. He was pushed face down on a table where his tormentors bludgeoned him, until he was limp. They dragged him onto the floor by his legs and, by kicking and beating, he was forced to stand up. Again, they demanded the names and addresses. Again, Eric refused. He was kicked repeatedly, this time in the abdomen. And then, the table treatment once more. He did not want to, but he could no longer stop himself from screaming. One of his captors placed Eric's head between his legs to silence him. Once more he was dragged onto the floor and then kicked into an upright position, again they demanded names and again Eric refused. The procedure was repeated, but Eric was in such in a bad way that only the continuous kicking kept him from falling to the floor. Close to collapse and continuing to refuse to talk, he was taken to a room with a bath, and stripped. It was the middle of winter, and 15 degrees below zero. He was put into the bath with his legs over the edge. One of his tormentors sat on his legs whilst the other, who held a bludgeon, filled the bath. He held Eric's head under water until he almost suffocated. Then his head was pulled up and the questions were repeated. Each time Eric refused, his head was pushed under water again. When he resurfaced a man in uniform yelled at him, 'Eerke, you will talk.' He was devastated.

The interrogator had used his Christian name, not the name that was used in his underground work, the name that had been used so far by his tormentors. He had hoped that the SD would only know his codename but now they called him by his own name. Did the uniformed man know him? Would his family and friends be implicated? The man hit him in the left eye. Eric lost consciousness.

He came to lying on the floor. His torturers threw a bucket of water over him to revive him and to clean him up so he could dress, and then they took him to an interrogation room where they were giving his fellow resistance fighter, Harry Diemer, the same table treatment. Eric was produced as an example of what would happen to him if he did not answer their questions.

Eric was taken back to the table where he had been previously tortured but he collapsed. Lying there, he heard one of the interrogators swearing at the others for making it impossible to get any information out of him. A guard took him back to cell 30. It was pitch dark. None of the other prisoners there could do anything for him. When daylight came, the blood was washed off with the only thing available, a dirty rag. Eric's left eye was totally closed. The corner of his eye was torn, as was the skin under his eye. His right eye was blue, half closed. All of his body was black with bruises.

Later that morning a guard took Eric to the interrogation room again. He was confronted by Kindel, the German officer in charge of the House of Detention. But Kindel did not interrogate him. Instead he asked who had beaten him so badly. Eric described the man. Kindel said that the man was a collaborator and that he would order him to stay away from the House of Detention in future. Kindel told Eric that he condemned these methods and that his wounds would be attended to. Indeed, after some time back in his cell, a nurse appeared who dressed Eric's head. His initial fear was that he would not be able to see again with his left eye but after a week some vision came back, and after another fortnight he could more or less see again. He was relieved that his glasses were intact.

Further arrests continued throughout February. The cells were overcrowded. Each day names were called and people were taken away to make room for new prisoners. Eric was interrogated, but for shorter periods and with decreasing frequency. His torturers changed tactics. They no longer beat him but instead threatened him with execution by firing squad.

In February 1945, Dresden in eastern Germany was destroyed in a firestorm that followed a massive aerial bombing by the Allies. Early in March, Germany launched a major offensive in order to prevent the loss of oil fields in Hungary but this failed. Cologne fell immediately thereafter and then the Allies crossed the Rhine at Remagen, between Bonn and Koblenz. On the eastern front the German army was in retreat. In Poland, Russian troops had entered Danzig, Gdansk. Things were not going well for the Germans. Many senior Germans officers began to realise that the war would be lost and became concerned that they might be identified as war criminals. Hitler ordered that no prisoners were to fall into the hands of the Allies. He charged the head of the feared SS, Heinrich Himmler, to execute the order. This suited the commanders of the prisons and camps in which atrocities had been committed. They started to clean up and remove evidence, and they had to get rid of the prisoners before the Allied advance arrived.

On Saturday 16 March 1945 in the middle of the night at the House of Detention cell doors were opened and names were called:
'Diemer, Johann Heinrich'
'Laning, Pieter'
'Van der Laan, Eerke Jacob'
In all, eighty six names were called and the prisoners were taken downstairs. It was an anxious time. There would be a transport. The following evening they were taken by bus to the railway station and split into two groups. The train, which had started in Amsterdam, consisted of cattle wagons. At every station, more prisoners were forced into the wagons. By the time the train reached Groningen all 25 wagons were full and conditions were appalling.

The prisoners were loaded into the crowded wagons. They were told that if anyone tried to escape ten others would be shot. Guards occupied a large part of the space, leaving standing room only for the prisoners. Piet had a suitcase, which he had received from his family. He found himself next to Harry, the biologist arrested with Eric, and three church ministers. Harry, with his unbreakable courage, managed to keep their spirits up. For hours on end they endured the pain of uncomfortable positions that Harry described as biological experimentation. They smoked Piet's cigarettes.

After the German border railway traffic was chaotic. The tracks were damaged. There were stops and starts and waiting. When British planes whined overhead, the guards scrambled out and, after locking the wagons, ran to find safety. The prisoners prayed and hoped that they would not be bombed. They passed Hamburg. It had been reduced to ruins. Finally at midnight, after three days in the train, they pulled into a camp, the last transport to arrive.

KZ-Neuengamme, Germany

The prisoners in the wagons can hear dogs barking and above the commotion the yelling of, *'Aufstehen! Aufstehen!'* They scramble out. There are bright lights shining and there are guards all around, machine guns pointed at the ready. In front of them is a large stone building and a portal with the sign, 'Hamburg Neuengamme'.

Main entrance KZ-Neuengamme

One wagon after the other is emptied into a huge central yard. The prisoners find themselves surrounded by tall buildings and high barbed wire fences. Exhausted and hungry, they are hurried along a concrete path to the large brick building and directed with beatings down a flight of stone stairs into the far end of a cellar. Several hundred people fit in. Kapos, criminals and murderers, in charge of keeping order, freely wield police batons. After more than ten years in prison these prisoners, long-serving criminals who receive privileges in return for supervising prisoner work gangs, have little humanity left. It is depressing.

Finally, names are called. In groups of fifty the newcomers are beaten upstairs and trundle through the dark to a large hall. They have to undress. Possessions are taken from them, rings, watches. Piet watches as his suitcase disappears. They may keep their shoes, toiletries and tobacco. They receive a numbered metal tag with a string to hang around their neck. There is a lot of shouting and noise. In the confusion, a Kapo seizes Piet's 200gram pack of tobacco and shoves him into the next room. Piet can do nothing. He has already learnt to give Kapos a wide berth.

The washroom has benches on one side and showers on the other. Naked, standing in a line, the prisoners watch as their friends go through the coming ordeal and anxiously wait their turn. One by one they face the first Kapo, who shaves their head. The following station is for lathering the next body parts to be shaved. They lie on the bench to get shorn like sheep, and humiliatingly bald are beaten towards the shower. Treatment is fast. Forward motion conveys them into the dressing room, where Kapos shove old underwear and a pile of clothes at them. The ragged outfits are either too small or too big and are made of different kinds of material. Still wet, they pull on the ill fitting garments and, without having noticed it, they are suddenly standing outside in the cold and dark. They don't recognise each other. They are marched to barracks furnished with row upon row of bunk beds three high. Piet and Harry get a bunk to share. They are lucky, some share with two others. There is a toilet, *Kiebel*, in the corner. There is no privacy. Sleep is impossible. They are totally disheartened and churn the past days' events over and over and over.

The macabre motto of the camp is 'Annihilation through labour'. Each day starts in the dark with a lot of noise and shouting, 'Aufstehen, aufstehen!' and '*Schnell, schnell!*' Hundreds of men start to move and the beatings start again. Standing outside in the central parade ground in rows of four for roll call, they endure hours of endless counting of heads. Those too weak to stay upright fall into the snow. Nobody is allowed to touch them.

Back at the barracks they are given breakfast to share between two: one thin slice of bread and a bowl of surrogate coffee made from malt and roasted wheat. A Dutch doctor warns them, 'Don't drink the water. It's contaminated.' He explains it's bad for the intestines. Indeed there are many ill men, all with dysentery, lying three to a bunk in the *Revier*, the hospital. Every morning the corpses are collected and thrown onto a wagon on their last journey. The crematorium operates day and night. It is always hungry. One day, the sole survivor of the Heidema intelligence group that Piet worked with tells them that the whole group was hanged in a bunker. Devastated, they cannot get it out of their minds.

A fortnight after arriving, the new prisoners are given cloth tags with the letter H, for Holland, and numbers, which are sewn onto their jackets and trousers, H77369... H77412... H77417... H77454.... A red triangle signifies a political prisoner. H77389... H77394... H77407.... These sixty four men are separated from the group. They receive another haircut. A strip known as the *Autobahn* is shaven from the front to the back of their head. They also receive a green band that must be worn on their left arm. It has *Torsperre* written on it. These easily identified prisoners are allocated to Barrack 10, which has its own electric barbed wire fence surrounding it. These prisoners will not leave the camp alive. They have received the death penalty and are waiting for the execution order to come from Berlin. Eric is one of them.

The Torsperre prisoners are not allowed out of the camp, not even under supervision. Each morning they collect the dead from the Revier and wheelbarrow the corpses to the crematorium. They clean the parade ground and the barracks. While doing this they steal or scrounge whatever food they can find, from scraps in the kitchen waste to nettles and dandelions growing in the yard, to supplement the never changing watery turnip soup. Unlike other nationals, the Dutch are not allowed to receive any Red Cross parcels. Danish and Norwegian prisoners, who are allowed parcels, save many Dutch lives by sharing theirs.

Whilst work groups leave the camp each day to dig trenches and repair the railways, the Torsperres spend most of their days in the damp, dark cellar making rope, cutting tyres for camouflage nets and waiting for the Friday execution orders from Berlin.

Friday 13 April 1945

By the end of March 1945 Piet, Eric and Harry were labouring in Neuengamme. Jan was in Helgoland. Tom had returned from a mission in Holland and was in a province to the south, Frank was constantly on the move in Groningen, Bob was hiding in a village just north of Groningen and Ep had gone to his home town, Veendam. As more and more leaders were unable to operate, Ep's friend, Gerrit, OD leader for six city neighbour hoods, became the OD Commander for Groningen. Although his direct contact with Tom, Bob and Ep was broken, Gerrit continued to work with Bart and Eric's successor, Arie.

Bart carried on working with the Packard group. It had not been infiltrated and it was able to recover despite the setbacks caused by the betrayal of the MI6 agent, and the rounding up of hundreds of resistance workers over the previous months. The Packard group managed to re-establish transmitters and was able to transmit reliable information on German troop movements and other military data to the Allies.

With every new wave of arrests, the SD gathered more and more information on the new OD leaders. Gerrit's home was raided, but he was hiding in a shop in the centre of the city. Ellie, his wife, was arrested again and taken to the House of Detention. Constantly on the run, Ep had been shadowed in Veendam when he travelled to his younger brother Jurrien's house. Someone betrayed him. On 1 April at five in the morning the SD came to Jurrien's house with two Dutch traitors. They knocked on the door.

'Are you Mr Pinkster?'

'Yes,' Jurrien replied.

'Gehen Sie mit!'

Jurrien pulled on his coat and put on his hat. The SD ordered him out of the house and pushed him into the street. They marched him down the road. Fifty metres further on Officer Bouman shot him from behind. He was dead. They'd shot the wrong man. That same day Ep's oma died.

Frank Haan had evaded the SD for eight months since his betrayal, moving from place to place, but they were on his heels and intent on catching him. They found out where Frank lived. They raided his house. Not finding him there, they detained his wife and took her away.

Bart continued to be on the SD radar. He kept on coordinating and liaising with remaining resistance fighters, getting vital information to the Allies. Bart knew the Allied liberators were moving north, coming closer and closer to Groningen. He kept Bob informed. On 7 April the SD visited Bart's family home again. Still they didn't find Bart. Instead, his older brother Jan was taken to the Scholtenhuis for interrogation and then incarcerated in the House of Detention.

Bob knew he could rely on Bart. Despite the continued activities of the SD, Bob decided it was time to risk a return to the city. Carefully, and as unobtrusively as possible, he cycled to the house where his family was hiding and was reunited with them.

A few days later Gerrit's wife, Bart's brother, Frank's wife and the other prisoners, in the House of Detention and the Scholtenhuis, were released just as the Canadian armoured tank units rolled into Groningen.

It was Friday 13 April 1945.

Three days of heavy urban fighting in Groningen's narrow streets destroyed much of the inner city. The beautiful facades of the Grote Markt lay in ruin. Shells had made gaping holes in the iconic Martinitoren. The bells had been hit. Great fires obliterated city blocks and large parts of the city were beyond recognition. Devastation was everywhere. The Scholtenhuis, where the Executioner of Groningen had reigned, was consumed by flames and burnt to the ground. But the destruction of the hated SD headquarters was a symbol of triumph over the Nazi oppression. On 16 April 1945, almost five years after the German invasion of Holland, Groningen was liberated.

Special edition of Trouw, April 1945

Grote Markt, Groningen, April 1945

The start of the Cold War

The Russian army was advancing into the heart of Europe at an alarming pace. Ten European capitals were in Soviet hands in April 1945. Germany had lost the war and the only thing that was unresolved was the way in which the country would surrender. The war in Europe was to last only a few more weeks but in this short time the destruction was fearsome, and there was a great deal of suffering. The people in the western part of the Netherlands were dying of hunger, but no precious time or resources could be lost in their liberation.

Speculation was rife in the western intelligence services. Both Roosevelt and Churchill worried that Germany had beaten the Allies in the race for an atom bomb. The prime concern of the nervous Western Allies was the threat of a Nazi weapon of mass destruction falling into Russian hands.

Churchill worried that the powerful Secretary of the Central Committee of the Soviet Union, Joseph Stalin, could not to be trusted. He had asked the armed forces to investigate what Britain's position would be if it came to a confrontation with the Russians. The results of the investigation were not encouraging. The Chiefs of Staff were concerned about the enormous size of the Soviet Army in Europe. The Russians would have more than three times as many troops on the ground and twice the number of tanks by the start of July 1945. Winning a war with the Soviet Union would not be possible.

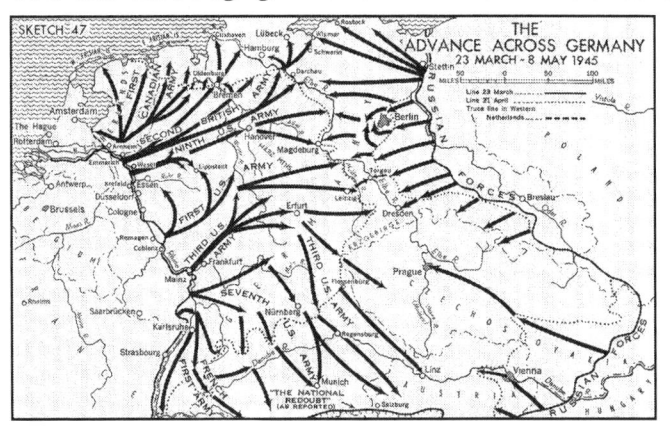

When President Roosevelt died and Truman came to power Churchill hoped that the new President of the United States might be able to start a thaw in their relations with Russia by declaring his friendship for that vast country. But Truman did not.

SS chief, Heinrich Himmler, had been aware for some time that the war was lost. He offered Churchill capitulation. This would have given the Western Allies the opportunity to move east rapidly and halt the Russian advance. However, Great Britain had a military agreement with the Soviet Union not to come to a separate peace deal with Germany. Himmler's offer was a windfall for Churchill. It gave him the opportunity to ingratiate himself with the Soviet leader. He sent a telegram to Stalin saying that he had received an offer of capitulation from Himmler but that he had declined. His telegram had the desired effect. Stalin replied quickly; and Churchill informed Himmler that the only acceptable surrender was unconditional on all fronts to the United States, Britain and the Soviet Union.

As the Russians progressed along the shore of the Baltic driving before them tens of thousands of refugees, German ships fled west. They gathered close to Denmark in the bays of the Baltic, where the remnants of the German fleet were assembled. The great German battleships were gone, but there was a new kind of menace, E-boats. These were large torpedo boats, with a reach of more than 1100km and so fast it was almost impossible to eliminate them. These boats were twice the size, and more suited to the open sea, than their British and American nearest equivalents. Furthermore, there were still hundreds of submarines, U-boats, and an unknown number of miniature submarines about. These so called 'Seals' could go virtually anywhere, could be very destructive and were difficult to trace. Churchill, himself a navy man, feared the German fleet and for good reasons.

The Nazis still controlled the north of Germany, Denmark and Norway. Denmark controlled the narrow straight giving passage from the Baltic to the North Sea, generating the suspicion that the Nazis and the German fleet might make a run for Norway.

British forces, on the banks of the river Elbe, were ready to push through to the Baltic, and to isolate the north from the rest of the country. It was inevitable that the Russians would take the German weapons research facility at Peenemünde, on an island to the east of Lübeck. British intelligence had become suspicious of Peenemünde in 1942 when aerial photos, showing torpedo like objects and black patches in the grass around an airfield, were studied. It was thought they were rockets. When some months later a conversation between two captured German generals was overheard, one telling the other that he had seen an experimental rocket launch, Allied intelligence was spurred into action. The Peenemünde facility was bombed. The air raid set back the German weapons work, but it did not stop it. Research and development continued; test launches resumed and manufacturing activities were moved to underground tunnels in the Harz Mountains. Two years later, Germany was bombing Britain with its first ballistic missiles.

The Allies worried over the mobility of the missiles. Adolf Hitler had alluded to submarine-towed platforms and successful tests with submarine-launched rockets. With technical personnel of the German navy, who were captured by the Soviets, being invited to join the Russian navy, the Allies were determined to prevent the German fleet from falling into Russian hands. As British Field Marshall Montgomery spurred his army to reach Lübeck, and the bays to the west of it, Berlin fell to the Russians.

Suddenly, there was news. Adolf Hitler, the Führer, was dead.

It was 1 May 1945. The German radio announced Hitler had died the day before '...fighting to his last breath against Bolshevism'. When Churchill heard this, he said: 'Well, I'll have to say he was quite right to die in such a way.'

An avalanche of events followed Hitler's death. Hitler had chosen Admiral Karl Dönitz, a master in naval warfare, not SS chief Himmler, as his successor. Both Dönitz and Himmler were in northern Germany, not far from the Baltic. Churchill, still without any response on capitulation, needed to act quickly... and decisively.

The British pressed ahead against attackable strategic targets in the north, while American troops pushed east. Earlier, whilst overrunning central Germany, they had found a nuclear stock pile in the Harz Mountains. Nearby was a plant that produced heavy water, a key ingredient in the production of atomic weapons. Shock waves went through the Allied secret services when the Technical Director of the German rocket programme surrendered to the US army. His team of expert weapons scientists had been secretly planning their surrender, but after being transferred from Peenemünde to the south of Germany they were closely guarded by the SS. The catch was special. The Americans learned that a vast quantity of secret documents was hidden in underground tunnels in the eastern Harz Mountains. The area was occupied by the Allies, however it had been agreed with the Russians that it would be part of the Soviet zone. Two days before the Russians moved in to take over the Allies succeeded in collecting fourteen tons of hidden material and transporting it to the safety of the future American zone, just in time!

In the north of Germany, the harbours of Hamburg, Kiel and Lübeck were bombed and the RAF attacked the fleet that had gathered in the bays of the Baltic. The control of Hamburg was fought for house to house, as the 11th Armoured division raced towards the Baltic.

Typhoon with four 20mm cannons and two 1000lb bombs being prepared for attack

The fight for the Baltic

In Neuengamme, a rumour goes around the camp. It is put about that Groningen, 300 kilometres away, has been liberated, that the Americans have crossed the Elbe, the French have overrun the Black Forest and the Russians are heading for Berlin only 175 kilometres from Neuengamme. There is speculation and uncertainty about what looms ahead. Slowly but surely the number of prisoners in the camp has been reduced. Harry has been transferred. Piet has been moved.

Uelzen, the sub camp of Neuengamme where Piet has been transferred to, is in chaos. The town is suffering heavy British bombing. Hundreds of men, women and children, each carrying a few possessions, file out of town away from the shelling. Each morning the prisoners file in the opposite direction to the ruined railway yard, walking over dead bodies and body parts to defuse unexploded bombs and clear broken rail tracks whilst bombs rain down. At the sugar factory, where the prisoners are camped, there is no power, no water. The Russian prisoners become bolder and bolder and force their way into the factory store, taking suitcases, clothes, shoes and sugar that they haul up to the attic for trading. One night eight of them escape through a small window in the attic. Then another group escapes. There is the threat of a massive breakout of prisoners, a severe danger for the civilian population. What could be worse than marauding bands of hungry escaped prisoners? The commandant shoots and kills some Russians. As punishment there are hours and hours of roll call and the meagre food rations are withdrawn for the day. Planes continue to bomb, but the days pass without the longed-for liberation. The prisoners are highly strung. They fear that the guns will be turned on them before the Allies arrive. Piet considers escape, but it is too risky.

Finally on 17 April the sugar factory at Uelzen is cleared and the starving prisoners are loaded into cattle wagons, headed for Hamburg. Many are ill. The stench is unbearable. In the night the Uelzen prisoners arrive at Neuengamme. The dead are left on the train. With beatings and shouting the prisoners are pushed into a dark cold cellar that is thigh deep with water. Everyone is exhausted and depressed. They pray to find the will to stay upright and alive. In the morning, Piet discovers that his belt and precious piece of soap has been stolen from him by the Russians during the night.

Without warning or explanation, the prisoners who are still alive are herded back into the wagons, which then stand at the sidings for three days. They are without food and water. There is no fresh air. People are begging for relief and praying to die. The SS guard the carriages with bloodhounds. At the end of the third day the train starts to move and after a night of travel they arrive at the port in Lübeck.

At Neuengamme, the Scandinavian section of the camp is emptied and 4,000 Scandinavians are taken away in the white buses of the Swedish Red Cross. Parcels of food from the Red Cross are left behind in the barracks. The starved Dutch Torsperres break into the empty barracks and take whatever is left. They feast greedily on the rich food: bacon and sausage, butter, sugar and syrup. They are oblivious to the nausea, stomach cramps and diarrhoea that they will suffer from afterwards. They find Chesterfield cigarettes and smoke, wondering what is to become of them. The gallows have been dismantled. The Revier has been emptied. They have spent the past two back-breaking weeks digging through the thick concrete of the parade ground to make a rose garden.

The camp commander, Max Pauly, is following Himmler's orders, removing all the evidence of what has gone on there. Whilst Piet and thousands of others are still locked in the cattle wagons, the Torsperres are delegated to stripping, clearing and cleaning up the camp.

Soldiers on parade at KZ-Neuengamme

On 23 April, the roll is called. Numbers and names are checked. At midday, the remaining one hundred men, guarded by two hundred guards, leave the camp on foot. They walk for seven kilometres. Those who cannot keep up are shot. At the first railway station, the prisoners board cattle wagons and are told they are going to Lübeck. The railway lines are badly damaged. The weakened men often have to walk. The holdups in the train journey are solved by these death marches. This journey is worse than any previous one. The suffering and the cruelty are beyond description. Death is everywhere. Although as the crow flies Lübeck is no more than 80 kilometres away, the journey takes two days. Finally, they walk the last few miles to the port where they are loaded back onto wagons for another day.

The port in Lübeck is overcrowded. Train wagons are overfull. Thousands of prisoners are packed onto the quay. The freighters Thielbeck and Athen are docked at the wharf. SS guards load the prisoners onto the boats. The Dutch prisoners are sent fifteen metres down an iron ladder into the fore-hold at the bottom of the 5,000 tonne freighter Athen. There are already hundreds of prisoners there, mainly Poles and Russians. It is pitch dark and icy cold. It stinks. There are no buckets in which to relieve themselves. Piet manages to get hold of a thin blanket and tries to sleep, but there is not enough room to lie down. People lie criss-cross over one another, shivering. Nearly everyone suffers from dysentery, raw hips and bad colds, and many cough continuously. It is indescribable. The boat sails, but to where? The prisoners suspect what this means. They fear that the ship might be taken out beyond the shallow bay to the deeper Baltic, to be sunk. They will die like rats in a trap and evidence of what happens to them will vanish.

Within a few hours of having arrived on the Athen, Piet is woken by Russians coming down from the hold above to steal food. Together with some friends, Piet seizes the opportunity to struggle up the narrow ladder to reach the higher hold. One by one they reach the hold where they feel a little safer, but there are hundreds of sick. The worst dysentery sufferers lack the strength to pull themselves away from the corners where the Kiebel would normally be found. They are skeletons, covered in dirt, without desire to live.

Each morning a rope is lowered and the ones who have died are hauled up. Then meagre amounts of soup are lowered down. Those who don't have the strength to fight for their food simply go without. At night the Russians gang together, stealing in packs and taking whatever they can get hold of: bread, shoes, even gold teeth. Few have the strength to resist. The thirst is unbearable and the only drink is seawater. In exchange for bread, Piet's sick friends are offered water by some Russians. It is urine. The inhumanity is heartbreaking. It makes many question if they will survive this horror. As the days pass in the darkness of the holds, the bond of friendship, talk and prayer encourages them to hold out. After five days of sheer terror they are moved from the Athen.

It is a bright sunny, calm day and they find themselves, disorientated, on a 15,000 tonne passenger liner, the Cap Arcona, a luxury boat that used to sail the Atlantic between Hamburg and South America. After hours of roll call, they make their way down the stairs. Hands slide over the mahogany railings of the Persian carpeted staircase. The ornate dining room has walls lined with Victorian brocade. The grandeur, the richness of gold and brass is ironic. Piet crowds into a cabin for four with nine others. It is clean. There is a wash basin with running water. The prisoners do nothing but clean themselves and their clothes, which are covered in black powder that has become viscid. They realise what the bloodsucking red crab lice have done to their itching, inflamed bodies, and delight in picking them off. Food rations remain meagre, but morale has improved. The prisoners hear fragments of what is happening in the world outside. Nobody knows for sure, but it appears to be certain that Germany is losing the war.

From the porthole they can see the shore, but they have no sense of direction. The boats in the vicinity keep bringing more and more prisoners onboard. The passageway is full of the sick. More men join the cabin and they end up with three to a bunk. No one can make it to the nearby toilet in time. There are now hundreds and hundreds of prisoners in the passages. It looks like an ants nest. Dead bodies are everywhere, some friends amongst them.

By the end of April, the ships are overloaded with human cargo. For the Germans in charge, it is a logistical nightmare. Nobody knows how many prisoners will be coming and what categories there will be. The sorting and grouping requires to and fro movements of prisoners, who are continuously taken from one ship to another. Then administrative communications stop. Nothing comes through, nothing happens.

Suddenly, there is a roll call on deck of the Cap Arcona. Six metres below, the Athen is tied alongside. About 2,000 nervous prisoners, mostly Poles and Russians wait in the usual rows of four. They sense that the SS are up to something. More prisoners are put on the Cap Arcona and the prisoners on the deck are ordered back onto the Athen, the ship of horrors. Piet, leaving behind many friends, finds himself back in the pitch dark of the lowest hold of the Athen with other Dutchmen and Belgians. One machine gun in the opening of the hold and not a soul would survive. Disheartened they agonize over if they will ever see their loved ones again. Some are rapidly losing strength and feel that their end is coming close. They turn to God for relief from this living hell.

The Athen continues ferrying between the harbour and the ships, bringing provisions and removing the dead, which are thrown in the sea. Towards evening four Russians lower two buckets of soup into the hold. It is said it is poisonous. Nobody knows for sure. Everyone gets his one-third litre share and the soup is eaten, poisonous or not. A suggestion is made by the soup-bringers to join the other holds in overthrowing the ship. The decision will be known when the corpses are collected in the morning. They spend the night restlessly, half-lying, half-sitting on cold iron. The walls are wet with condensation. Piet climbs the ladder to have a look. It is still dark.

In the morning, the prisoners are woken by the sound of the engines. They are moving again. More friends have died. The corpses are hauled out of the holds. They ask if they will have food. It is thought not. The ship no longer moves. The engines idle. Those spying on top of the ladder declare it is calm. The Athen anchors not far from the coast. Small motor boats set out for the harbour. The prisoners wonder if the crew are being changed. They receive soup, more water than beets, to last until tomorrow. They fight over the soup; no more talk of poison, they are alive. The body collectors say something will happen. The resistance committee advises everyone to be prepared to attack. The captain has promised to try to overpower and disarm the SS. The attack signal will be three strikes of an iron bar on the steel framework at the bottom hold of the bow. The prisoners doze, drifting in and out of sleep, losing all sense of time.

They can hear the drone of planes. The SS and crew man the guns. All hell breaks loose. The clatter of anti-aircraft guns is deafening. The Athen groans and trembles in all its joints. Tracer fire races back and forth over the deck, flashes light up the hold. The ship bobs up and down like a cork. The prisoners scream and believe their end has come. They worry they will be torpedoed and drowned. They try to climb the ladder, but no one can get to the top. They are thrown on top of each other. Two Russians are shot and tumble through the hatch into the dark hold. Four Russians rush up, but are quickly pushed back down. Every prisoner who tries to climb the ladder is pushed back. More than twenty prisoners lie injured at the bottom, but the prisoners persist in trying to get up. The shooting reduces and the noise abates. The ship stabilizes. The prisoners calm down. It is said a submarine close to them was hit. It is cold. The wounded Russians are screaming in pain.

By morning, everyone is choking with thirst and they wonder if it is the soup. A barge carrying prisoners from the Stutthof concentration camp draws alongside. 300 female prisoners are put onboard the Athen. Planes fly over the ship and prisoners in zebra striped uniforms are ordered on deck. The planes disappear.

Suddenly, the ship's engines run at full speed. She heads for Neustadt and moors at the quayside. In the fore-hold the prisoners hear one knock on the steel frame. Is this the signal to get ready? Planes suddenly fill the sky and fly low over the bay. Bombs are dropped. The SS guards open fire on the attacking aircraft. The noise is overwhelming. There is a rumble of artillery in the distance and shots are fired from the shore. But, it is not as bad as yesterday. Do the British know that there are prisoners onboard? From somewhere the will to live encourages them to hope for a miracle. The atmosphere is charged with longing and fear. The signal goes! Some prisoners attack the hold guards and find their way up onto the upper deck. The crew help the prisoners to attack the SS and throw them overboard.

Piet gets onto the upper deck. There are not many people and he can't see any SS officers. Another spurt of bombs and explosions sends Piet lunging for shelter. In the distance he sees three pillars of fire. The sky is full of planes and ships burn like furnaces. Piet knows the friends he left behind on the Cap Arcona must surely die. They must choose between the flames and the water: burn or drown. It is horrible to look at. The Athen gets a volley of shots that hits the crew's quarters, and a rocket that takes out the anti-aircraft gun, blasting a hole in the ship. An explosion seems to throw the Athen into the air. Piet is knocked out.

The Cap Arcona lists. The lights are out. The Captain orders that they abandon ship. For the prisoners, the remaining life boats are in pieces or on fire. The fire hoses have been destroyed, the davits are damaged. There are no float vests. Prisoners race from the fires to jump into the cold water. They are machine gunned from above and from rescue boats that refuse to take anyone except German guards and members of the crew. The water turns red. Some prisoners manage to swim to land, but SS men, naval personnel and the Wehrmacht shoot at them as they reach the shoreline. A few are rescued by local fishermen.

The deck is wet and slippery. Some prisoners manage to hold onto the railings and struggle to keep their grip as the ship lists. As she capsizes she creates whirlpools that are impossible to escape from. Some escape the fire and smoke through the portholes, enduring the searing heat of the metal beneath them and struggle to keep from slipping off the smooth surface into the sea. They are exhausted. Time for them has stopped.

The Athen is hit in the middle. There is confusion, crying and screaming. People clamber up the ladder to get out of the holds. Many are wounded. Piet comes to as the injured come on deck. He fears the ship being hit again.

He rushes for the gangway and into the gun barrel of an SS soldier. He turns and races to the front of the ship. To the left and to the right, the deck is covered in blood. The moaning and crying is horrendous. Death is all around. Piet sees his chance! The mooring rope! A rush of adrenaline powers his body. With new found strength, he shins up onto the railing, menacingly high above the jetty, grabs the rope and slides down until the jetty looms close. He jumps, and runs. Others follow.

The harbour is in uproar. There are dead floating in the water and at the water's edge wounded, sloshing for attention. On solid ground, there are hundreds of men, women and children in striped clothes, all of them dirty, skinny, panic stricken and trying to get away from the harbour. Piet sees one of his friends. He has stripped his clothes of the damning Torsperre badges. In the crowds, they bump into another friend, also running away from the pandemonium in the harbour. The three of them go looking for a safe place. They run towards Neustadt. They pass the U-boat shed where there are many badly wounded, half drowned people, some heavily bleeding, others severely burnt. They ignore the yelling of the Grüne Polizei and SS officers shouting the hated camp roll call order, 'In rows of four!'

Tiredness and hunger forgotten, Piet and his friends have one aim - to get away from it all. Passing the Submarine School they go up a hill. In the distance they see tanks approaching fast and, afraid, they hide in a ditch. As the tanks come nearer, there are sudden outbursts of shouting and calling. They watch as the tanks roll on to the harbour and realise that they are British!

'The English!' they shout. Prisoners throw their hats in the air, hop around and hug each other. Everyone is kissing, crying and jumping, all skeletons dancing in the midst of misery. Skeletons on their knees thanking the Lord, skeletons at long last free. What a macabre sight! Thank God for the miracle of their survival!

A Dutchman, who was forced to work for the Germans in a hospital close by, offers Piet and his friends a place to stay. They gladly accept. He feeds them bacon and eggs, bread, butter and jam: a banquet! The next day they venture into Neustadt. They ask British soldiers for news of Groningen. Disappointingly there is none, but they are given packets of cigarettes and chocolate. They stumble into a warehouse where they find bottles and fill them with wine. Piet catches a chicken and puts it in a bag. At the U-boat shed they pick up some tinned fruit and, exhausted, they head back to their lodgings. They have been starved for months. They cook and eat the food, but it is too rich, and in the middle of the night a doctor has to be called. They are admitted to hospital. Each of them weighs less than 50 kilos.

In the hospital their filthy clothes are burnt. They are washed and scrubbed. It is painful. They are put to bed with clean sheets, but the mattresses are too soft. They cannot sleep. The doctor has seen thousands die of their conditions: lack of food, exhaustion and mental strain. Completely weakened, they realise they are well on the way in the same direction if they do not do adhere to the program.

Whilst the air attacks are going on, British troops move north from Lübeck along the road that follows the shore of the bay. The first troops reach Neustadt at 4pm. When the Naval Liaison Officer arrives at the navy barracks, he orders that no vessel whatsoever is allowed to leave the port, preventing German military personnel from escaping. It is not until 6pm that the British officer hears that there are prisoners on board the ships. He immediately sends rescue boats.

The Cap Arcona has settled in the shallow bay, on her starboard side, half submerged. On board it is quiet. The few surviving prisoners cling onto the ship. Physically exhausted and mentally drained, one after another weakens and falls into the seven degree water. By evening no one in the water is alive.

Some prisoners set fire to the Athen, the ship from hell, during the night. A rescue team is sent and finds prisoners still on board. When it is thought that all the prisoners who have survived have been removed from the ship, it is towed into the bay to prevent it from setting fire to the wharf.

Eric is rescued from the Cap Arcona by the British. He is taken to the barracks of the Submarine School that has been taken over as a hospital. He is in a terrible state. He is given blue German marine pyjamas and put to bed. For the first time in many months he receives proper food, on a plate, and he is cared for.

Four days after the Neustadt Bay disaster a simple memorial service to honour the dead is held in Neustadt. A group of prisoners who have survived the calamity gather on the square in the centre of Neustadt. Dressed in their striped clothing or civilian clothes that they have been given, found or stolen, the ex-prisoners follow a small troop of soldiers to the beach northeast of Neustadt. Two mass graves have been filled with the hundreds of bodies that have washed ashore. The silent procession is joined by a small number of Germans. Some of them are forced to help bury the dead. There are a few women with flowers. At the graves the procession stops and soldiers fire across the water. The shots can be heard from the hospital. It is a very sad and sombre occasion.

Cap Arcona
54°3'52"N   10°49'34"E
3 May 1945

Years later Piet wrote in his Memoirs of Neuengamme Concentration Camp:

Even now, after 35 years, all are in our thoughts. The terrible things that have happened have stayed with us all along. No day passes without us thinking of those who have not been blessed in the same way as we who were able to return.

The years after the war

Throughout the Netherlands, the men and women who had fought in the Resistance and had survived tried to pick up the pieces of their shattered lives. For many, life would never be normal again.

Once the Canadians had liberated Groningen the measures that the OD had discussed during the war to maintain public order and avoid chaos were implemented. The movements of Groningen's citizens were limited. Without a new permit one was not allowed to leave or enter the city. Checkpoints manned by the OD were everywhere. German citizens and soldiers, some dressed as civilians, Nazi sympathizers and other suspects were rounded up.
    Mother was desperate to find father. He had been arrested on the 24 January 1945. In the previous seven months she had seen him twice, fleetingly at opa's funeral and a few weeks later on their wedding anniversary, the day she was arrested. We were still living in the cottage in Zeegse, some fifteen kilometres south of Groningen. Mother needed a permit to travel. She was amongst the first to receive one and be allowed in and out of the city. The document for unrestricted freedom of movement, dated 28 April 1945 and signed on behalf of the LO, declares that she was known to the LO as a good patriot, and that the LO had no objection to her entering and leaving the city. From that day onwards she searched for father. Each morning she cycled from Regina Cottage to the city and queued with hundreds of others. Each day there was more horrifying news of concentration camps, the appalling conditions, and what had gone on there. Each day the lists of names were checked. Each day mother was hoping and praying for good news. Each day was a repeat of the previous. 'Sorry, we have no news.'
    Some weeks later, we returned to our home in the Koninginnelaan. After we were evicted it had been allocated to strangers. The people who had been living there were now gone. Almost all of our furniture, except some odd bits and pieces, was gone but they had left a sideboard that wasn't ours. Anyway, it didn't matter. We were home!
    Every morning mother went to the Red Cross to see if any word had come through of father. Every evening I had to console her: 'I'm sure he'll be back.'

Information about missing resistance workers and ex-prisoners was scant and often incorrect. Lines of communication were chaotic and inefficient, and the news filtering through from Germany was not encouraging. Ep was frustrated by the situation. He was concerned about the welfare of missing ex-prisoners, colleagues and friends. He knew that if they were still alive in Germany, they would probably be too ill or too weak to be able to undertake the journey home by themselves. Transportation was hampered by a lack of vehicles and a shortage of fuel. The infrastructure was in ruins. Many bridges and roads were impassable and the railway network was in chaos.
    Ep discussed the problem with other members of the OD and together with Gerrit planned a mission to Germany. Ep was leader and Gerrit looked

after the paperwork. Ep's brother Jan managed the transport and a doctor agreed to accompany them. They set out in convoy to search camp hospitals in Germany for survivors and to compose lists of missing Dutchmen. They travelled first to Wilhelmshafen in northern Germany to look for and collect as many ex-prisoners as they could. The trip was a success. Ep was determined to carry on with the work.

While Ep and Gerrit were in Germany again, Tom and his young family returned to Groningen and learnt that Bob and Frank and their families were back in the city and all in good health. Bart, Ep and Gerrit and their families were well, and had also returned to their own homes. Jan arrived safely back from Helgoland. The children did not recognise their dad, who had left suddenly eight months earlier. Once back in Groningen, the group of Resistance friends learnt that the whereabouts of Piet and Eric were still unknown.

It took three weeks of nursing before Eric was discharged. He was restless and yearned to be home. His body was bony and he still had symptoms of hunger oedema. His face was gaunt. His glasses hid his deep, dark eye sockets. He had no hair. He was not yet well but he felt sufficiently confident to leave and decided it was time to try and make the journey back to Groningen. He was given an old pair of shoes, trousers and a jacket, which he put on over his blue marine pyjamas. He tucked the red, white and blue striped flag into his coat pocket. He put the fork and spoon he had used to eat with in hospital into the inside pocket and left for Groningen, 382 kilometres westwards.

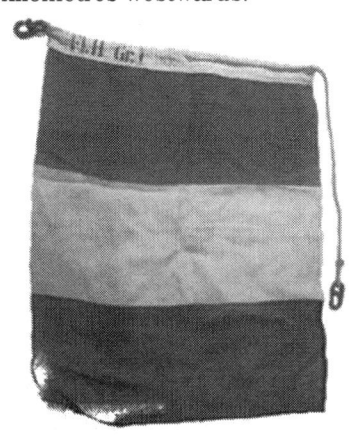

Everything was in post-war disarray. Using the flag to show he was Dutch or French, he was able to get food and hitch lifts, first south to Belgium then back northwards by train to the south of Holland. In Eindhoven ex-prisoners from Groningen convinced a fellow Groninger bus driver to take them home. Finally after four days of travelling father arrived by bus with other ex-prisoners on the Grote Markt and walked the last mile to the Koninginnelaan. In the middle of the night, he rang the doorbell of the sleeping house at number 19A. He was home! It was 1 June 1945.

The hospital in Neustadt that Piet and his friends had been taken to by the doctor was visited one day by a British colonel. The colonel talked with Piet, who told him that he and his two friends had belonged to the Groningen intelligence service. Sometime later, his story confirmed, he learnt to his delight that he and his friends would be regarded as British soldiers. The colonel promised they would be treated as such, and it was not long before they were transferred to the 74th British Clearing Hospital. Piet was still weak, but with special treatment on Sister Elliot's ward he recovered enough to be able to go home by mid June. Piet and other ex-prisoners were flown from the Lüneberg Heath to Eindhoven in a Dakota. In Eindhoven they were issued new clothes and put on a bus to Groningen.

Ep and Gerrit spent two months getting the tracing and rescuing of ex-prisoners really moving. They collected information largely based on the few remaining German records. Ep obtained permits from the Canadian army authorities in Groningen, enabling the team to be supplied by the Allies with food, accommodation and fuel when travelling through Germany. One Groninger recalled his luck at being picked up south of Bremen. He was walking back to Holland, and looking for a bridge to cross the river, when Ep and Gerrit rolled up in their battered van. They were returning to Enschede, with Dutch ex-prisoners who had survived the march from the Sachsenhausen camp. Would he like a lift?

By 18 July 1945 a larger team was equipped and ready to go. This team included two doctors, a nurse and a clergyman. Within a month the team succeeded in repatriating 150 ex-prisoners in conditions that ranged from very sick to more or less healthy. However, their work was not officially approved and recognition of the team by various authorities at times caused problems. Ep approached the Dutch Red Cross. It was agreed that he could represent them and it was agreed that extra members from the Red Cross would strengthen the team. The next team of sixteen persons was less successful. Differences of opinion developed between the original group and the new Red Cross team members. This resulted in Ep having to write reports about what exactly did and what did not happen, a most frustrating task. After the adrenaline-fuelled work in the Resistance the return to bureaucracy was like a wet blanket. And there was another factor. The ease with which the Canadians had supported their efforts seemed to be a symbol of the so much desired freedom for which they had fought so hard. Whereas Ep's earlier team had received every possible form of cooperation from the Canadian side, the now re-emerging Dutch administrative system was only prepared to follow bureaucratic procedures.

Frustrated and disappointed with the situation, Ep changed focus. During the German occupation, relatives of resistance fighters captured by the Germans were always somehow taken care of and kept financially afloat. The Foundation 1940-1945, which Ep and Eric had helped to set up in Groningen in the last months of 1944, was determined to support and maintain the solidarity of the ex-resistance fighters. Ep continued his involvement with the war victims through the Foundation, serving as director for Friesland, Groningen and Drenthe. Together with Gerrit, Bob, Bart, Frank and others they concentrated on tracing ex-freedom fighters. Their names were submitted to the Foundation and its membership and activities expanded rapidly. In the province of Groningen many more resistance members had been arrested than in any other Dutch province. Of the 2,000 active resistance fighters in Groningen, 393 lost their lives. The fact finding and piecing together of stories by those who worked with the Foundation helped many families to find closure. Bit by bit, stories emerged. There were families where the fathers and mothers had died in concentration camps. There were the wrecked survivors of the camps, people who had been physically or mentally mutilated. Of those Dutch men and women sent to internment camps, only one in ten had survived. There were families where members had disappeared after being arrested. Bodies were found and mass graves were uncovered. For months and years following the end of the war, people were reburying the dead.

It fell to the WWII Crimes Investigation Team, led by Major Till, to investigate what had happened to the prisoners from Neuengamme.

Neuengamme camp had included 80 sub-camps spread across northern Germany. Till noted that Neuengamme's reputation was amongst the worst of the Nazi concentration camps. Many medical experiments were carried out there. Of over 100,000 inmates, half died. Between 20 and 23 April 1945 the last of the Torsperre prisoners were taken from Neuengamme to the docks of Lübeck, where they joined thousands of prisoners from other concentration camps. Despite the chaos of the final days of the war, Pauly completed the evacuation of the camp and destroyed all the records before the Western Allies got there. When they arrived at Neuengamme it was empty. Everything was clean, neat and tidy.

There were hundreds and hundreds of boats of all types, shapes and sizes anchored in the countless bays and inlets of Schleswig Holstein, south of the Danish border. In the Neustadt Bay to the north-west of Lübeck the merchantmen SS Deutschland and the SS Cap Arcona lay at anchor. The Cap Arcona had worn out engines, a skeleton crew and little in the way of fuel. The Deutschland was being refitted as a hospital ship. The SS Thielbeck was moored by the quayside and the SS Athen was used to ferry the prisoners to the Cap Arcona.

When the Athen, laden with 2,352 prisoners and about 225 guards, arrived for the first time alongside the Cap Arcona, her Captain, Bertram, refused to take the prisoners on board as he had not received any orders. The Cap Arcona only had lifebelts for its crew and he considered it unsafe for thousands of people to be on the ship and to be exposed to the dangers of air and U-boat attacks. The German Navy told Captain Bertram that his ship had been transferred to the Commissioner for Sea Transport. That authority insisted he accept the prisoners, yet when the Athen drew alongside the Cap Arcona again he refused to take the ropes and the Athen left. On 26 April, German officers boarded the Cap Arcona, handed Captain Bertram an order to accept the prisoners or he'd be arrested and shot.

In Lübeck, the presence of the prisoners was no secret. Allied journalists and the Red Cross knew about it. As a result the Red Cross had arranged to transfer about 1,250 prisoners to three small boats that left for Sweden on 30 April. About 2,000 prisoners, including very sick ones, were loaded onto the SS Thielbeck and she was towed out into the Neustadt Bay not far from the Deutschland. Within a week the Athen ferried 6,500 prisoners to the Cap Arcona and all the prisoners that had been on the docks had been loaded onto the ships.

On 2 May, as Berlin fell to the Russians and the 11th British Armoured Division entered Lübeck their commander was told by the Red Cross that there were some 8,000 prisoners on board the ships in the bay. The commander phoned the message through. The next day, a wave of planes reached Neustadt Bay but turned back because of poor visibility. At quarter past two, eight RAF Typhoons appeared and attacked the ships with 60lb rockets and 500lb bombs. The Cap Arcona was the first ship to be bombed. Lurching, ablaze and full of smoke the Cap Arcona capsized and sank within an hour. Ten minutes after the attack on the Cap Arcona, the planes returned and dropped their cargo of explosives on the Thielbeck and the Deutschland. Deutschland sank, but the crew were able to escape. The Thielbeck sank in a matter of minutes.

Witnesses estimated that fewer than 350 people had escaped from the Cap Arcona and only a hundred from the Thielbeck, although most of those from the Athen had survived. Many from Neustadt had no idea the SS had imprisoned the prisoners on the ships. The crews of the planes that bombed the ships thought that the people they attacked were German military men. A pilot of Fighter Squadron 193 flying a Typhoon 1B said:

> We used our cannon fire on the chaps in the water... we shot them up with 20 mm cannons. Horrible thing, but we were told to do it and we did. That's war.

Till concluded in his report that the Germans who placed the prisoners on the ships did so with such a degree of negligence of safety that it was akin to manslaughter, and had many resemblances to murder. He pressed for instructions to the British Army to prepare a fitting burial ground for the proper burial of the corpses that had been buried so far, and for those that continued to be washed ashore and were being buried without distinction in unmarked mass graves on both sides of the harbour.

Till's investigation was interrupted twice by higher authorities. In his report he states that because of these diversions his team's investigation had not been thorough enough. The available RAF reports were not the most important source of information. A nameless Intelligence Officer with Group 83 RAF, who came to visit the team twice, volunteered information that on 2 May a message had been received that these ships were laden with prisoners. There was time to warn the RAF, but they attacked the following day. By '...some oversight...' the message was never passed on. Convinced that the British had been advised that there were prisoners on the ships, Till concluded that an enquiry was needed and, as military rules defined, the responsible authority would be the RAF.

If an enquiry was held, its conclusions have not been made public. The cause of the Neustadt Bay tragedy continues to mystify as there are few records relating to the incident in the public domain. The material is under a 100year embargo. Under the British Public Records Act of 1958 and 1967, records may be kept under lock and key, albeit for a limited period of time. This may be 30, 50 or even 75 years but a 100 year secret is extreme and very rare. It is the maximum allowed under the Act. By 2045, a hundred years after the tragedy, any remaining secrets will have to be revealed.

More than 7,000 people lost their lives on 3 May 1945 in the Bay of Lübeck, one day before the German troops including all the naval ships in the north of Germany, Denmark and the Netherlands surrendered. Four days later, Victory in Europe was celebrated.

Victory had been achieved, and the soldiers were going home. But the worry about Russia remained. For the Groningen Resistance fighters who came back from the concentration camps the worry, the fear, and the angst were real. Jan in Helgoland, and Piet and Eric first in Neuengamme and then on the boats, had encountered Russians under the worst imaginable circumstances, gangs of knife-wielding thugs terrorising their fellow prisoners and stealing their last crusts of bread. After the war, many ex resistance fighters feared having to face an oppressor once again - this time the Russians. The withdrawal of American troops would leave Europe dependent on the goodwill of the Russians and Stalin might not be able to resist the temptation to invade Europe over a destroyed German Reich. Their anxiety was no different from the trepidation that dominated Allied decision making in the final days of World War II.

Many from the Resistance were dead, but they were not forgotten. Each day brought news of fellow fighters and ex-prisoners. Ep's brother: shot dead. Eric's courier, Kieft, did not survive the camps. In the Sandborstel concentration camp Drenth, strong in his convictions, had followed his course calmly. He had helped people who no longer felt they could go on by writing passages from the Bible for them, on small pieces of paper which they could keep close. One day he had collapsed on the parade ground. No one could help him. He died after two years of captivity. Eric recalled the inspiration that Drenth had provided and that had kept on inspiring them even after he had disappeared.

The doctor who had warned them on arrival in Neuengamme not to drink the water didn't make it off the Cap Arcona. Harry Diemer, Eric's friend who had been arrested with him, survived the camps and was liberated by the Americans but died in July 1945 in Sandborstel. At Neuengamme, Harry's optimistic view point had cheered many fellow prisoners. He often paced the prison yard while solving a problem and the theological conclusions that followed gave prisoners much pleasurable discussion during the hours and hours of prison boredom. Eric wrote his obituary.

By the end of the summer 1945, Groningers were trying to get back to normality.

Eric resumed his employment at the NNZ. Throughout his months in prison, the NNZ had never ceased to pay his salary. Eric's responsibilities had grown in scope with the growth of the company and on his return he was appointed deputy manager, holding power of attorney for the company. Leendert Boot was there, but his brother Marinus had not survived. He died in a camp in the vicinity of Buchenwald and was buried in a mass grave.

Eric continued his involvement with politics and became treasurer of the AR party. He was appointed a member of the post-war tribunal in Groningen that judged people who during the war had collaborated with the Germans.

Tom returned to his job at the Municipal Council.

Ep was elected President of the Foundation 1940-1945, and Bob and Gerrit helped the Foundation in Groningen looking after the victims that the war had created.

Frank went back to the laundry and Jan reopened the tobacco shop.

Bart restarted his painting business.

Piet left the bakery and joined Heineken's as a sales representative.

Within the circle of friends from Groningen deep friendship and trust in each other had developed through the years. The comrades-in-arms all worked together out of a sense of justice and a sense of idealism, something they never lost. They knew what they were doing. They knew the dangers involved and chose to accept them. There were no regrets afterwards. Strong bonds grew from challenging circumstances. They seldom, if ever, spoke about their role in the Resistance. Those who had been taken prisoner rarely disclosed what had happened to them in captivity. For many who returned from the camps the experience was something that couldn't be passed onto or shared with others. How could anyone who had not met with the horrors understand?

People all over the country were dealing with their problems and trying to cope with the situation. It seemed that nobody was interested in the returning prisoners and ex-fighters. The system allowed some collaborators to escape punishment. They got their jobs back and picked up their lives again as if nothing had happened. Some of those who were responsible for the deaths of as many as twenty people escaped punishment altogether or were sent to prison for just a few months. To come face to face with those who had betrayed their countrymen and caused pain, suffering and death, was a moral dilemma and a mental struggle for many ex-resistance fighters. Some of them found it difficult to return to their previous jobs and to have to work with those who had betrayed them. Many had serious objections to the prevailing form of justice.

When Eric's interrogator at the House of Detention faced trial, the prosecutor asked Eric to write a statement concerning his experiences there. In this document, he described what happened to him:

> ....In the end, the man hit me so hard that I became semiconscious. He had injured my left eye so I could no longer see with it. I was bleeding heavily. The water in the bath was entirely red. I thought my end had come. I had no strength left and allowed myself to sink into the bath. I swallowed the water in the hope that I would be relieved from my suffering.
>
> After having tasted the delights of the House of Detention for seven weeks, as well as the torture at the hands of the monsters that were there, I was sentenced to death and transported to Neuengamme.
>
> It was only after the liberation that I realised who the man in uniform was, who had behaved so brutally. I recognised him from a photo shown to me as being O. Bouman.

I am prepared to swear this on oath. 2 September 1946

It was not until 1948 that the story of the Eric's betrayal came to light. Sister Faber, Eric's courier, had kept extra milk rations for her child. Eric protested. When Lehnhoff's men arrested her for possession of the illegal food coupons she claimed authorship of the anonymous letter which had led to the arrest of Eric and Harry. Her claim was confirmed and she was freed after paying a fine of 1,000 guilders, and promising to deliver Eric's successor, Arie van der Kaaden, to the SD. Sister Faber was arrested a second time and was released after another 2,000 guilders were paid and she promised again to deliver Eric's replacement. However, the SD was unable to capture Arie van der Kaaden and he continued with resistance activities until the end of the war. Council for the prosecution called for a ten year sentence. The judge delayed sentencing for eight days and then the court ruled that the woman had been in a state of diminished responsibility. Sister Faber escaped the ten year sentence.

Eric was the first victim of the interrogator Bouman. The interrogation turned into a frenzied attack, and Kindel removed Bouman from the interrogation team in the House of Detention. Under Lehnhoff in the Scholtenhuis, many resistance fighters subsequently suffered the techniques Bouman had learnt in Germany. He received the death sentence and was executed in 1949. The Executioner of Groningen, Lehnhoff, received the death sentence and was executed. Kindel was never brought to trial. He suffered a brain haemorrhage and died in prison in 1948. Before being questioned Knorr committed suicide in prison. Lighthouse reported to his unit and was given the opportunity to plead his innocence. In 1949 he was freed of all blame. To many in the resistance, this was inexplicable.

A year and a half after the end of the war, there was a mood of disquiet. The Dutch were struggling to cope. Many freedom fighters felt hopelessly trapped in a dead-end existence. The atmosphere was stifling. They had expected something different from the hard-won peace, something that would inspire them. The memory of the behavior of the Russians, and the terrors that they had caused, lay on them like a dense fog. The Red Army was only 250 kilometres from the Dutch border. After the fast moving style of *blitzkrieg* tactics that the Nazis had used in Europe, people knew that this distance meant nothing. As the cold war unfolded, many people feared yet another foreign occupation and the real possibility of another World War.

For those who came from a Reformed Protestant background, the post-war years brought yet another problem. Faith had helped many to withstand the unceasing tension, worry and despair, and the bewildering problems of war. During the dark years of imposed curfews and with little or nothing in the way of recreation, people spent time debating and bickering over religion. There were endless differences on matters of theology and canon law. In 1944, when there were enough other things to worry about, a schism took place in the Reformed Church and the consequences of this rumbled on long after the war.

Many of those who fought in the Resistance were exhausted and unsettled. They had managed to survive by the sheer force of their ideals.

They were disappointed in the new system that was emerging. They had hoped for an environment that would have space for their restlessness. Many queried the direction of the post-war Netherlands and they started to question the country's future.

There was a pressing need for reconstruction but the coffers of the Dutch treasury were empty. Industry was in ruins. Holland was without natural resources such as iron and timber and had lost access to the former Dutch East Indies that in the past had contributed so much to the prosperity of the Netherlands. The country had to tighten its belt.

There were three all pervading problems: food, fuel and housing. As in the rest of Europe, there was a shortage of food. Mother was not happy. Food rationing made it impossible to improve father's health. When mother heard an announcement on the radio encouraging those who had returned from concentration camps to apply for extra food rations from the authorities, she encouraged father to write. The letter he wrote is brief and is held in the archives of the Dutch Institute for War Documentation, NIOD:

> In reference to your radio announcement of today, that ex-prisoners of a German concentration camp would be supplied with extra food ration cards, I am writing to inform you that on 24 January I was arrested by the SD, was imprisoned until 17 March in the House of Detention and from there transported to the concentration camp Neuengamme. I left this camp on 23 April and after some wanderings by foot, then in railway wagons, was loaded onto a ship, on which I cruised the Baltic for 6 days and after many deprivations was liberated on 3 May in Neustadt in Holstein. I left there on 28 May and arrived 1 June in my place of residence in Groningen.

4 July 1945

As soon as the extra coupons were received, I was sent to the horse butcher to buy steaks. These were recommended as being the most nourishing. A real steak, what joy! But only for father, who proclaimed that it was the best steak he had ever eaten. We were a bit jealous of him. In 1946 the meager rations were even further reduced, and rationing continued long after the war ended.

The winters of 1945 and 1946 seemed to be colder than anyone could remember. To keep warm we put layers of newspaper under our jumpers. As there was a serious shortage of fuel many people burned furniture. Homes lost their plinths and architraves, internal doors were hacked into firewood. Two days after Christmas in 1946, our sister Nicky was born, our Christmas present. Premature, and very small, she had to stay in hospital in an incubator for four weeks. When mother brought her home she needed warmth. She was put in a cot in the dining room where the hearth was kept burning day and night. I have no idea where the coal came from. It was probably bought on the black market.

The most urgent of all problems was housing. During the five years of war vast numbers of houses had been destroyed. There was near-complete destruction in the bombardment of Rotterdam. In the west, whole towns and villages were destroyed. In the east, countless homes were lost in the battle of Arnhem. In the north, the liberation of Groningen exacted a heavy toll in houses.

The population of Groningen had swollen by a fifth in the last months of war. The accommodation situation was catastrophic. Often a number of families lived under one roof and newly-weds had no hope of finding a home. Throughout the country there was a feeling of too many people, of claustrophobia.

Economic recovery was a priority, but the price of the recovery seemed unsustainable. Not everyone agreed with government policies. For years counting the cost continued. Taxation was high and access to foreign exchange was virtually impossible. More and more rules suffocated the sense of relief that the liberation brought. Despite the fact that the reconstruction of Holland required all hands on deck, migration was encouraged by the government as a way of easing the strains on housing and the economy.

With the growing fear of a Russian invasion, New World countries appeared to offer promises of a future free from the legacy of war. Places where there was freedom and where peace reigned seemed increasingly attractive. Still filled with the spirit of adventure that had emerged during the war, and with sentiments of dissatisfaction, many Dutch spent the cold winter of 1946 in discussions on migration.

Sketch by Dirk Bolt, 1945
Martinitoren on the Grote Markt.
The ruin in the foreground is what remained of the Scholtenhuis.

Starting a new life

Starting a new life in a new country appealed to the group of comrades from Groningen so much that they decided to explore the feasibility of emigrating together. As they had come to know each other under extreme circumstances, they knew that they could rely on each other completely. They were all from the same cultural background and as Protestants they were all convinced that the Christian belief should be the basis of their association.

The research started seriously. Throughout this phase they sought answers to many questions. The first ones were where they would go and what they would do. The men and women of the group attended lectures by speakers from Canada, Australia, South Africa and South America, Suriname and New Guinea. These lectures were organised by the Dutch Emigration Department so that intending migrants would have some idea of where they might go.

I remember the lectures and the jovial discussions that followed, punctured with Piet's sense of humour. Most of the meetings were held at our house in the Koninginnelaan and it was once more a hub of activity. Crowded in our living room were Gerrit and Ellie, Ep and Klara, Frank and Tjits, Tom and Els, Piet now married to Dineke, Bart and Douwien, Bob and Annie, Jan and Tinie, my father, my mother and I. Fully backing their men folk, wives showed the same commitment and brave support as they did during the resistance.

The provisional choice fell on Australia, although it seemed impossibly far away. Despite the distance, there were good reasons for choosing Australia. In the wake of World War II, Australia actively promoted immigration. The government realised that the country was very vulnerable because of its small population. 'Populate or perish,' the slogan said. Australia needed more people for defence and economic growth. Australia had immigration agreements with the Netherlands and there were provisions for assisted passage for ex-servicemen from Holland, Norway, France, Belgium and Denmark.

Internationally, Australia was in the forefront of countries seeking a better global future. The Australian Minister for External Affairs, Dr Herbert Evatt, had been elected President of the General Assembly of the United Nations in 1948. That same year the country signed up to the Universal Declaration of Human rights. Then, in 1949, when the group was about to decide where to migrate to, two important developments took place in Australia. Firstly, the construction of the Snowy Mountains Hydro Electric Scheme began. For years to come, this mega project would seriously tax the national construction industry. Secondly, the Nationality and Citizenship Act was passed. For those who met the eligibility requirements the act offered Australian citizenship. Previously, immigrants would have become Britain subjects. Australia was in the exciting phase of becoming aware of its own identity.

The Australian government welcomed new arrivals. The small amounts that the country contributed towards their fares were a good investment. The approved immigrants had to be healthy and this was checked by doctors, so that their burden on medical services was minimal. All members of the Groningen group had families, important from the point of view of the immigration authorities. Young adult immigrants were at the peak of their economic performance. Attracting them saved the cost of their education and training. The older children of the group were well on their way in their education. It would not be too long before they too would begin to contribute to the Australian economy.

At this stage, the group came into contact with Mr William Higgie, who was an immigration officer at the Australian Embassy in The Hague. He was very helpful to the group from Groningen and over time became their trusted adviser in many migration matters. They realised they would be leaving behind steady, secure jobs, but they also believed in freedom where hard work would lead to prosperity. The positive response from the Australian side encouraged the group to continue. There were no guarantees. It was indeed a gamble.

A key question was how they could export capital. Access to foreign money was severely restricted. Money for the import of materials, equipment and machines that were so badly needed for reconstruction in the Netherlands was short. A bachelor emigrant was allowed to take out £10, the equivalent of 100 Dutch guilders, and a maximum of one cubic metre in personal goods. Heads of households were allowed to take £35. The members of the group would largely need to pay their travel costs as the Australian contribution towards this was not substantial. Subsidies that were applicable were limited and subject to many restrictions.

The group agreed that they did not want to go to a big city. Tasmania had been mentioned as a destination. It was known that Dutch people had migrated to Burnie, in the northwest of the island. The 'Beautiful Isle', as Higgie called it, was large enough. At two and a half times the size of the Netherlands it was perceived as enormous by the would-be immigrants. At the same time, the population of Tasmania was comparable to that of the province of Groningen. Its system of governance and its institutions would be on a familiar, human scale. The climate looked good, temperate and with many more hours of sunshine than they were used to.

By chance, they met a Dutchman, Jan Boot, who had lived in Tasmania for thirteen years. He initially worked for Philips, but later became involved in finance. Jan was renting a house in Drenthe while completing a PhD degree in textiles. He happened to meet Eric, who was familiar with the practical application of materials in packaging. Jan was about the same age as Eric and they got on well.

Jan gave the group first hand information. He lived south of Hobart, in Taroona, on the road to a place called Kingston, which he suggested might be a suitable location for settlement. Everyone was interested in Jan's suggestions and he endeavoured to answer the many questions put to him. Being Dutch, we knew that Indonesia was a long way away, but Australia was far beyond these tropical islands and Tasmania was altogether on the other side of the world. Java to Hobart, the capital of the Island State, was as far as from Amsterdam to Karachi! The globe was looked at with new respect. We all began to realise that, if we chose to go to Tasmania, it would be unlikely that we would ever see Holland again.

With the attention of the group focussed on 'Down Under', the ball started to roll. There were a series of meetings with a lot of discussions and questions.

'Jan Boot said that there is an urgent need for housing and that there's a shortage of builders.'

'Why not start a building company?' This seemed like a good idea.

'What about tradesmen? Plumbers, carpenters and electricians. We don't have a clue about building!'

'What about calculating and submitting tenders?'

'We definitely need someone who knows about building!'

An idea on what they might do gradually took shape. They realized that they would have to look outside their group for construction skills, knowledge and building experience. More meetings followed. I was at some of them. A broadly painted picture of the future was emerging and the missing parts were being filled in. I remember how the perception of migrating became a clearer and clearer vision.

In March 1950, the research and planning had advanced so far that the time for talking was over and it was time to act. They needed confirmation that their concept was sound. At one meeting it was decided that an advertisement should be placed in the local papers to advertise for the position of a builder contractor to join the group.

Geert
Geert de Haan
1911

In the late 1940s everything in Winsum was in short supply. The local building industry could not move ahead because all available building materials were needed for the national reconstruction effort. Geert, a young local contractor with a carpentry background could not really get started in business. When he saw the advertisement in the local paper that a building contractor was wanted to join a group of people who were migrating, he responded immediately. Life took a new turn for him, his wife Tetje and their four boys; Geert, Douwe, Willem and Anno.

Tom, Bob and Piet had spent many days in Winsum on various missions. They knew the town well. It lies sixteen kilometres north of the city of Groningen and is in the midst of rich agricultural land. It is a picturesque rural town with an old trading centre along the canal, an ancient church, decorative facades, bridges, and two 19th century windmills for grinding grain. Surprisingly, amongst the traditional village style buildings are beautiful houses that were built for retired farmers with clearly sufficient means to engage leading architects of the day. There are architectural masterpieces from the 1920s and 1930s that are so modern that they make much younger buildings look old fashioned. A walk through Winsum is a walk through time.

Things were gathering momentum. Within a week the group had a professional builder in their midst. Brick by brick, the foundation for the venture was laid. A letter was sent to all the families. This was really exciting.

Groningen, 11 March 1950
To the families: B. Folkerts, F. Haan, G. Kuiper, E. J. van der Laan, P. Laning, E. Pinkster, J. Th. Steen, J. de Vries, G. Zuidland

Dear Friends,

Our migration plans for Australia, which up till now only had an investigative character, need to take a concrete form. Right now a definite decision has to be made. To that end, we invite you to a meeting on Thursday 16 March at the home of E. J. van der Laan, Koninginnelaan 19A at 8 pm.

Below is a plan with a rough calculation that you need to study carefully. In general, this needs to be kept to but details can be changed as we discuss it. Each one of you has to decide if he is prepared to continue participating or in case one is not sure about it, then one needs to say so now. The ones remaining will then proceed. The plan is based on the participation of all!

The above nine persons will start a community of interests, for the time being for three years. They promise to assist each other in all ways. A contract will be drawn up in which the manner of capital, method of working and distribution of profits will be specified. Each of the partners will soon have to declare how much money he expects to be able to contribute.

Provisionally, we need to transfer an amount of 1,000 guilders each. This amount needs to be deposited immediately after the community of interests has been founded. After the reduction of the fares that we calculate at 1,350 guilders, the remaining capital will be available to the community of interests. Two people will leave in June, in service of the community of interests, to do the preparatory work to enable the rest to follow. Their task is to find the most suitable place to settle, to establish contacts and lay the foundations for our interests. We think that these two people should have the use of a good second-hand jeep and camping gear in order to cut costs of transport and accommodation. The two families of the scouts will be dependent on the community.

Budget for two families for six months
Dutch guilder 250 per month   f. 3,000
Accommodation costs Australia   f. 1,000
Purchase of jeep and gear   f. 2,500

Unforeseen   f.   250
Total   f. 6,750

This comes to f.750 per family.

The first task is to ensure accommodation for the coming families. Furthermore, a start needs to be made building houses for the market. This can best be achieved if, soon after the departure of the first two, as many tradesmen as possible follow together with young unskilled labourers who can help with the building. They will be employed by the community and will be given certain guarantees like wages and lodging. For the time being they will have to be content with board and keep, as the payment of wages can only happen after the first income has been derived from the houses to be built. The plan to build houses stands and falls with being able to provide funds for it. We will be able to work on this as soon as it is known how much capital we have in total. We will need to investigate what possibilities exist for the transfer of further funds. Perhaps we can to talk with Mr Boot about this.

You may think the above is not positive enough, but the experiences of the scouts will be the deciding factor. It is only possible to solve things locally, not here. Here we can only decide to go or not to go but when we have decided to go we can tackle the business with full force. G. Kuiper, E. J. van der Laan, E. Pinkster and J. Th. Steen have declared to be prepared to act as scouts. Think about whom you would like to go, as we will decide it next Thursday. Also, think about ideas that can help us. If possible we would like to receive these on paper beforehand to enable us to have an orderly discussion.

See you next Thursday.

The above notes are the result of discussions between Kuiper and Steen, and Van der Laan and Steen.

On behalf of you all,

E. J. van der Laan
J. Th. Steen

Geert was invited to the next meeting. It was a significant day when on 16 March 1950, eight of the ten men founded the Tasmania-bound community of interests and signed the Deed of Contract in the following order: Bart, Frank, Eric, Piet, Ep, Tom, Jan and Geert.

The broad plan that had been discussed and adopted over the winter months had suddenly grown into a detailed formal agreement. In the Deed of Contract, the members of the group confirmed that they would support each other during the remaining preparations for the migration, during the journey and after their arrival in the new country. They knew they could trust each other and a solemn promise was made, as if on oath, that their agreement would be implemented in the same spirit of trust that formed the basis of friendship and cooperation during the war years. Although Geert did not have the same background of active participation in the Resistance, his skills, knowledge and experience in the building industry were very important to the other members of the group. He was the only building professional amongst them.

Upon arrival in Australia, the community of interests would found the Australian Building Corporation. The ABC would build houses for its members use and for sale to others, and undertake any other activities that might be profitable. The duration of the ABC would be at least three years, whilst the duration of the community of interests was to be unlimited. The capital of the ABC would be 20,000 Dutch guilders, divided into equal shares that the members would deposit within a month. It was agreed that any passage, subsidies or other funds that members were able to transfer to Australia, would be lent to the company to increase its capital. Loans would return an interest of four percent and be secured by the properties that the ABC acquired. Everyone agreed that after three years a quarter of the loans would be redeemed and a similar amount each year after that. To increase the company's assets, the houses built for the partners and their families would be the property of the company and when the assets were no longer needed these could be sold at cost price to the members on terms agreed by all.

Everyone agreed to work full time for the company for at least three years. They accepted that if the cash resources of the ABC were insufficient to pay their wages, they would be partly paid and the balance credited to their accounts. The needs of the families would be decisive in determining the wages that would be paid in cash. As soon as it was possible, members would be insured for health and occupational risks. In case of death, the company would look after the wellbeing of the bereaved family. In case the family could not provide for its needs the company would help it to become sufficiently independent.

The members would form the management of the company, with the chairman, secretary and treasurer running the day to day business. Two signatories would have the necessary powers and proxies of the company. Any two members could ask the chairman to call a meeting and he would be obliged to do so within seven days. Unanimity was desired for any decision though it was not obligatory. With the exception of amending the agreement, which required at least two-thirds of member votes, a majority was all that was required for its decisions. There were other provisions in the agreement, including rules regarding the financial year, the balance sheet and profit and loss accounts. Profits would be equally shared. It was agreed that the members would determine the amount of profit or would to lend it back to the company if liquidity issues necessitated it. In sum, all foreseeable matters and circumstances were considered and the related actions agreed to. The i's were dotted and the t's were crossed.

The days following the meetings in March were hectic. One of the very first decisions that the group took was that Ep and Eric would be the scouts. Ep resigned from the Foundation 1940-1945. Father handed in his resignation to the NNZ, the company he had worked for for 25 years. The remaining men continued to work. In case the scouting venture was unsuccessful, only two families would be affected. Everyone had to find buyers for their houses and larger assets. Bart, Jan and Frank had to sell their businesses. Exploring how the capital raised could be exported would be the task of those remaining.

    Preparations for the scouts' departure went quickly. Medical examinations and X-rays were compulsory, passport photos were taken and the mountains of paperwork were completed. In less than a month of taking the decision, on 13 April 1950, the application to migrate was submitted. A jeep was bought for transport, and a tent and camping equipment for their accommodation. These would be sent as soon as the scouts found a promising area. Had they not read how sunny it was in Tasmania and that the average temperature was much higher there than it was in the north of the Netherlands? Nobody realised that in the south of Tasmania, winter storms move in straight from Antarctica and that there is no warm Gulf Stream to modify temperatures. After the scouts arrived in June, in the middle of winter, they found very quickly that the clear skies which revealed the amazing sights of the rich southern constellations and the magic southern lights, meant very cold nights.

    The scouts would need help with building the first houses before any other members of the group and their families could come to Tasmania. For this, the group sought young tradesmen, possibly bachelors, who would be willing to rough it in the first phase and to get started without the support of the usual range of domestic comforts.

The group found four young men who were willing to undertake the adventure. Although not members of the ABC, the four were regarded by Eric as an integral part of the undertaking. He also referred to them as his 'brothers-in-arms'. Jetze Schuth and friend Reinder Doedens had both been engaged in illegal activities during the war. After it, they volunteered to join the Dutch army and had served in Indonesia. They learned of the venture from the Sikkema brothers. The youngest and fresh from high school, was

Henk. After his mother died, his father remarried. Henk had just finished high school, received his diploma and was ready for something new.

Henk and I had gone through high school together. We had known each other since we were 13. He was often at our place, knew my father and mother well, and we shared the air of excitement that preceded our emigration.

Henk and I spent hours studying the map of Tasmania and found familiar names: Zeehaen, Maatsuyker Island, Cape Frederick Hendrick, Maria Island and the name Tasman was in many places. The island was discovered by Abel Tasman, who was born in a small village called Lutjegast, near Grootegast, some twenty kilometres west of Groningen. Both villages had been resistance hiding places during the war.

As early as 1606, the Dutchman Willem Janszoon had found the Gulf of Carpentaria and named the land that he discovered New Holland. Ten years later, Dirk Hartog visited the west coast of Australia. Abel Tasman had sailed to Java when he was in his thirties and by 1642 was placed in command of the Heemskerck, a 120 tonne three-mast war yacht, and the 200 tonne Zeehaen. He was given the task of exploring the mysterious southern landmass. His journey was to be one of a long line of Dutch explorations of Australia, putting parts of the continental puzzle together. Tasman's navigator conceived a bold, clear plan. Why not sail from Java all the way to Mauritius, then turn east and use the trade winds to reach the southern limits of the assumed land mass?

In November 1642 they sighted land. Too stormy to go near the shore, they tacked into the wind, sailing southwards then eastwards, and rounded the tip. At Stormy Bay they were blown out to sea again, but a few days later the ships sailed close to shore until they found a good place to anchor - for which the naval council thanked the Almighty God.

It was agreed that they would go ashore where columns of smoke had been seen. The next morning a party of eighteen men set out. It was a cool day, with a stiff, south easterly wind. They collected fresh water and samples of greenery from the strongly scented trees. They saw trees hollowed out by burning, the bases lined with mud, and assumed them to be shelters. After returning to the ships, the council reconvened and it resolved that they would take formal possession of the land.

The ship's carpenter made a monument in the form of a pole with carvings that included the initials and trademark of the Dutch East India Company, VOC. The flag of Prince Frederick Hendrick of the Netherlands was attached to the top. As the party neared a small rocky bay, the breakers were so powerful that they couldn't go nearer without risking the sloop breaking up on the rocks. It was decided that the carpenter would swim through the surf with the pole and the flag and that he would erect the pole near four tall trees that stood near the centre of the bay. Tasman named the island Anthoonij van Diemenslandt in honour of the Governor General of the Dutch East Indies who had sent him on the voyage.

The continent continued in its little known state until in 1770, when James Cook reached the eastern shores of the supposedly rich southern continent. From 1789 onwards Bass, Baudin, Flinders, Peron, Mortimer,

Fourneaux and other explorers would sail the seas south of the Australian mainland. Step by step, they made Van Diemen's Land better known to the world. In 1856, it became a self-governing colony of the British Empire and, in honour of its first European discoverer, Van Diemen's Land was renamed Tasmania.

Once the decision to go to Tasmania had been made, it was exiting to know that a little more than 300 years later we would soon be discovering this island, our new home, for ourselves. It was agreed that Henk and his older brother Wim, who was a mechanic and had useful knowledge and experience, would join Jetze, a carpenter and joiner, and Reinder, a plumber and electrician.

3 May 1945 Memorial, Neustadt. 3 May 1950, Piet and Eric, Toni laying a wreath

The group did not want to lose momentum. The scouts had to be on their way and to save time it was decided that they should fly. Just before father left for Australia, he, mother and Piet travelled to Germany and visited the memorial that had been built in Neustadt. It might have eased their painful memory of the misery of the victims if the disaster in the Baltic Sea helped stop the military advance of Bolshevism and prevent the horror of another war that many so feared.

Eric and Ep's day of departure was set for 28 May 1950. About fifty relatives and other well-wishers came to Amsterdam's Schiphol to wave goodbye. We travelled very early in the morning from Groningen. Some came by car, some came by train.

Schiphol is one of the world's earliest commercial airports and is the base for the world's oldest airline, the Royal Dutch Airlines, KLM. The first civil aircraft lifted off from its tarmac in 1920. Today it is Europe's fourth largest airport with large shopping centres, an art gallery, casino and a train station with direct connections to European capital cities and, to the north, with Groningen. In 1950 it was not like that at all and the journey to the then still small airport was quite an undertaking.

KLM was no stranger to Australia. Before the war, KLM had an eight day service from Amsterdam to Sydney. Although in 1950 KLM was carrying more than 350,000 passengers, the airline had lost planes in 1946, 1947, 1948 and 1949. Flying was not without danger, but the alternative, to travel by boat, would take too much time. For the long distance flight to Australia, Eric and Ep would be flying in a four engine Douglas DC4. Thanks to the range of the DC4 fewer refuelling stops were needed, enabling the scheduled flight time from Amsterdam to Sydney to be reduced to five days. Everybody was anxious to hear from the scouts and how they would fare in Tasmania.

KLM Check-in, Schiphol 1950

Checking in was simple. Eric and Ep registered at the counter for KLM flight 2. Toni and Klara accompanied them. The passengers were weighed and this was jotted down. The baggage and the hand luggage were also weighed and recorded. There was chatting and laughing, camouflaging the rollercoaster feelings and racing heartbeats. Then the time to say farewell was all too quickly upon them. Needless to say, it was very emotional.

KLM Weigh-in, Schiphol 1950

95

Eric and Ep disappeared. Toni and Klara joined the group who would be waving them off. We stood behind a low fence next to the apron where the departing plane was standing. The plane, *Zeeland*, looked impressive in the early morning light. It wore the blue livery of the KLM, with the words 'The Flying Dutchman' proudly written above its oval windows.

The passengers emerged from the terminal one by one and made their way across the tarmac. At the foot of the boarding stairs, they were met by the chief steward. Eric and Ep turned to look at their families and friends. Everyone realised that it was not just Eric and Ep who were leaving. Others too would be departing from the land and the people they loved, and had fought for, and that they might never see again. Spontaneously, in tears, those who would leave joined those who would remain behind in singing the national anthem, each expressing their personal sense of loss.

KLM flight 2, Chief steward with Eric and Ep

Then, as Ep and Eric slowly mounted the steps to the door of the plane the anthem of their home province, which had become so popular during the war, filled the air with gusto and pride:

> From Dollard to the Lauwers Sea
> From Drenthe to the brine,
> There thrives a green and golden land
> That frames a city fine.
> It's Groningen that is the name
> Of *Grönnen's* gem and golden frame.
> It's Groningen that is the name
> Of gem and golden frame.
>
> There roars the sea, there howls the wind
> Along the Wadden's mire,
> But people quietly toil all day
> Around St Martin's spire.
> It's Groningen that is the name
> Of meads and fields that we acclaim.
> It's Groningen that is the name
> The *Grönnen* we acclaim.
>
> There people speak in openness
> Their will is strong as steel.

There means the heart what words do say
Their purpose they reveal.
It's Groningen that is the name
The *Grönnen's* North, from which we came.
It's Groningen that is the name
The North, from which we came.

Moved, they turned once more, smiled, waved and disappeared into the aircraft. There was no turning back.

Grönnens Laid

Gronings Volkslied

Teis/Jager
arr: Jan Wolters

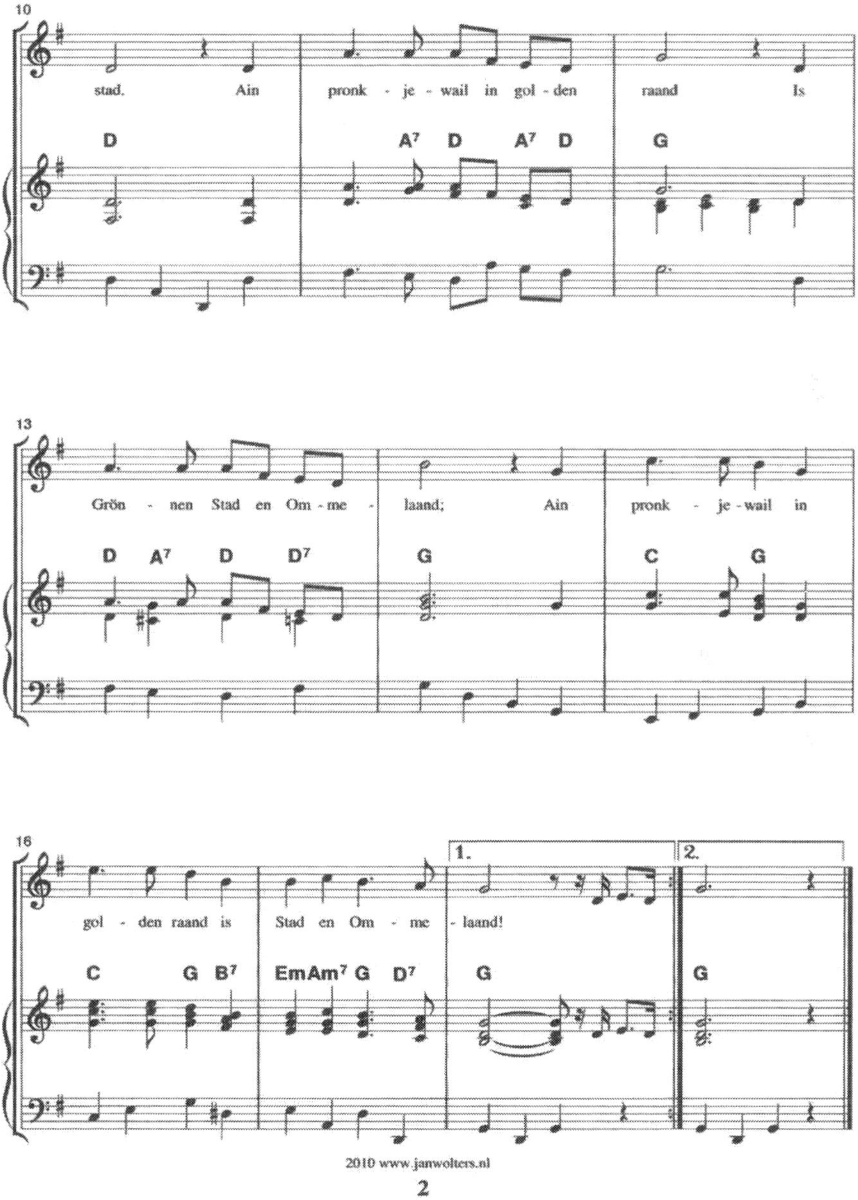

2010 www.janwolters.nl

2

Jan, Tinie, Piet, Dineke, Gerrit, Wicky, Kusha, Ellie, Dirk

Kusha, Ellie, Dirk, Bob, Annie, Toni, Ina, Hidde, Klara, Frank, Tjits

Part Two

Little Groningen

En route to Tasmania

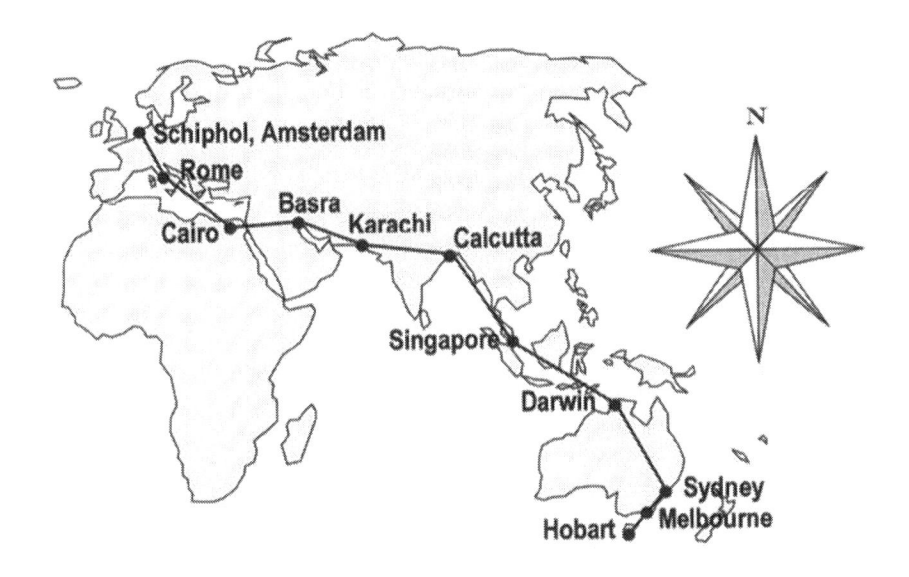

Sydney, 3 June 1950

Dear friends,
When we heard you so proudly singing the *Wilhemus* and then the *Grönnens Laid* we were deeply touched. We sank into our allocated seats on the right hand side of the plane, three seats in a row. We tried several times to wave to you. I have no idea if we were successful.

Soon the warning light 'Fasten seat belts – no smoking' appeared and we took off. It was a wonderful sensation taking off for the first time. Instinctively, you feel somewhat anxious but it doesn't take long to feel safe in this mighty bird that flies higher and higher and makes the earth literally shrink away. We see very little of Holland as it disappears in mist and rain. Friends, Ep tells me to explain the warning light to you. It's in English and says, 'Fasten seat belts – no smoking'. The sign, turned on, means you must fasten your seat belt and you are not allowed to smoke. The light only appears on taking off and landing or when the plane flies through heavy rain and storms, then it can make peculiar frog like leaps.

At first it was very cold. Oh, I must tell you that at taking off and landing you are given a packet of chewing gum to make you swallow. Your ears start ringing because of the change in air pressure and you become more or less deaf. When the plane reaches the cruising height and speed the warning light disappears and you are offered a cigarette with the compliments of KLM. After this first experience of excellent service by the charming and beautiful stewardess, you start to feel at ease and it's time to have a look around.

The seats are adjustable. You can lounge in a comfortable position and there's a cushion so that you won't get any bed sores. You can easily spend hours on end in this chair.

In addition to Captain Haas and a crew of nine, there are seven children, a one year toddler who runs like a lapwing, seven women and forty two men. For the kids, flying is ideal. They are not bothered by anything and are allowed to play in the aisle. You hardly see anything of your neighbours in front or behind you. Seating is in rows of five, three-aisle-two, and so you have most contact with the passengers in the same row. You can walk about if you wish, but Ep and I stay quietly in our seats most of the time. I sit on the right hand side, Ep in the middle and next to him at the window Miss Truus Reimerink from Hilversum who is going to get married after her arrival in Sydney. We have a lot of fun with this sweet bride-to-be. She places herself under our protection, Ep is Pa to her and I am Opa, roles we happily undertake. Across the aisle from me is Mr Vermeulen, who is in the diamond cutting business, and next to him a barkeeper, who is going to try his luck in Sydney. I have forgotten his name. Now you can imagine the scene. We are on our way to Australia!

First stop, Rome. The first we see of the landscape are the French Maritime Alps, a mighty sight but from a height of 3,000 metres, very small. Over Nice we leave solid ground, and flying over Corsica we approach the Italian coast, as flat as a Dutch polder. In the distance we see the domes of St. Peter. The first sensation of landing soon dispels the pleasure of the sight. Landing is a little like getting a flat tyre in a car. We are both figuratively and literally brought down to earth when we arrive at the airport because the runway, consisting of perforated metal steel plates and sand, is such a stark contrast to our beautiful Schiphol. It is hard to imagine this is the gateway to the eternal city of seven hills, the centre of Roman Catholicism.

In the airport restaurant, black-eyed Italians feed us soup followed by some kind of chicken, which tastes very nice and on which I burnt my tongue, on a hot pepper. After exactly one hour we are back in the air, off towards Naples. 'See Naples and die!' they say. We saw it! Contrary to the adage, we didn't die! Vesuvius looks to us like a bit of a molehill. Capri is beautiful, like a mosaic beneath us. With Ep's binoculars we look back towards Europe and joke about seeing as far as St. Michel, but we see nothing. Then, we fly over the foot of the boot of Italy with its impressive mountains and after that the long haul over the Mediterranean. For hours we see nothing but water. Our bird flies this leg stately and serenely.

Here comes Egypt! There's Alexandria. In the light of the setting sun we can see the mighty delta of the Nile and then the lights of Cairo. We land in pitch dark. Passport control is by dark-skinned men in red fezzes. The formalities are quickly over. The restaurant, KLM Oasis, gives us the first impression of the Middle East. Big ceiling fans cool us. We are served by numerous servants in long white frock coats with orange cummerbunds round their waists. Two enormous steaks each, Truus offers us her steak as well, but that would have been a bit too much. It is sultry hot and we are dripping with sweat.

Everything here is very generously built. Servants take us too our sleeping quarters housed in long pavilions in a garden. Truus finds it rather creepy being escorted by an Egyptian stranger with bare feet, nevertheless she risks it. Ep and I are parted for the first and last time. A lovely five minute shower cleans us from sweat but the transpiration soon starts all over again. Afterwards, in the garden of the hotel we are offered a whisky soda, which we did not like and which has to be drowned by a gin and lime, for lack of a Bols genever gin. We are captured by the enchantment of the East. Five of us sit in easy chairs on a small lawn a little apart from the rest of the company. The full moon bathes the garden in soft light. The ghostly white dressed servants move silently around us. It is romantic, it is really beautiful.

Twelve o'clock, to bed. Four o'clock, reveille. Then, on our way to Basra. The Red Sea. We are thinking of the Israelites who went through it to the Promised Land. And then beneath us the desert with nothing but sand and brown hills, sand, sand and sand again. Just before Basra are the first palm trees. Basra, where the Euphrates and the Tigris flow together. It is an impressive idea to fly above the cradle of mankind.

The air in the plane is always cool and sometimes when we fly very high and it rains, too cool. At taking off and on landing the ventilators don't work and you sweat a lot. This is alleviated by great quantities of Boldoot eau de Cologne which the stewardess pours over our handkerchiefs.

In a big restaurant, we try to enjoy a piece of mutton which is obviously from an old sheep. Even Ep with his determination and mighty jaw muscles is unable to demolish it. I have no idea what the rest of the meal consists of, but it is tasty enough. As dessert we are given a large box of dates labelled with the message that they are from The Garden of Eden. The small Persians who serve us are even darker than the Egyptians. They wear the same white garments, but for variety with blue cummerbunds and turbans.

There is just enough time to have a look outside the airfield. We see date palms everywhere. We see women in long colourful robes. Everything is strange and exotic. In the meantime, the temperature soars so close to boiling point that we can't even be bothered about stopping the sweat. And so quickly, we start with the Boldoot again.

Just after leaving Basra we spot an American warship and many tankers in the Persian Gulf. Long pipelines for supplying oil meander over the earth and the mighty rocky mountains under us look grotesque. Until we reach Karachi we gaze over a landscape so desolate that it becomes frightening.

In Karachi the waiters also wear blue cummerbunds. We are well looked after in the large KLM restaurant and are served bean soup with garlic and meat. After dinner it is time for a shower. We sleep four to a bedroom, ours is part of a large arcaded pavilion complex. One of our roommates who arrived earlier complains there is no water. Thanks to some knowledge of taps we make the shower work and we all feel much revived, even though the water is always lukewarm. Here as in other places we are offered free drinks and so we enjoy a few glasses of gin and lime.

After a few hours sleep we are on our way in pitch dark to Calcutta. We can't distinguish much, but India seen from the air seems a gentle landscape of green fields and forests. Early in the afternoon we approach Calcutta, Ghandi's city on the Ganges. Below us we see the mighty river with its countless tributaries and then we land. We are taken by bus to the centre of the city. It is incredibly hot. Near the airport we see beautiful trees with orange blossoms and then we pass through the outskirts with dreadful hovels, swarming with people. Every possible trade is practised here in small shacks with no windows. Thousands of people of all colours and races live here crowded together. This whole trip is a sensation for us and there are no words to describe it. We are just flabbergasted by it all.

The Grand Hotel is an immense palace, situated in the inner city area at a main road that exceeds anything we have ever seen in terms of traffic. People swarm like ants. A glass of beer revives us, then dinner. We are served a creamy spinach soup and an Italian mushroom omelette, which Ep labels 'beard stubbles'. It tastes nice, but it is hard to define. After dinner we go into town with Vermeulen and Truus. By now it has become dark. We don't dare to venture very far. Beggars cling to us like glue. A small boy pulls at Ep's trousers and calls, 'Mamma, mamma', rubbing his stomach. Ep is successful in getting rid of him, but then he starts on me. Whatever I try, I can't lose him. He keeps hanging onto my trousers. At long last I see a policeman and just as I go to ask for help an Indian cuffs the boy's ears and so I am free at last. Hours afterwards, I could still feel that little boy hanging onto me. We have no money, so cannot give anyone anything. Later we are told that if we had given something we would soon have been followed by a herd of beggars.

Our impressions of the city with its seven million people are so many that I am finding it impossible to describe them. The terrible poverty in contrast to the fantastic garments of the Indian women, the thousands sleeping in the streets and amongst all this the grey white cows that walk or lie down amongst them everywhere, even on the footpaths. And, that dreadful stench.

Then again, a few hours sleep cooled by the big ceiling fans. In the middle of the night we leave the hotel travelling through streets with sleeping brown people. A city we will never forget.

From Calcutta to Singapore is a long stretch. We do not go via Bangkok. We fly over the Indian Ocean until we see land at Malacca, around the mid-point of the Malaysian peninsula. Nearing the land mass, the plane starts to heave more and more, and when suddenly the Fasten Seat Belt sign lights appear, we are rather scared. The steward was in the middle of lifting our spirits by serving strongly fortified drinks when there was an enormous jolt. Half of my genever was spilled over my trousers and the rest had to be used as a dry cleaning fluid for Ep's spilled port. Well, after that incident we thought a song to cheer us up might be appropriate and we sang about Holland, 'How beautiful and sweet thou art'. After the song one of the passengers in front of us, a real sour puss, turned around and asked why we should want to migrate if we thought that Holland was so wonderful. Well lady, the answer to that is well entrusted to us.

As we fly over the beautiful landscape of Malaysia, our anxious moments are soon forgotten. Malaysia is a wonderful patchwork of cultivated fields, rice paddies, tin mines and forests. When we land in Singapore we are struck by the enormous difference between here and Calcutta. The airfield is a lovely grass field with clean buildings. The people are friendly, helpful and immaculately dressed in a variety of colours. The city is as clean as Groningen, well planned, new cars, new bicycles, on the whole a picture of prosperity.

In Singapore the passengers are divided into three groups. Our party goes to the Adelphy Hotel, a first class hotel. Just after our arrival at the hotel we meet the Veersemas, a Dutch planter and his wife who treat us to a sightseeing taxi ride and afternoon tea. We had an interesting conversation with them. They live alone on an island in the Riau Archipelago. For shopping and provisions they take their motor boat to Singapore. They had no knowledge at all of the current troubles in Indonesia and they were obviously pleased to meet a couple of boys from Groningen.

Before dinner we take a short walk through the town area. We like this beautiful city. Again, in an enormous dining room, dinner consists of dishes that are unknown to us but we dine well and enjoy it. We thought we were allowed three free drinks in our expensive hotel. It is here, for the first time during our trip that we discover a real Bols. When we come back from our after-dinner walk we want to down our third drink allowance. It comes, but with a bill. They charged us $3.25 for it. This led to an embarrassing encounter with the hotel manager, who in the end lets it go as we have no money. We confess all this to the KLM stewardess who thinks it's rather amusing and decides that the KLM is a good enough customer anyway.

At the early hour of a quarter to two in the morning, we are off again for the big jump to Darwin. Eleven hours of flying in one stretch. Of Indonesia we only see parts of Borneo, Flores and Timor, and for the rest just sea, sea and more sea. Towards the evening, we near Darwin.

Australia! The country of our dreams! Goodness, it took two hours to pass customs. Passports, health papers, documents. Everything was checked. Dates and oranges were confiscated. By now we were very tired. We went by bus to a restaurant to have a meal. The airport restaurant was very primitive.

Darwin, which we had imagined to be a big harbour city, turns out to be a town of only 3,500 inhabitants. Its houses are scattered. There are a couple of good hotels, but being the tourist season there is not enough accommodation for all the KLM passengers and the crew. The captain wanted to fly through the night to Sydney but this plan is abandoned because the flight from Singapore to Darwin had been exhausting due to the headwinds. The result is that seven of the crew and ten passengers have to overnight in the aircraft, whilst the rest of the company is being spread out over three hotels.

But first, let me tell you about dinner. This was done in three sittings. Up until now everything had been KLM organised but from here onwards others took over. The first party has just finished when our party arrives. We feel like we are in the middle of a prairie. The restaurant resembles a wild-west bar, a ramshackle building with shaky tables and service is by a couple of blondes. Lemonade is served with dinner! You know, this kiddies' drink! The meal is some sort of a stew with carrots and a few pieces of cabbage. The meat is fried in sheep fat! It is so unexpected we wonder whether this is customary in Australia. Even the KLM crew are surprised about the standards, but after that things improve. The pineapple for dessert makes up for the rest of it and we end up in a super, open plan hotel with a good bedroom and mosquito nets over the beds.

When we arrive at the hotel there is dancing in a large pavilion, guests are sitting in the garden. It is a lovely sight. Ladies are in wonderful evening gowns, gentlemen in fine white shirts. We join the people in the garden, but for us there are no drinks. Our stewardess takes pity on us and at our instigation after some negotiation with the manager she manages to arrange that we can order whatever we like. For our first time, Australian beer! It certainly quenches our thirst.

It is a beautiful night, so lovely we have never experienced anything like it in Holland. Can you imagine this hotel in the middle of no-where, the garden romantically lit, exotic trees, a gently sighing breeze, shadows cast by the light of the moon and the sound of the sea? At eleven the music stops abruptly, and we have to stand up for 'God save the King'. So odd, after a dance party!

Ep, Truus and I go for a short walk towards the sea, but we don't have any chance to get near the beach because it lies some forty metres below where we are, and it is rather steep. So we sit on the edge of the precipice and let our thoughts wander to Holland, ten thousand miles away. Despite the earlier disappointment with Darwin, we've had an absolutely lovely evening.

The rest of the night, we don't sleep much. I make the mistake of not closing my mosquito net, so I get bitten, although it doesn't bother me all that long. Those who slept on the plane have been up for some time because of the heat and the mosquitoes. Despite the short night, we are all in good spirits. We thought it an act of sacrifice that the captain and his crew after the long flight from Singapore had stayed on the plane. Hats off!

From Darwin to Sydney is a ten hour flight. There is little variation for the first half. We fly over sheep country but there is not a lot to be seen, just brown fields and later hills and forests. Approaching Sydney it looks much nicer. Just before landing we get our last Bols and a delicious cold lunch. It was really remarkable how the stewards and stewardesses could produce all these delicacies from such a tiny kitchen. It was like magic. Excellent coffee and tea, cold lemonade, soup, cold meat, ham, you name it! They have had a full-time job and we admire them.

We express this in a declaration signed by all the passengers. After landing in Sydney it is handed to Captain Haas, who in turn expresses his thanks on behalf of the crew, and with three cheers we take our leave. We have reached Sydney!

Just before customs Truus' fiancé jumped over the fence and embraced his bride-to-be. We were invited to look them up in Manly, close to Sydney.

Customs in Sydney was easy and quick. No problem at all.

Everything is fine. Till our next report, sleep well!

Eric   Ep

Eric and Ep spent a few days in Sydney attending to business matters. They needed to get to the Union Bank to access their funds and to get Australian money. Armed with letters of introduction they visited the bank and various people in order to improve their understanding of the building industry in Australia. Some of the people they called on were clearly surprised that they had chosen to go to Tasmania.

The response in Sydney was disappointing. In general the people they met weren't very enthusiastic about their plan to start their own business and they were given little chance of success. After all it was only possible for a family to bring £35 from the Netherlands and this was entirely insufficient to set up a business. Almost everyone held the view that they start as labourers first. Immigrants could only begin to think about setting up their own business after a number of years. At some of their contacts they were offered work right away, they could start as labourers the next day!

Eric and Ep had other plans and left for Melbourne, arriving on 6 June. They stayed at an immigration reception camp. This was an obligatory first stop for new arrivals. From here immigrants were distributed to places of work, where they would then have to find accommodation. Eric and Ep were exempted from this procedure because Jan Boot had agreed to sponsor them and to guarantee their initial accommodation in Tasmania. However, this would not apply to the next members from their group. Until the Immigration Department agreed that the group itself could guarantee work and provide approved accommodation the next immigrants, including their families, would need to stay in the camp.

They would be able to issue the required employers' certificates themselves, as soon as the building firm had been registered. However, they would only be able to issue housing certificates once the houses were in fact there and met the requirements of the immigration authorities. It was then that Eric and Ep realised that the support Jan Boot had provided was very valuable, and that finding accommodation for the fifty or so people who were to follow would not be an easy task.

After they had sorted out the formalities at the migrant camp and had become clear on the procedures there, they decided to pay a visit to the family of Mr Higgie, the young immigration official at the Australian Embassy in The Hague who had been so helpful to them. Higgie had explained that his family lived in Macleod. He said that this was located in Inner North Melbourne. The address was Thyport, Argyle Street, Macleod. Being in Inner North Melbourne, Eric and Ep imagined it would not be far from the city centre and that they would be able to walk there. It was a beautiful day and they looked forward to seeing something of Melbourne on the way. However, after finding a map they realised that Macloed was but one of very many suburbs of Melbourne.

'We'll drop dead if we have to walk that far.'

'Well Little Man, what now?'

They went to the station and found the Hurstbridge railway line that would take them to Macloed. Some places they passed sounded familiar, like Heidelberg West, or very English, such as Greensborough, which they couldn't pronounce, or very strange but poetic, names like Bundoora and Yallambie. They tried pronouncing them, with limited success. After 17 stops they got off the train. 'G'day mate,' a fellow passenger greeted, touching his wide brimmed hat.

Macloed station appeared to be in the middle of the bush. It had three platforms. There was a small brick building with a waiting room on the first platform and, at the end, a place for stabling horses. Between the second and third platforms was a small shack, where some sprawling bushes with yellow brushes that looked like bottle cleaners poked out. There was little else to be seen. They started their search for Argyle Street. The strong fragrance of eucalyptus was overwhelming. They found the street, then the house. Strangely the house had no number only a name, Thyport. They knocked on the door.

They were welcomed by Higgie's sister and introduced to her parents. After some small talk they were shown into the living room where a table set for afternoon tea. Mrs Higgie asked them if they would like some tea. Well, after their long journey they would love a cup, of course.

Ep tried to hide his surprise as Mrs Higgie poured milk into the cup... and then the tea! Milk in tea? Tea in Holland is usually drunk without milk, except in tea for children.

'What about a bit of cake?' They were offered a huge slice of light sponge, cut in half, filled with strawberry jam and cream and the top dusted with icing sugar. They'd never seen such a lovely home baked cake before. They loved the afternoon tea ceremony, so very different from the traditional *koek* and black tea with a few drops of lemon that was normal in Groningen.

Mr and Mrs Higgie were so glad to hear news of their son. The Hague was so far away... What was Holland like? They were asked all kinds of questions, more than they could answer. When Mrs Higgie curiously asked if her son had found a girl friend in Holland, they could not tell her and on that note they all had a good laugh. It had been an enjoyable time with the Higgie family and they were pleased to have made the visit. They had to get used to the way the Australians spoke English, it was very different to the English they heard spoken after the war.

It wasn't until the two weeks later that they could send a letter to Mr Higgie telling him of their visit to his parents.

Hobart Town

Hobart at the foothills of Mount Wellington with the floating bridge over the River Derwent

Eric and Ep flew to Hobart, Tasmania, on 11 June 1950. Dropping down below the clouds before landing they saw a rugged coastline with long wild beaches and protected sandy coves. At the airport Jan Boot's manager, Gerard Rhee, who was Dutch and his Australian wife Margaret were there to meet them. They invited Eric and Ep to stay at their home in Taroona, which was gratefully accepted.

From the airport they drove over a rough metal road through pine forest then eucalyptus woodland. It was winter but leaves were still on the trees, so odd. At the rise of a hill, their first view of Hobart, Australia's second oldest city. It lay along the estuary spread out over the foothills of the snow capped Mount Wellington behind. The world's longest pontoon bridge, with its elegant upstream curve, connected the two shores of the River Derwent. The car clanked over the bridge sections for nearly a kilometre.

They passed through a large park, the Queen's Domain. Margaret pointed out the Botanical Gardens that were Australia's second oldest and Government House that was considered to be the finest in the British Commonwealth. Tasmania boasted many of Australia's first establishments: the brewery, the army barracks, schools, the public reading room, the public park and the zoo. Australia's first golf course and the oldest surviving bridge were not far away.

They continued down into Sullivans Cove where Hobart Town began life as a British penal settlement less than 150 years ago. After Bass and Flinders' discovery that Van Dieman's Land was an island, the British were eager to prevent the French from forming a colony there. Its isolation proved to be attractive and a colony was started with 178 convicts, 13 settlers who chose to migrate freely and 70 men, women and children sent by the Crown.

111

The Governor granted land to free settlers and exemplary, pardoned ex-convicts and allocated one convict per 100 acres to help clear the land for timber and farming. The terrain was problematic; the bush was dense. Conditions were tough. The incomers were ill prepared for the cold climate and found the hot summer droughts unbearable. There was a lack of tools, supplies were short, and the arrival of supply ships often uncertain. Tempers frayed. Land pressure led to commonplace violence and wars with the indigenous population. Contact with the settlers introduced the Aborigines to diseases to which they had no resistance. Their population declined rapidly and, when there were only a few hundred left, they were relocated to Flinders Island.

By the early 1830s Hobart Town's population was around 7,000 with free settlement double that of convicts. Agriculture, whaling and support industries were booming. The economy was thriving. Hobart Town had grown into a prosperous harbour settlement and a quaint picturesque town. Landowners, who soon after arriving had created a new privileged class, dominated the progressive and class conscious society. Under Governor Franklin Hobart grew. Elegant public and private buildings were constructed. The first Royal Society outside Britain was formed, Australia's first synagogue started. The educational, spiritual and cultural facilities available matched the very best of British society. The worst was matched by the notoriously seedy area around the docks.

Government offices, Hobart

Transportation of convicts lasted for 50 years. In that time 67,000 convicts had been sent to Tasmania. Transports stopped after local lobbying, which progressed to demands for self government. When this was granted, the town became Hobart, the capital of Tasmania. By the turn of the century, after new lobbying, Tasmanian women were granted the right to vote, nearly twenty years before the Netherlands and Britain.

Constitution Dock, Hobart

The site for Hobart had been chosen for its deep water harbour. It dominated the centre of town. A Norwegian whaler, some supply ships and the most beautiful sailing yachts were anchored there. Margaret explained that sailing was a popular sport in Tasmania. The Hobart Regatta, Australia's oldest sporting event, had been held every year since 1838 and a new event, the Sydney to Hobart yacht race was started a few years ago. Yachts left Sydney on Boxing Day, sailing some of the roughest seas known, and arrived in Hobart days later, in time to enjoy the New Year celebrations.

On into the town, they passed grand Georgian sandstone buildings and shops with awnings that extended over the footpaths. There was not a bicycle in sight, not a horse and buggy, not a flag – instead trams, new cars and signboards.

The road rose, dipped and twisted past charming pastel painted wooden houses with verandas and decorative detailing. They drove south, skirting the shore of the Derwent, with its beaches in the middle of town and houses facing the estuary spread out over the hillsides. At last they reached Taroona, the place named by the Aborigines after the molluscs that thrived on the rocky foreshore.

Taroona was best known for its Shot Tower, built to produce lead shot. Molten lead was dropped from a colander at the top. As the lead fell down the shaft it cooled and formed droplets, which hardened on impact with the cold water at the bottom. Past the Shot Tower, the road wound its way around the hills to the small settlement called Kingston. Soon after Hobart was founded, a Scots botanist Robert Brown visited a place where a group of Aborigines collected shellfish, fished and hunted wallaby and kangaroo around the tannin-rich river. The area became known as Brown's River. The first white settlers to live there came from Kingston on remote Norfolk Island in 1808. Norfolk Island was being closed as a penal settlement and settlers were offered land in Tasmania as compensation. Thomas Lucas was a Freemason and ex-marine, and his wife Ann was an ex-convict. Her sentence had been 7 years for stealing a petticoat, apron and baby bonnet.

The Lucas' were granted 530 acres of land at Brown's River. Until the mid 1830s the area remained thinly populated. Dinghies were used to load and off-load goods from ketches that plied the coastline between Hobart and isolated villages to the south. The construction of a private track to Hobart, quickly declared a public road by the Government, improved communications. A regular coach service came into being, over-land postal services were established, a school was started and St Clements Anglican Church was built. Most development was on Lucas land. A large red brick Georgian-style house overlooking Brown's River, the 'Red House' was built by the Lucas' son, Nathaniel.

In 1851 Police Magistrate, Lucas' son, Thomas, renamed Brown's River, Kingston, and after a public petition the settlement was declared a town. With improved connections to Hobart, Kingston became a popular seaside and holiday resort. By the 1880's, shops, lodges and boarding houses had sprung up. The town offered an array of sporting activities; tennis, cricket, football, hunting and fishing, rowing and sailing, swimming, surfing and golf. George Lucas built the Australasian Hotel, and offered accommodation with packaged activities. Kingston Beach now had a jetty and barges and ferries called in daily. Sunday became a special day, ensured by a steady stream of affluent day trippers, many seeking to circumvent the drinking laws. Only travellers, those who had travelled 7 miles or more, could legally drink on a Sunday. The Australasian Hotel by the beach was well placed to cater for the tourists. The 'Red House' became the clubhouse of the Kingston Beach Golf Club and by 1924 Kingston had its own regatta, culminating at night with a bonfire on the beach and fireworks display.

Motoring became popular; the jetty dilapidated and, after WWII, it was pulled down. Gerard explained that significant change had come to the area. Thousands of young men, who came back from the war expecting they would be able to start a family, found there was an acute shortage of houses. Construction had stopped during the war. The Government made Crown land available to soldiers who were certified to be qualified, if they remained resident for 5 years. Rural activity in the area increased: especially timber, orchards and soft fruit, dairy and meat production. Challenges presented; housing was poor and there was a lack of labour. Some ex-soldiers were succeeding. Many walked off the land.

Eric and Ep realised that, irrespective of where they would ultimately settle, they first and foremost needed to cater for their own accommodation. They needed tradesmen who were prepared to work hard and machines and equipment necessary for building. Getting capital out of Holland, in whatever form, was crucial. To achieve that would require significant organisation.

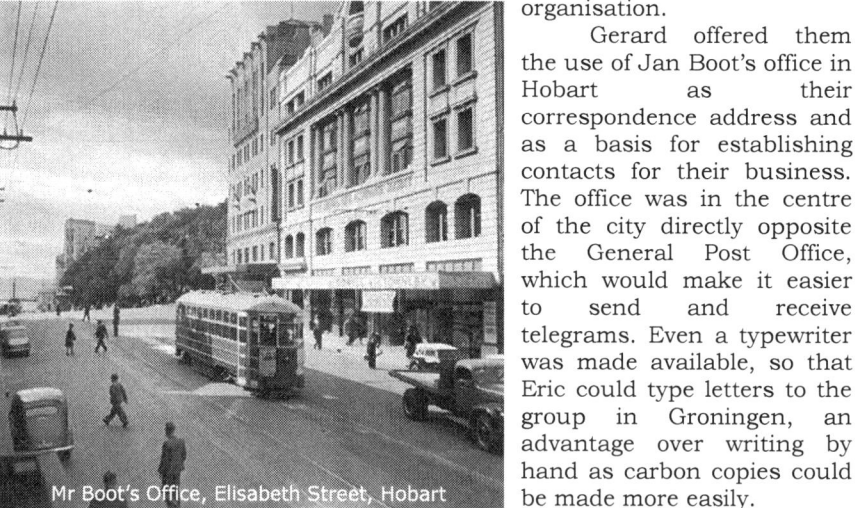

Gerard offered them the use of Jan Boot's office in Hobart as their correspondence address and as a basis for establishing contacts for their business. The office was in the centre of the city directly opposite the General Post Office, which would make it easier to send and receive telegrams. Even a typewriter was made available, so that Eric could type letters to the group in Groningen, an advantage over writing by hand as carbon copies could be made more easily.

Mr Boot's Office, Elisabeth Street, Hobart

Back in Groningen, family and friends waited anxiously for further information from the scouts. The members of the group who stayed behind had lots of things to do: sell assets, source equipment, secure funds, undergo medicals, complete applications and get visas approved. The women especially had to deal with the emotions and the very many large and small complications of emigration. What had they started? They had to suppress doubts. They had to find solutions. Was it actually true that their future was going to be in that faraway island, Tasmania? News came, and they read with excitement.

General Post Office, Hobart

Letters from Tasmania

Hobart 14 June 1950

To the ABC club,
Dear friends,
We've now had time to explore Hobart, so below follows the first letter from Tasmania.

The Docks at Sullivan's Cove, Hobart

There is plenty to be built here and we think it is possible for us to get work in the building industry. It's a great pity that our building expert Geert is not here because we need his experience as a contractor. Ep and I have insufficient technical knowledge. We cabled you this morning saying that, apart from members of our group, we need skilled carpenters as well as machines for woodworking and other joinery and builder's equipment. We also mentioned that the idea of importing prefabricated houses is potentially very important. Some of the smaller woodworking machines that we need could be sent over as part of the household goods as at this end there would be no problem importing these. Have a look to see what can be done in this regard. For a good start we need to be well equipped.

The reason we sent the telegram was that yesterday we found that there are very liberal credit facilities here. We think that we could come to an agreement with a bank. The Commonwealth Bank in Hobart is prepared to give us credit to match our own resources, which includes our Jeep and building equipment at valuation, so these can serve as security. Furthermore, the bank is prepared to help finance the import of prefabs. This credit facility is very important because it helps us to overcome the stumbling block of not being able to take money out of Holland and hence being short of cash.

The way the building industry works here is that when we build on the basis of a contract and the building is completed, we receive 90 per cent of the cost of materials and labour. The balance is not paid until the end of the maintenance period. So for at least six months, and usually for a year, we would have to wait for part of our money. Nevertheless, the conditions are such that we, initially on a small scale, should be able to make a good start. There are practical difficulties, for instance in obtaining roofing materials and even nails. Also, water supply pipes need to be ordered a long time before they are needed. In general there are very long delivery times. We will therefore now discuss the import of prefabs.

As soon as possible, we need quotations for the supply of prefabs that comply with the requirements listed below. The quotations must include insurance and freight CIF Hobart. If it isn't possible to get quotes for shipping to Hobart directly then make it to Melbourne, we can get local prices for shipping the goods from there to here. To get these, we need to know the volume and weight of the consignment.

For prefabrication of houses, we are thinking of the six firms in Holland with whom we have already had preliminary discussions. Their quotations need to be accompanied by complete drawings and specifications. The imperial system of weights and measures is used here. The drawings need to show dimensions in feet and inches and the specification must be in English. There is a lot to do here in the prefabrication sector. Everything depends on whether or not we can perform in terms of quality and price. If these are competitive we will certainly succeed.

We would like to see a number of alternative designs by different manufacturers. The houses need not necessarily be rectangular as people here like the so-called L-shape type of dwelling. A typical house has a living room with a special corner for dining, two or three bedrooms, a large kitchen, so people have the option of eating there, so small kitchens are a disadvantage, and a bathroom in which there is also a toilet. In addition, there is always a *laundry*, which is like a second kitchen just for doing the washing. Affluent people here have a Bendix, which is a big automatic washing machine, but in our prefabs we should offer an ordinary laundry in which there is space for a set of two washing basins, named a laundry *trough*, and a connection for an electrical washing machine. The laundry need not be big and should be next to the kitchen.

In general, people look for minimal hall space because a hall is considered a waste of space. Although in the houses here one usually enters directly from the outside into the living room, there is in most cases a small, enclosed intermediate space for reaching the bedrooms and the bathroom.

Everybody wants an open fire in the living room. The construction of open fireplaces is an art that our bricklayers will need to acquire as we have rarely seen such fireplaces in Holland. We are used to cast iron stoves that are fitted directly to a chimney. Clearly, an open fireplace that is poorly built will cause problems with smoke. Chimneys are built on the outside of the houses. Construction bricks or even rough lumps of natural stone are used. The chimneys don't need to be as tall as in Holland. We have seen chimneys that protrude only slightly above the roof. The Dutch drawings that we had with us did not find approval because, it was said, the chimneys were too tall by far. The fireplaces are not to be included in the prefabs as the drawings only need to show where they are to be added on site.

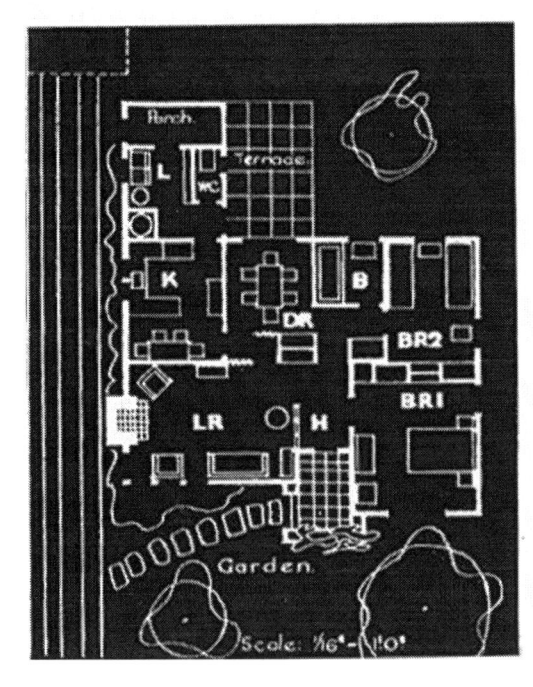

Typical Australian house design from 1950

The roofs on the Dutch drawings were considered far too steep. They enclose too much space under the roof. This is considered a waste of money.

Therefore roofs should have a low pitch, eaves should be narrow and there should be no verandas. People add these themselves if and when they are needed.

We assumed earlier, in view of the warmer climate, that people here would prefer smaller windows but this is not so. They like large windows, especially in the living room. The front door needs to be of a better quality than the internal doors, and most people like a small porch. We will leave this aspect to the imagination of the prefab manufacturers, as they will know how to make the houses look attractive on the outside.

Concerning technical matters, electrical wiring needs to be included in the delivery but without light fittings and light bulbs. There is no need to use electrical conduits, cables alone are used instead. In the kitchen allowance needs to be made for an electric stove including a very large oven, for which a heavier cable is required, and for hot water, for which people have a *boiler*. As these are subject to special regulations they cannot be supplied from Holland. We think that it is best to prepare offers on the basis of houses that are complete with electrical wiring and plumbing but with a separate price that includes bath, WC and stove. We think that it would be a good idea to include the Jeltes extraction fans that we saw in Holland in the bathrooms. This could be something special and increase the attractiveness of our offer.

As I type, Ep is sharpening his brain. Here come the results. In the kitchen we need deep cupboards on both sides of the sink. Directly below the sink are drawers, below these are cupboards with hinged doors. The sink itself is always in polished stainless steel and this must be included in the offer. In the other rooms we need cupboards and wardrobes. The bedrooms here do not have hand basins. In Australia a basin is only provided as part of the bathroom. Like the bath, the basin has hot and cold water. A shower is fitted above the bath. In larger houses there usually is a separate shower cubicle, in which case the shower above the bath can be omitted.

Paint and glass are difficult to get. We will leave it to the expertise of Bart to decide to what extent the prefabs should be pre-painted in the factory. If Bart would like us to take a look at doing the paintwork locally we would need to have specifications and quantities of materials and labour so we can prepare a cost figure. Just like the door and window furniture, roof gutters and drainpipes need to be included in the prefab prices.

We should mention something about ants. In Holland we had heard that white ants are a real problem in Australia. We now understand that this is the case on the so-called *Mainland* but that this is different in Tasmania because of its cooler climate. There are apparently no white ants in Hobart and woodworm is not considered a serious problem. Yesterday we saw a house that was under construction by an English builder and he was using ordinary pine for the external walls. We asked if there was not a danger of woodworm but he did not think so and also said that, in any case, there are treatments for reducing the danger. We hope that the information will help you in obtaining the necessary quotations. Geert, could you please calculate the man-hours required for erecting the prefabs, except for the concrete footings and the masonry parts of the buildings? We can then calculate at what order of cost the houses can be put on the market.

Concerning permission for export of the prefabs, the Ministry of Economic Affairs in The Hague should be interested in developing export to Australia. At the ministry, Mr Terlouw recently received a visiting Australian mission that was looking at the building industry overseas. He accompanied them on a tour of the Netherlands. No doubt he would support the granting of the necessary permits for export.

Before we tackle this we need to have the quotations. These would enable us to start working on the export permits from this end. For the cost of freight you could enquire at the Holland-Australia Line. Even if you are able to organise that we get enough tradesmen and machines here to start our own workshop, we would still gain from the import of prefabs. It would provide us with the experience we need for making our own. As for this we need a mix of skilled and unskilled people, so there is also a need for those of us who are not yet skilled craftsmen. In your view, what would the proportion of carpenters, painters, bricklayers etc. and unschooled personnel need to be?

As we will soon have our own Tasmania-registered business, we will be authorised to issue our own employment certificates. We have discussed this with the immigration officer in Hobart, Mr Mellor, and he has promised us his complete support.

The Commonwealth Bank is prepared to lend us money to enable us to buy land for a so-called *subdivision*, on which houses can be built. Such land needs to be prepared by removing the natural shrubs and trees, which is called *clearing the bush*. You should see the kind of wilderness we are talking about! Where there is insufficient access, roads need to be constructed. The bank is looking at the extent to which they could provide us with credit that would be covered by the value of our assets in Holland. We discussed this previously with the Union Bank in Sydney but that did not get us very far. Now Mr Jim McCusker of the Commonwealth Bank in Hobart, to whom we have explained our position, is having a look at what his bank might be able do. In the meantime, we would need to know what the position is with your various businesses in Holland and concerning such assets as might be available over there. In general, it can be said that we have developed good relations with the best people in Hobart, so please support us by sending the requested information as soon as possible.

Ep and I are both in good form, although Ep's nose drips like a tap, he yearns for a genuine borreltje, and so do I. Perhaps we should have some samples for local testing sent over by one of the distilleries in Schiedam, because only drinking Australian tea gets a little boring! Despite our efforts, we have not yet succeeded in finding accommodation. Today we tried to see a Tasmanian architect for drawing some house plans for us but that has to wait until next week because tomorrow we go north.

We look forward to seeing more of Tasmania. Gerard Rhee will take us to Launceston. This will save a few pounds on the cost of the trip. In Launceston we will take the bus to the northwest coast and Burnie. We hope to meet a Dutch carpenter there. Who knows, he may be willing to work for us. In Burnie we will go to the Union Bank that, as you know, is our initial correspondence address. We very much hope to find a sign of life there from all you people. However, from now onward we would like you to use the address of Jan Boot's office, as our temporary headquarters are now in Elizabeth Street, Hobart. We will be back there at the start of next week, when you will hear from us again.

Many greetings to all our friends, especially our little wives, who you no doubt will inform about this letter. So long, and the very best.

17 June 1950

Dear brothers-in-arms,
Here follows the tale of the two young men who went to Burnie. They woke at five in the morning on Thursday 15 June.

It was bitterly cold. We had planned to leave at six but due to all sorts of circumstances were delayed. After traditional ham and eggs for breakfast our host started the car. At that time it was still dark. In June it is winter, how strange. At this time of the year dawn is around eight and by five it is dark again.

To conserve as much heat as possible the three of us sat on the front seat of the car. The winter mornings here are icy. This is aggravated by the fact that cars in this country don't have indicators. To change direction the driver puts his hand out of the window and indicates that he is about to turn by waving. This is better than an indicator, at least according to local opinion. Of course, we agree, even though it costs whole of tubes of aspirin because of the consequential colds. You now understand why we squeezed into the front seat but that can be taken with a grain of salt because in Gerard's big new Ford there is room aplenty for three. However, the writer of this had bad chest troubles this morning and Ep, in the declining stages of a cold, was coughing only slightly less. The first kilometres I sat on the right hand side and nearly died of the cold. Then, Ep with his self sacrificing spirit kindly offered to swap places. We did, but it didn't help much. It was still freezing. Amazingly, Gerard Rhee seemed to be immune to the cold.

From Hobart to Launceston the road climbs and then drops continuously. Especially as the road goes over the ridge of a hill it twists and turns in all directions to reach the other side, a thousand bends like one. Sometimes you're so high that your ears remind you that you're passing through thinner air. The Tasmanian landscape is quite different from the landscape that we are familiar with. It has an undeniable charm, although the yellow-brown colour of the steppe-like grazing lands seen in the hills cannot yet efface my memories of the fresh green meadows of Holland. At the same time it is fair to say that we should not have too many comments on colours because the frost had covered everything with layer of white! Despite the cold and the sight of landscapes that we have to get used to, it was a beautiful trip and as we approached Launceston the sun broke through.

Launceston lies in the valley of the river Tamar. The city is built from the Tamar up into the surrounding hills. Since it lies in a hollow it is often covered in mist until late in the morning. As we came down from the hills we saw a white blanket that covered the Tamar and the adjacent parts of the city. In Launceston we entered the local office of Gerard's organisation absolutely chilled to the bone. Fortunately the ladies there ensured some warmth was restored to our frozen limbs with the welcome help of a cup of hot coffee.

Our first visit was to a baker from Groningen who had exhibited at the bakers' exhibition there. He liked it in Launceston. When we arrived he was in the process of baking apple dumplings, something that is not available here and for which he had found a ready market. He intended to start making Dutch biscuits with a machine he had ordered and which he expected to arrive anytime.

We went back to meet Mr Broek, who was in charge of the Launceston office of Mr Boot's company. Margo, the secretary, produced more coffee and we talked to Broek. He is an old colonial who has lived in the Netherlands' Antilles. He reads the Dutch weekly *Elsevier* regularly and will send it to us after he has read it. Coffee was served with little hot meat pies, a pastry that is popular here. It has a finely baked crust with some sort of filling which is not identifiable but tastes rather peppery. After lunch we just had time to visit a timber merchant I had written to for information about timber prices. When he heard my name he suddenly remembered that he was almost ready with his reply but that he was still waiting for some prices. We suggested that he might as yet write to us in Hobart but I don't expect that we will ever hear from him again.

At a quarter to two the bus left for Burnie. We would shortly see this land of promise, about which we had heard so much, with our own eyes. We were anxious to see how this would compare with the south. The bus went via Deloraine, Devonport, Ulverstone and Penguin. As we left Launceston the landscape became friendlier and appeared greener and more fertile. To our left, the mountain tops rose high into the sky, an imposing sight that never fails to impress our Dutch eyes. The soil here is red, something we find very strange. As a consequence the sheep look as if they are dyed. The cattle also differ from the black and white Friesians we know. The cows are Jerseys. They are smaller and thinner but good milkers. We were told they produce milk with as much as five per cent fat, but in lesser quantities. The quality of the milk that is served is good and the taste is excellent. After Devonport the road follows the line of the shore. To the right is Bass Strait, a sea that seems to disappear into infinity. The coastal strip was actually quite narrow in places. Everything was rocks. On our left the hills rose sharply, at times almost directly out of the sea. There are no waves to speak of. Every now and then we saw a small beach. Nature is beautiful here, and very impressive.

Just before Burnie is a big pulp and paper factory that seems to dominate all of Burnie. You could almost say that the factory was Burnie. At six o'clock we arrived at the place of our dreams, the little town and this part of the earth already covered in a blanket of darkness. In Hobart we had pre-booked our overnight accommodation. We had said that it shouldn't cost a great deal, so we were booked into a so-called *guesthouse*. We had to pay a pound in advance. The slip of paper we had been given said, '167 Main Street, Upper Burnie'. We assumed the address would be in the centre of town. As we got out of the bus we almost stumbled on the toes of a very large but friendly gentleman. When we asked for directions he suggested we take a bus, as the place was about two miles away, uphill and a bit too far too walk. The bus would arrive shortly. It did and our ample friend gave the bus driver directions as to where to deliver us. As the road became steeper and steeper the bus developed breathing problems and went slower and slower up the hill. I was so glad we were not walking and bless Fatty, because if you had to walk this climb you would need different legs to mine.

The driver had problems finding the place. He had to leave the bus twice to ask for the family French, first in a shop and then at a garage. When we finally got as far as the end of the bus route it turned out that the place was right there. It was pitch black by now and you couldn't see a hand in front of your face. There was only a bit of light from the stars and no matter how hard we tried we couldn't find the Great Bear, so we did not know where north was.

We pushed open a little gate and found our way down a concrete path. We saw light, pushed open a door that had a key in it, walked down a corridor, went through another door that stood ajar and there we were... in the kitchen. Australian sounds greeted us and after some guesses we surmised that the lady was asking us if we still needed to eat. 'Yes, indeed!' Ah, but that was not possible, she only catered for *bed and breakfast*. So where could we eat? In Burnie of course! Good grief! Ep ran back through the corridor and along the concrete path to see if the bus was still there and yes, it was. The driver would wait whilst Ep found his way back to collect me. A few minutes later we were back on the bus and on our way to Burnie.

After some searching we ended up in the Bay View Hotel where, in a rather stately dining room, many distinguished people were dining in grand style, soon to be humbly followed by us. The food was good. And now I must refer to another matter. I do so to prevent you from being caught out, as Ep and I, innocent as we are, have been. Not only was the food good in the Bay View but this place also gave us an altogether different reason for satisfaction, namely that we could find 'it'. You should know that in Australia this is not always an easy task as they are far and wide in between. There are numerous milk bars and cafés and although these sell drinks that quench your thirst they give no attention to corresponding needs. You sit yourself down to drink something and to use the convenience you start looking around... but bad luck! So now you have the advantage of having been warned!

After dinner we asked ourselves what we should do next in this dark place. We looked in our notebook and found that we had intended to meet one of the carpenters employed by somebody called Jennings, but where was Jennings? After a while we saw a sign that said Police and decided to ask there. We went into the building and arrived on the first floor of what turned out to be the town hall. The lights were on but there was nobody there. Eventually we located an officer and he directed us. We had to be in Upper Burnie, so the long haul back up the hill started again. Each time we reached the top of a crest I thought we would be there but Ep would just smile and, of course, he would be right. After asking three times we finally found the entrance to the Jennings works. There, everything was in darkness. We followed a path and came to a barbed wire fence. Risking our lives by scaling it, we came to a big store full with timber and workshop equipment but not a person in sight.

We were just considering going back when we saw some people in the distance. We went to them and asked where the Jennings camp was. We were looking for a certain Peter Onrust. Well, as it happened they knew Peter and could take us there. Armed with torches they guided us downhill and lo and behold, there was a camp. There were some fifty huts, mostly for two persons each although they were very small. Peter did in fact turn out to be the Mr Onrust we were looking for. When we arrived at his hut it was about time, I could no longer put one foot in front of the other. My chest was hurting and my back had given in. Fortunately I could rest on his bed, so I was soon all right again. Peter told us a great deal about the Jennings organisation and the way in which they ran their business. They were building for the Agricultural Bank, which supplied the material and paid the wages of the workers who were supplied by Jennings. Jennings also supplied the technical resources and management. For their services they were paid ten per cent of the turnover. Well, we could do that too, if only we had our men!

We talked to Peter about the materials that were used and the work conditions. All timber used is *hardwood* obtained from the gum trees. It is difficult to work with. It is also very heavy, which leads to a slower pace of work and less production. Skilled persons earn £10.15.0 per week and receive a living allowance of £2.12.6. For boarding they pay £2 to the camp. Jennings is Melbourne based, so workers receive a three monthly allowance for travel to Melbourne. In fact few workers ever go there, so for most of them that's sheer profit in their pocket. All-in all, they end up with a saving of about £10 a week. For bachelors, and most of them are, that's good. Our Mr Onrust is very adaptable and has a way with words. It doesn't seem to matter that he's not a qualified carpenter. He has managed to gain a position as interpreter between the Australians and Polish and Czech workers. No wonder they don't want to do without him.

At half past ten we returned from our outing and were back at Mother French's guesthouse. She kindly gave us a drink of warm milk into which I mixed three aspirins. In the middle of the night this caused me great concern and I had no option but to open the window and offer the contents of my stomach to the flowers.

Breakfast the following morning was not bad at all. The highlights were cornflakes, ham and eggs, toast and, of course, tea. After such a good start we happily walked in the early morning sunshine down and up and down the hills again to Terrylane-Montello, a suburb of Burnie. You should know about the suburbs in this country. Every self-respecting town is surrounded by suburb after suburb, suburbs in front, suburbs behind and suburbs at the sides, often with weird names and additions to names.

We were on our way to see what Jennings was doing there. We saw how new roads were made with bulldozers and how houses were shooting up like mushrooms along those roads. As the site was quite steep, the parts between the natural ground and the floor levels of the houses varied a lot but were always built up in masonry placed on stepped concrete strip footings. The external timber walls are placed above the lower masonry walls. Masonry piers support floor bearers, joist and internal walls. The walls are erected as large, pre-assembled timber fames that are load bearing and support the roof construction. The roofs are covered in corrugated galvanised iron. The external cladding is in so called *weatherboards*, like the framing, all in hardwood. The construction is dead simple. A tradesman would soon know how to do it, for Geert a piece of cake. As far as we can see he would be able to pick it up in a day.

Everything is put together rather roughly. Perhaps that could be improved. People complain about how difficult it is to work with the green hardwood. It is apparently quite an art to nailing it properly. The timber warps in all directions. After the frames have stood for a few days and before the cladding is put on all kinds of corrections are made, for which axes are used. With this kind of construction a good axe is hailed as a most useful tool. For the masonry large cement blocks, or so called *concrete blocks*, that are about five to six times the size of ordinary bricks are used. As a wall can be built rather rapidly this way the blocks might not be a bad idea. By the way, we heard from our solicitor, Fred Mitchell, that he has invented a new kind of machine for making concrete blocks. We will have a further talk about it next time we see him. How on earth is it possible that a solicitor would get involved in something like this, it beggars belief! This is exactly how Australia is. Anybody can do anything. Today a farmer, tomorrow a carpenter!

At the Jennings site we also talked to a Dutchman called Westra who was a resistance fighter in Friesland during the war. At first we thought that we might try to interest him in our venture but in the course of the day things worked out rather differently.

From the Jennings site we went to the centre of Burnie to go to the Union Bank to pick up the mail. To our surprise there was no mail for us at all! We had so longed to get a sign of life from the motherland but we hid our disappointment bravely. As usual, the manager of the bank received us well and was very friendly. We told him our story. He would, of course, provide us with every kind of assistance but for a start we would need capital. That was difficult. In Burnie there would be enough work, Burnie would be better than Devonport. He did not personally know many suppliers of building materials but he could introduce us to a timber merchant. No, he had heard nothing from Sydney about the possibility of credit on the basis of securities that we would provide. We thought it better to not try and develop this very much further, clearly Jim McCusker, of the Commonwealth Bank in Hobart, would be more able to assist us.

From there we went to the shipping agent Stephens and impressed on the people there that we were in a hurry to get our Jeep. They would let us know as soon as possible. Actually, from all quarters we heard sombre talk about having things shipped from Melbourne. This might take up to eight weeks! We will try everything we can to improve this but cannot be too hopeful. Australians rarely have a sense of urgency.

Near Burnie we had a quick look at the foreshore and then went off to see if we could meet a retired captain of the Dutch merchant navy, who apparently is a fountain of local knowledge. It turned out that he was on holidays in Adelaide. A great pity, we would have liked to talk to the old sea dog. However, at his place we met a certain De Bruin, a young man of 36 who has already lived here for two years. He told us a lot of stories, which we were not sure what to make of. Initially, he had been a farmer and made good money that way but he is now managing a dairy factory. He took us through the plant, which is a modern establishment. He had bought a large piece of land, as much as twenty acres, complete with a house, for £200 per acre. The house had been valued at £2,000, therefore the land cost him only £100 per acre. Although it was beginning to get dark he insisted on showing us the site. He drove like a maniac, at times he reached 75 miles per hour, but we survived. It was a beautiful piece of land. He calculated that it had space for sixty-six homes and wanted to start building with Westra and a Dutch building contractor, who presently was employed by Jennings as a foreman. We met him and found him a bit tedious but he certainly had brains.

Finally, we ended up having to listen to endless gossip about other people from Holland, which was not to our taste. We were told again, and in no uncertain terms, that as newcomers it would be impossible to get started, if only because of the lack of business contacts. Before you could even think about starting on your own, you would have to work with somebody like Jennings. We did not comment but kept our thoughts to ourselves. We'll see. At De Bruin's place we were invited to join them for dinner, which was delicious. His wife is an excellent cook. She is very refined and civilised, something that could not be said of some of the men we had met. Some of them swore like troopers.

By the time Ep and I were in our beds we had both come to the conclusion that Burnie was not the place for us. Hobart appears to offer many more possibilities. The people there are ready to help and some of the people we have met have influence. So we decided the next day to go back to Hobart and we have now returned to the hospitable family Rhee.

Ep and I still have a cold, so for the journey back to Hobart we thought it wise to prepare by putting on our newly purchased pyjamas underneath our clothes, in the hope that this would help us to keep warm. As the colourful pyjamas made us look the part we performed an Apache dance yesterday in front of the landlady's mirror.

I now close in the hope to have a chance tomorrow to write about things that need to be done in Holland. Our work here is first of all to find our own accommodation and then to find accommodation for you people. So there's plenty of work to be done, but there's enough courage left!

Good night and sleep well.

18 June 1950

I could no longer put pen to paper yesterday but here follows the summing up of our trip to Burnie. Incidentally, you shouldn't think lightly about distances here, they are considerable.

We started the bus journey at 9.30 am and did not arrive in Hobart until 6 pm! It takes a whole day, and even longer if you take the train. Travel is not cheap. The bus tickets cost us £4.8.6. This means that, while still in Holland, you should try and pay as much as possible for all travel because you can still pay in Dutch guilders. The people at the travel desk in Holland tend to belittle the cost of local travel and leave it up to you to pay for it here. However, for the group as a whole this amounts to a lot of money, so please insist on it being included in the pre-paid travel. The best thing is to travel from Melbourne to Hobart by air. It costs £6, but in the end it is cheaper as you save on accommodation and other costs. So I suggest you travel by air and pay for it with guilders, and in advance. The Dutch finance authorities accept this form of money export, so please do not forget!

We heard in Burnie that big removal cases take much longer than smaller ones. The reason is that there is a shortage of bigger lifting equipment and there are problems with local transport. As cases of 10-15m^3 give problems it is better to have cases made that are not bigger than 5m^3. These are easier to transport and will get here long before the others. There could be exceptions. For instance you may need larger crates in order to be able to pack machines with your household goods.

It is essential to bring sturdy tools and implements such a spades and shovels, we will need strong tools for clearing the ground. We also heard that nails are imported from Holland. So rather than pay for Dutch nails here it is better to bring them. I think there is factory in Belmond. So please fill all the nooks and crannies in your cases with nails! The concrete blocks that are used here measure about 4 x 16 x 6 inches. Do you have any idea how these are made?

Now that we have spoken to more people we found that some paints are not of the desired quality and some paints, especially matte paint, are not to be had for love or money. Filler is altogether unavailable, one does not even know of its existence. Putty is used instead but that does not look very suitable to us. Also, linseed oil is scarce and hard to get. Concerning electrical wiring, a correction of what I wrote earlier. Different kinds of cables are not only used for stoves and for other fittings but also for light fittings, two core, and for power points, three core. The timber flooring of the prefabs needs to be good because floors here are of excellent quality. However, it is currently very difficult to obtain flooring boards that have been sufficiently dried. As long as this is the case, import is an attractive option.

We will not yet attempt to describe the land and its people to you. So far we have not yet had enough chance to really get to know Australians. We have been too busy talking to all those Dutchmen. However, it has become clear to us that everything is, of course, different and that in many areas we will need to adapt to the new environment. This is a further reason why we should all be here soon, so we can adapt at the same pace together. At the same time it will be desirable to retain some aspects of our national character and culture and that will certainly be possible. I will write more about this later.

This morning we went to the Presbyterian Church in Taroona, which is the suburb of Hobart where Gerard and Margaret live. The service was held in a small hall, with about twenty people there. To join in singing with the congregation is easy because we know most of the tunes. One aspect of the service was interesting because it was new to us. The minister first spoke specifically to the children, a very good idea. His sermon was simple but orthodox. We both enjoyed it. One of these days we will visit the minister.

Tomorrow we will start our search for accommodation. It will not be easy as there is a crying need everywhere for living quarters. We will need a bit of luck to find anything at all.

Dear people, the very best and warm greetings.

19 June 1950

This morning we received Tom's letter with great joy. We are so pleased that your thoughts run parallel to ours. Since the letter was written we have already answered some of your questions in our previous letters. We will deal with the rest here.

As we have not yet found accommodation we have written to Mr Higgie that we have no objection if our families would initially stay in the immigrants' camp in Melbourne. This means that things can keep moving. Enclosed is a copy of the letter. On the same note, we expect that we will find accommodation in the meantime and that there will be no need to make use of the temporary facilities at the camp. Therefore please book and pay in Holland for flight connections from Melbourne to Hobart directly after arrival in Melbourne. Concerning the departure of Geert, Bart, Jetze Schuth and Reinder Doedens, we think it is much better if instead of coming by sea with the Sibajak, that they take the plane. It will cost more but we will earn that back in time. We need to be able to make a start here as soon as possible and without them there is not very much that we can do.

We agree of course to the purchase of a concrete mixer and to getting it here as soon as possible. This is entirely in our line of thinking. Bart too should bring whatever he needs in the way painting equipment. Everything will be useful here. We do not know details about the prices of the various items but that is not important at this stage. Importing equipment means for us that we are importing capital. If this implies that the goods work out to be a bit more expensive we'll happily take that on board. Whatever we can pay in guilders and not in pounds can be regarded as profit. Perhaps a weird logic but that's how it works out under the circumstances.

We are pleased that you are looking into the matter of prefabs. We had almost forgotten about the firm in Enschede but if something can be achieved there, go ahead! You have the basic requirements for the houses so you should be able to get quotations. We will try and arrange the financing from this end as soon as we have sufficient information. When looking for tradesmen, there is no need to insist on very high levels of traditional trade competence as many things here are different anyway and require knowledge, skills and experience that can only be acquired locally. What is important is that the men are willing to learn and to work and that they agree to support us in building up the organisation. On the immigration application forms please state clearly that those who are coming are carpenters, bricklayers or other basic tradesmen, as people who work with their hands are needed and therefore readily accepted. There is no need to take much notice of the high level diplomas etc. required by Dutch emigration officials. They are good at paper bureaucracy but not at understanding situations that prevail in this part of the world. Nevertheless, take care that they remain your best friends because, after all, you do need them for your papers.

Please use the time you still have in the Netherlands as well as possible for the purposes of our goals here. Don't worry about the expenses. In our case, costs come before profits. We look forward to signs of life from Holland. It's always good to hear from you, it strengthens our task.

Good luck dear boys, and see you soon.

```
19 June 1950
Mr W.A. Higgie,
Immigration Officer, Australian Embassy,
Stalpertstraat 66, The Hague, Holland
```

To whom it may concern

The undersigned E.J. van der Laan and E. Pinkster hereby certify that they agree that their wives T.A. van der Laan-Bandholz and K. Pinkster-Jager and their children after their arrival in Australia will make use of the reception centre facilities for migrants offered by the Australian Government.

Dear Mr Higgie,

As we've had a very busy time after our arrival in Hobart, we've had no opportunity to write to you earlier. We had a very interesting trip by plane to Sydney. The KLM service was excellent and we were very pleased to have made the journey to your country in this way.

We spent some days in Sydney and on the 6th of June we arrived in Melbourne. On the 9th of June we went to Macleod to visit your family and they gave us a really warm welcome. Your father, mother and sister were very pleased to see us and accepted your greetings with great pleasure. They asked us many things about you, more than we could tell and your mother especially was very interested to know whether you had a girlfriend. Unfortunately we could not inform her about that. In any case, we had a wonderful time with them.

We trust you are able to get passage for our families on the Sibajak in July, so that we'll have the pleasure of having them here towards the end of August. It will be necessary for them to fly from Melbourne to Hobart and we'd appreciate it if you would also give this your attention. We thank you very much for acting the intermediary in these matters. We were most grateful that we could make use of the reception centre facilities in Melbourne and herewith enclose a separate letter confirming this. We trust that by the time our families arrive we will be in a position to organise the necessary accommodation ourselves.

Furthermore, we can tell you that we've already made many friends who are prepared to assist us in any way on this side of the globe. Several authorities have welcomed us here and we can rely on good support for furthering our building activities. The most important objective is to get all our friends here as soon as possible, especially the skilled labourers De Haan, Folkerts, Schuth and Doedens. If you can assist in their early departure at all, this would be highly appreciated not only by us but also by the authorities here. A quick start of our business will be to the benefit of all.

With most kind regards, we are,
Very truly yours,
Van der Laan, Pinkster

Thursday, 22 June 1950

Dear friends,
We received a letter from Piet. It was a great pleasure to read it in our language of the North. Speaking of languages, before you leave Holland, all of you will need to learn English as much as you can possibly squeeze into the time that is still available. If you speak English you have very many advantages. We notice it every day.

There is not enough time this morning to write a complete report on all that has happened since our last letter. The reason is that we're in the process of buying a *block*, a piece of land, for £200, on which we can build two houses. This morning we will be looking into the implications of this. When we build on the block it will not be for sale at this stage but for our own use.

View of Mount Wellington from the block at Hutchins Street

This is the only way in which we can get the necessary accommodation. Yesterday we opened an account with the Commonwealth Bank in Hobart. For the time being the account had to be in our own names because the Australian Building Corporation is not yet officially registered but that is being attended to.

Concerning the prefabs, we are gradually becoming more familiar with the local building regulations. As far as the toilet is concerned, we referred previously to this as being in the bathroom. That is indeed often the case but this alone does not meet the minimum requirements of the regulations. Such a bathroom toilet is an extra. There is a minimum requirement for a toilet in a separate space measuring at least 3 by 5 feet. This is often placed near the backdoor and laundry, which has the advantage that the toilet can be readily accessed from the garden. The regulations also require that a bedroom must have an area of at least 80 square feet, at least 8 by 10 feet.

We have been told that, in general, the cost of the materials of a house is 37½ per cent of the cost of building, and the labour cost 62½ per cent. That's good for us because it suggests that that there is money to be made with a good building team. The architect who we intend to ask to design the houses for us confirmed this. He is of the opinion that the big problem in building is always how to find the labour and that, although there is often a shortage, the supply of materials is the lesser problem. His name is David Hartley Wilson. He was also the architect of the houses of Jan Boot and the Rhee family. Gerard is of the opinion that he is one of the best in Hobart. Wilson gives the impression of being energetic and a man you can get on with. We have explained our plans to him and said that if we have a complete building team on the way we would be relatively independent from specialist sub-contractors. He thought that that was a very good idea. Today we will discuss the matter further. We'll keep you in the picture about how things develop.

The priorities now are to transfer the maximum amount of capital in terms of goods and equipment and to obtain quotations for manufacturers of quality prefabs. Concerning shipping, we have learned that the Port Line sails every two months from Antwerp via Sydney to Hobart. We will be given shipping rates here but it is important that you also make enquiries at your end. This route may be cheaper and more effective than trying to ship via Melbourne. In Holland, the agents for the Port Line are Burger & Co in Amsterdam and Rotterdam.

About our families, we have had word about the ship Toni, Klara and the children will be on. It is the steamship Sibajak, which will leave Rotterdam on 15 July and if all goes according to current plans it will arrive in Melbourne on 29 August. This is earlier than was previously expected. Ep and I look forward to the arrival of our families.

That's it for today. Warm greetings and strength.

For the second time today I climb behind the typewriter. When I wrote the first letter it was eight o'clock. It is now half past three. Ep and I have just come back from our wanderings through Kingston.

But, let me go back to Monday morning after I'd replied to Tom's letter in all haste. It was then ten o'clock when Ep and I went to Hobart. Ep, with his honest face, got a local driving licence without any trouble other than having to pay ten shillings. You have no idea how fast we spend our money. Now and then we bite on our tongues to stop us being frugal. Then, in a spending mood, we spend that shilling extra in order to have a good feed and feel full. Full in the acceptable sense of the word, although one's wife would not permit the use of it preferring the expressing, 'I've had sufficient.'

Our task for the day was to hunt for accommodation. First, to the Presbyterian minister, the Reverend Reid, in the hope that he might have some addresses. He was not at home. Come back at half past two. Then to the Dutch Consul, a Mr Swanton. He was not there either. Come back at four. Hobart is rather hilly with lots of ups and downs. Even if it is freezing your tongue soon hangs down to your belly button. It's a shame kangaroos aren't for rent! In the afternoon Reverend Reid referred us to the YMCA. No success there, although we could get accommodation for a few days in rather inhospitable rooms next to the tourist bureau, which gave us a printed list of hotels and guesthouses. A quick calculation showed us that in the Hobart area we could not expect much below ten pounds for the two of us.

We then saw Mr Swanton at his office. In order for us to have a quiet talk, he took us to a coffee place and treated us to coffee and toasted sandwiches. He's a very nice man, Australian. It turned out that he is the organist at St John's, which is the Presbyterian Church in Hobart. He is a director of a shipping firm that also trades in building materials, does insurance work and a host of other things. He rang a shopkeeper in Kingston Beach for us, who said he would be happy to let us know of any possibilities in that area. All in all, a lot of discussions but no tangible results yet.

Despair is not exactly a mood we indulge in, yet that evening we were edging towards it. We decided to turn our backs on the city, shake the city dust from our clothes and to resume our attempts in more rural surroundings. After all, had Jan Boot not suggested right from the start that we should look at Kingston? At that time we thought in the first place of Blackmans Bay, which lies just south of Kingston. In its vicinity was a block of land that solicitor Fred Mitchell might have for us and we thought that we should look at it. So, time for bed.

On Tuesday morning we set off for Blackmans Bay. In Tasmania you don't get anywhere much before nine in the morning, so at that hour we stepped out of the door of the Rhee residence. From there you turn north to Hobart and south to Kingston. Although our destination was decided, our plan was a blank sheet. As we saw no bus going in our direction we started to walk. It was still fairly cold and we walked and walked. When we arrived at the post office in Taroona, we had still not seen a bus, so we asked the postmaster. He said Kingston was a good four miles away, and added that if you were to ask any passer-by he would no doubt tell you that Kingston was just a quarter of an hour down the road! He rang to find out when the next bus was due, eleven twenty!

There we were, like the good boys we are, we had no option but to start walking again, up and down the slopes. Our corns sang with joy! We asked ourselves why we shouldn't try to get a lift... and that was it, boys... from where the inspiration came I don't know, but right then we heard the rumble of a car approaching. We put our hand up and low and behold, she stopped the car, or was it a he? In the car sat an elderly man and a black dog.

'Are you going to Blackmans Bay?'

'No, I am driving to Kingston, but come in...'

I now need to tell you that this man had never given anyone a lift in all his life. As this was our first time as well it was rather strange for all of us, nobody said anything at first. Then he asked what we were doing. We said that we were looking for accommodation. 'Well,' he said. 'I am a builder.' He said that he was building a house and if we would like to have a look at it that would be fine.

So we went with him to Kingston. He was building a house for an English lady on a piece of land just south of the village. Near the house-to-be he had built himself a small shed where he could sleep. At the same time it served as storage for his building materials. The shed was equipped with all kinds of conveniences. 'Would the gentlemen like a cup of tea?' 'Well, yes please.' Within five minutes he had magically produced tea, bread, butter, cheese and jam. In less than half an hour from having met we were drinking tea to our hearts content, eating bread and listening to a radio that happened to be there. Oh well, all very comfortable and the old boy was talking away. After thirty years as an inspector with the telegraph service, he was now filling in his free time building houses.

The view overlooking Kingston Beach and the River Derwent

He had a nice little weekend house nearby, would we like to see it? There was also somebody who had a subdivision for thirty-nine houses in the vicinity. He wouldn't mind showing that to us as well. Half an hour later we were in his car again and on our way to the *batch*, as they call a weekend house. We saw the subdivision where men were clearing the site with bulldozers. These machines can be hired at £3 per hour for small and £5 for large machines, or £35 per day. For sites that have a lot of trees you would need them! Some trees are so big that if Tom and Piet were to start on one of these immediately, I think that the job would be done by the time they were ready for retirement!

Well, we looked at the batch and found that it was situated in one of the loveliest places on earth. It is at the edge of North West Bay, in a cove of the Channel, which is wind free and the water is warmer than elsewhere. I should explain that everywhere here the water is ice cold because of cold currents, the reason they don't swim here. Bathing is restricted to basking in the sun for the ladies to be seen!

Nature is beautiful and that certainly applies to the place where our newly found friend, Archibald Henry Smith, has built his batch. But let me continue. Archibald, 'You'd better call me Archie,' asked if the gentlemen had made arrangements for lunch. No? In that case would we join him for a *rough lunch*? So on the way back, he called in at the butcher in Kingston Beach. In the shop Archie bought, apart from meat, some tins, and so we returned to the building site. The site is situated on the slope of a hill. To the north you see Mount Wellington, which looms so large that it seems close by. In between lies the valley, over which we have a beautiful view. In the valley are many green grassy fields, which give a fresh impression. And, you look right over Kingston.

For lunch, Archie lit a fire outside between some heaped bricks. 'Would you like two pieces of meat?' 'Yes, we would like that very much.' According to Archie the meat would get a special flavour by being cooked over a fire. He had a thick frame of steel wire mesh that was folded over and held together at a long handle. He then squeezed six pieces of meat in between and this was put on top of the bricks. There was a good fire underneath it. The whole thing erupted with flames shooting up as the fat in the meat melted and ran into the fire. Within half an hour lunch was ready. The result was excellent! The fried lamb tasted wonderful, better than we had tasted in any restaurant, boiled peas different in taste to ours, plus bread, butter, jam and tea. I believe that we each ate more than a pound of meat. And all that in the open air, what a feast!

After that we spoke about business. We told Archie of our plans and he immediately agreed to help us. Next to where he was building was a block for two houses, for which the asking price was £200. We saw it and liked it straight away and were very enthusiastic about it. Although we did not show each other too much enthusiasm, we both thought that this would make a perfect starting place. Archie had to attend to other business and we went to nearby Kingston Beach to look for the shopkeeper the Dutch Consul had spoken to about our accommodation.

The shopkeeper had gone into town and could not be contacted. So what now, little men? We decided to take our chance and walked into the next store to ask where we might find accommodation. They mentioned Greenland. We went there and yes, we could get a room for £3 per week including meals. The price seemed reasonable to us and we said that we would let them know the following day.

Greenlands guest house

Next, we decided to go to Blackmans Bay so we could take a look at the site that Fred Mitchell had mentioned. Two miles from Kingston Beach, we were told. As Archie had offered to give us a lift back into town at half past four, we reckoned we could just make it. The Israelites in the desert must have had it easier than us in those two hours. We raced hill up and hill down on a road gravelled with sharp, jagged stones, saw Blackmans Bay and arrived back in Kingston all sweaty at exactly half past four, just as Archie drove up. On the way back we talked about all kinds of things and it was agreed that we would meet again on the day after the next.

When we came to Gerard Rhee's house Archie, as he stopped the car, asked us a question, 'Do you know the first...' and then came a word that we did not understand. We did not understand it at all. He repeated the question and then asked if we had ever heard of Freemasons. We thought that the question might be some sort of identification for the brotherhood but as we had failed to answer Archie knew immediately that we were not. But never mind, just good friends. After this amazing encounter, which we saw as a godsend, we were in good spirits that night and by ten o'clock we were already in bed. People here go to bed incredibly early, but this gives us time to think about things. Ep is the master of contemplation. Of course, I cannot tell everything we discuss with other people. I already blame myself that the reports deviate too much, but take us as we are.

Wednesday, we went to town. We had many meetings. We spoke with the shipping agents. We had a conversation with the architect and we paid a visit to a certain Miss Van Lunsden and her sister. We talked to them about schools and the education system. According to the ladies, there is a desperate need for teachers of Latin, German and French. For those who can teach these subjects, there is a good chance of getting a job even if you don't have the necessary papers. We thought of Hidde, there could be an opening in this field so we will investigate further. According to the ladies, education is not half as good as in Holland. For the children it is certainly much easier. Homework is never given. They can choose the subjects that they will be examined in, so they only need to take those that they are good in.

At six o'clock we were back at the place of our friend Gerard, who felt it was time for a drink, a feeling that Ep and I had suppressed for some time! And so, we went to Wrest Point, the nicest hotel in Hobart, where we shouted each other brandies. Brandy is something like a weak cognac, but very drinkable. If you tried very hard you could say that it approached our national drink, and so we returned in a relaxed mood to the cosy fireside at Rhee's, very hungry and therefore delighted with the very good dinner our hostess had prepared. She is always happy when, in our best English, we praise the dinner by saying, 'It is very nice.'

First thing this morning Ep and I had a disagreement about what day of the week it was, Wednesday or Thursday. We concluded that the days flee from us like shadows. It turned out to be Thursday. At nine o'clock we caught the bus to Kingston, and half an hour later we set foot on Archie's building site. After all our pondering, to cut a long story short, we proposed to him that we buy the block of land for £200 if our lawyer confirms that we can build two houses on it. In theory it should be possible because the land is one third acre, about 13,500 square feet, and the minimum for a house is 6,000 square feet. We would help Archie to finish the house he was building so that it would ready by the middle of August, well ahead of his schedule. We would then rent the house as a temporary dwelling for our families, as we had understood from Archie that the lady he was building it for would have no need of it for another six months. As soon as her house was finished we, with the help of the tradesmen who in the meantime would have arrived, would build the two houses, which would be ready within six months. Archie did not think this was a bad idea at all. He was anxious to get the house finished so he could get on with other work. He thought it might also suit the owner. He was meeting her sister this coming weekend and would put the idea to her. In the meantime we could check on the number of houses that would be permitted on the site.

If this were to go ahead we would, from our point of view, kill three birds with one stone. We would learn how to build in Tasmania; our families would have a roof over their heads; and we would have two houses for our own use. We now have to wait. Keep fingers crossed! Our expectation is that it will be all right but perhaps we are too optimistic. Anyway, we see it as a unique window of opportunity.

At Greenland it turned out that the room we had hoped to get had been let to two Poles last night. There was one room left but this received no sun and was so cold and miserable that we hesitated to accept the offer. We went to Kingston Beach again and ended up at the Australasian Hotel, owned by a Mr Lucas. First we had dinner there, which was excellent. Then we asked about a room and board. That would be £5. We had to think about it. Ep and I then went to the beach, where we weighed up the pros and cons and we asked ourselves whether it was justified to spend so much money. I came up with a compromise by suggesting that we should try it for a week.

Kingston Beach with the jetty, as seen from the Brown's River

You should have seen Ep cheer up! We were scared to have to crawl into that cheerless Greenland. So we thought of a further compromise. We went back to the hotel and asked how much it would be if we did not have lunch there, as we could have that at work. Now, that would be £4. And so it happened that we arranged that the next Saturday we would move in. We reckoned that before too long the luggage that was coming by sea would arrive, including our tent. We could pitch it and sleep in it, once we had our own land. This assumed that all would go according to plan, which would be almost too good to be true.

As an interlude I should tell you that when we arrived at the hotel early this afternoon, we were absolutely frozen to the bone. Mrs Lucas said that if we would like to be warm we should go the bar. What she was referring to was the big log fire that was burning there rather than hot drinks. Of course you cannot expect us just to stand in the bar and stare at the fire! So we ordered, although with heavy hearts, a brandy and to our surprise were offered an extra large French cognac for not too much money. Before we had time to finish our balloons the barman came to us and said, 'The gentleman over there is the brewer here, he is offering you a drink.' So we enjoyed another of the same medicine, delicious! We drank a toast to the generous gentleman and had an interesting conversation with him. He was the manager of the Cascade Brewery, the biggest brewery in Tasmania. No doubt he saw us as future customers, although he drank port himself. So you see you meet unexpected friendliness, and that is nice.

E.R. Pretyman Photographic Collection, Tasmanian Archive and Heritage Office
The Australasian Hotel, Kingston Beach

On Monday, we're going to see the premier of Tasmania, Mr Robert Cosgrove. It was not easy to get an appointment but Gerard Rhee managed to get it organised. We shall see what this can do for us. In the meantime we're anxiously waiting for what Archie has to tell us, so much depends on it.

The arrival in Melbourne of the ship that is bringing the crate with our Jeep is now set for 30 June. We need transport so badly that we decided that rather than wait for it here, Ep should go to Melbourne to see if he can bring the crate to Burnie, then drive the Jeep from there. If need be, we will even get it over as airfreight, which is possible nowadays. It costs more than sending it by sea but we cannot wait forever, and pay frightfully high storage charges. So although it will cost extra we must get the Jeep here because without transport it is not possible to get started. Practically nobody walks here. The distances from one place to the next are simply too big, you would spend your days walking.

Dear people, we close for tonight and we'll see what tomorrow brings. Everyday there's something new and so far only good things. Be all warmly greeted.

27 June 1950

Honourable, Dear comrades-in-arms,
It's only Tuesday but already many things have happened since our last letter. As last impressions are the freshest, I will continue in chronological order and go back to Friday, when we were in Hobart.

In Tasmania, the Hydro Electric Commission supplies electricity. The HEC is also the authority that approves electrical installations. We had a meeting with the person responsible, a Mr Watchhorne. He told us that electricians are only allowed to work if they have a permit to do so. He can issue a permit if there is evidence that the person has the necessary qualifications. So our tradesmen Doedens and Schuringa will need to bring written proof, in English, that they are qualified. Perhaps the institutions that issued the diplomas could write letters to go with them, the letters stating what the diplomas are for. We have also asked if electrical appliances from Holland, such as vacuum cleaners and radios, can be used. According to Mr Watchhorne there is no problem, machinery too can be imported. We think that people who have the right papers will have no problem. Talk to Hidde about this, and don't let him fret too much.

Whilst in Hobart we saw Mr Mellor, the immigration official. This was useful as it gave us an opportunity to explain to him that we needed Geert, Bart, Schuth and Doedens urgently, and to discuss the problem of the delay that they had encountered at the Australian Embassy in The Hague in getting permission for their passage. As Mr Mellor had requested a letter setting out the circumstances we went to 'our' office in Elizabeth Street, wrote it and delivered it to him within the hour. We had to declare that we had accommodation for the men and, drawing a deep breath, we have done so. Mr Mellor assists us as much as possible but he needs to cover his back, officials here are no different from those elsewhere.

We spent Saturday 28 June in idleness as there is nothing to do here on Saturdays. Everything is closed. When I said that everything was closed, I meant it. We could not even buy cigarettes until after 6pm, when a shop opened up and we could treat ourselves to a box for three shillings. It was our last day with the family Rhee. At three in the afternoon Gerard took us in his Ford to Kingston Beach. On the way we looked at the block we thought of buying. Gerard thought it was a fine site and in a good location. While we were there we met the sister of the English lady, Miss Freeman, and were pleased to hear that if we helped to complete the house she did not think that there would be any objection to us renting it through to January.

A problem would be that of the roof covering. Corrugated iron sheets were very hard to get. We promised that we would try and find a solution to this. So, if all goes according to plan we will have temporary accommodation for both our families. It'll be a bit tight but as that would be only a temporary problem, we should be able to manage. From there we went to the Australasian Hotel where Ep and I enjoyed the evening meal. I think we can say that we are lucky because they really look after us here. As the place is so conveniently located others too can stay here temporarily after they arrive. It will cost a bit more, but at least they won't starve.

On Sunday Ep and I decided to go to the Methodist church, as there is no local Presbyterian church. In Kingston Beach, the Methodist Church had a notice outside saying that there would be a service at 11am. Nobody there when we arrived, so we walked to the Anglican Church in Kingston instead. All told there were five women including the organist and six young girls, apart from us. The service lasted an hour. The first forty minutes were used for singing and ceremony. This was followed by a ten-minute sermon and then again ten minutes of ceremonial singing. Not our cup of tea. The sermon was a nice little talk, not a decent thought provoking sermon. No wonder the congregation wasn't larger. An hour later we saw the minister painting his fence.

In the afternoon we paid a visit to a Presbyterian lady in Kingston named Mrs Geard, who was recommended to us by the Reverend Reid. He had thought that, as the Geards had a farm, they might perhaps have a *shack* that could be used for temporary accommodation. Our hotel is by the seaside in Kingston Beach. I mention this to explain the laborious trudging which was our lot that afternoon. From the seaside it was hill up and then hill down to get to the main road, but we had no luck in finding the house, even though the Reverend Reid had sketched a map for us. We had to ask a farmer. 'No, Mrs Geard does not live here.' She lived more in that direction… on the other side, up the hill towards Blackmans Bay. Again up and down, and we asked again. 'Yes, Mrs Geard did live here but now she lives up on the other side of the hill.' Such an ugly word! We had just come from there! I suppressed a rather ominous Dutch expression. My tongue was hanging on my shoes. Thanks to Ep's power of persuasion, I started walking again. We crossed the main road for the second time and we stopped at the first house on the next hill to ask again. A nice lady thought it very interesting to be talking to two Dutchmen and offered us a cup of tea. And did we need it! Her husband happened to be the building inspector for the Kingston area, so we had made another good contact. We talked for an hour or so and received some valuable information. Then, having been pointed in the right direction, we were again on our way uphill to the Geards. The Geards were nice people too. They were looking for a farm hand and were prepared to provide accommodation, although it was rather primitive. The farm is in a rather isolated place. '*In the bush*' is what they say here. It has 80 acres but part of it still needs clearing. This is no mean feat in a forest of gum covering hills and dales. Yes, they had a number of huts that we could possibly use. As it was getting dark, we could have a look at them later. Fortunately, Mr Exhausted managed to get the farmer to take us back down the hill to the hotel in his car. Ep saw an opossum for the first time. Of course, I did not.

That night we mustered the energy to take a stroll along the beach. We needed to think and decide. On Saturday we had already walked to the far end of the beach and clambered over rocks until we could go no further. Ep had wanted to continue the daredevilry but I was afraid he would roll into the Tasman Sea. This time, we walked in the other direction. There was light from the moon and the scenery looked idyllic. After a while we came to a place where we sat on rocks and smoked a cigarette.

The 'Thinking Rocks', Kingston Beach

The next morning, Monday 26 June, we took action. We first went to the Council Chambers in Kingston to find out if the block of land that we were after could be split into two. According to the town clerk there would be no objection but a certain Mr McInnis, who was the Town and Country Planning Commissioner in Hobart, would need to make the decision. At ten o'clock we got on the bus and took a return to Hobart, four shillings. Mr McInnis said he could approve it but he needed a letter from the council confirming that they had no objection. And that's how we are kept busy. We're working on it.

From Mr McInnis we went to the secretary of the Returned Soldiers League, RSL, to become members. To our surprise, he would not accept us. He said that that was not allowed. We discussed for half an hour. Had not the Australian government recognised our ex-servicemen status and yet the club of ex-servicemen would not accept us? Ep was furious.

Later we spoke to the Dutch Consul about it. He referred us to another person after he had said many kind things about us over the telephone. He's a wonderful guy, this Mr Swanton. We also asked Swanton about corrugated galvanised iron sheets. He said he might be able to get Japanese sheets for us, they were expected to arrive in Hobart in about four weeks time. He also had a permit to import sheets from the Netherlands but these had turned out to be more expensive than English sheets, so they had ordered sheets in England, even though the imported sheets were twice the price of the equivalent Australian sheets. We found it hard to understand why, under these circumstances, Holland could not compete. Therefore we would like you to try and get quotations. In our notes we could only find a firm near Rotterdam, but surely there are others. The corrugated galvanised iron sheets that are used have a standard length of ten feet and the other dimension we were told is 10 *gauge*. We have not been able to find out what that means but the manufacturer may know. We would like the quotes CIF please.

At half past two we went, respectably dressed, with Gerard Rhee to meet the premier, Mr Robert Cosgrove. The secretary announced our arrival. Mr Premier, as he is addressed, received us in a very friendly manner. His room was enormous. He sat behind a gigantic desk. He was very interested in our plans, especially because we were builders. We received promises of every possible form of support. The minister responsible for the building industry was not available but his offsider, Mr Plummer, was called in to assist. All we could do was to act, at least a little, as if we were big businessmen. Mr Plummer was requested to provide us with all kinds of information. We made an appointment with Mr Plummer to meet him in his office the following day. He would introduce us to the chief architect who would be able to answer all our questions.

That evening we spoke by phone to Archie Smith, who confirmed that the sale of the land would be in order. That too... it had been an eventful day!

The significance of our call on the premier is illustrated by the enclosed paper cutting taken from today's newspaper, a headline on the front page! This morning, as we came into the breakfast room at the Australasian Hotel a lady who is one of the guests pushed the newspaper under our noses. She announced, 'You have a headline in the paper!' Ep and I laughed about it, at first we did not believe her but yes, there it was.

The Mercury
Hobart, Tuesday, 27th June 1950
DUTCHMEN WANT TO BUILD HERE

Two representatives of a Dutch building group are inquiring about the possibility of bringing Dutch building tradesmen to Tasmania to erect homes. Yesterday Messrs. Vanderlaan and Pinkster, who came to Tasmania from Holland by air, discussed their project with the premier, Mr Cosgrove. They said they represented a big group of building tradesmen in Holland and would come to Tasmania and erect homes if work and accommodation could be guaranteed. They told Mr. Cosgrove they proposed to import pre-cut homes from Holland. Mr. Cosgrove said Messrs. Vanderlaan and Pinkster had conferred with the housing member of the Agricultural Bank Board, Mr Plummer, about the type of homes required in Tasmania

The Mercury

HOBART: TUESDAY, JUNE 27, 1950

SOUTH KOREAN TROOPS RETREATING IN CONFUSION

SEOUL, Mon. — South Korean troops defending Seoul, the capital, are retreating in confusion before terrific artillery fire from the invading North Korean forces.

The South Korean Defence Minister (Sihn Sung Mo) today described the situation as "alarming," and admitted that the invaders were within 12 miles of the capital.

JAP BISHOP HERE

Trail Of Death, Destruction

N.S.W. FLOOD EASES

SYDNEY, Mon. — Muddy floodwaters slowly subsiding in the water-ravaged district from Newcastle to the Queensland border have left a trail of death and destruction.

Defenders Reel

FIGHTER PLANES CLASH

Powerful Aid

WASHINGTON, Mon. — The United States, with naval and powerful weapons to back Korea in an all-out attempt to halt the Korean war today, it appears, on East-West conflict.

Toll Rises

DUTCHMEN WANT TO BUILD HERE

MASS ARREST OF NUNS, PRIESTS

VATICAN CITY, Mon. — Hungarian police broke into monasteries and convents throughout Hungary on June 9 and carried off 922 priests and nuns, Vatican sources said today.

- Editorial — Page 3.
- U.N. Order — Page 4.

● Homeless Return — P. 2.

'Ovaltine' is now better than ever

STATION WRECKED

BENDIGO, Mon. — A man was killed instantly in the Heathcote power station early this evening when a large flywheel attached to a generating engine disintegrated, wrecking the power station.

N.Z. Pilot Starts Solo Flight

DRIVE-IN BANK LATEST U.S. IDEA

Coal Rationing Begun In N.S.W.

At half past nine we were at the office of Mr Plummer, who introduced us to the chief architect, Mr Harding. He took us on a tour through two of Hobart's suburbs, Moonah and Glenorchy, where the Agricultural Bank was building houses for the state government. The houses would be made available to workers on favourable financial terms. So the Bank is really a kind of large housing developer, with architects, workshops and whatever is needed for their enterprise. They are interested in us because they are looking for companies that can erect prefabricated houses for them. We talked it through and said we would get back to them after we had been in touch with our colleagues in Holland.

Ep and I think that in case we would be unable to get work through lack of funds, or by not being able to get materials, we could always go and work for them. They would supply all the materials and we the labour. The houses that are built by the Agricultural Bank are good. We have looked through some of them in detail. The joinery work is well finished. We also looked at the workshops where the prefabs are being made. About a hundred and fifty people work there. They were putting a new model together for the first time, so we saw that too. It was clad externally with timber, lined internally with Swedish hardboard and the ceilings were softboard. We enclose two drawings of houses that are built by the bank. In both cases the floor area is 9.8 *squares*, which is 980 square feet.

Just now the Australian Broadcasting Corporation rang us. They had read the article in the paper and would like to have us for a radio interview. Accepted! We are a bit nervous about it, so this part of the letter is a bit disjointed. It's now half past two and they will collect us at three o'clock. What is in store for us now?

We have also learned that there are good opportunities in Tasmania for three kinds of industrial enterprises: a wood-working workshop, a brick factory and a factory for making glazed pipes for sewers. For each of these we could get government support. We should have a quiet think about this to see if it suits our plans and if so to see what it is that we could actually do. In any case we need people: carpenters, joiners, bricklayers, electricians, plumbers and plasterers. We can always place them. Also, for our own information, please take a look at what kind of skills are needed for making bricks and have a discussion with an expert in this field.

That's it for now. We will continue soon and look forward to signs of life from you. We know nothing of what's going on in Groningen. So long and the best.

5 July 1950

Since 27 June we have had no time to write to you. We now live at the hotel in Kingston Beach and have no typewriter there. So tonight we went to the family Rhee. I can write there on Gerard's typewriter, here we go. We were pleased to find four letters at his place, from Klara, Bart, Piet en Geert. Many hearty thanks. We needed that, because it's depressing not hearing from you. Before I start answering the many questions I will try to continue the chronological account, so you are up to date.

I ended the last letter with the rather terrifying prospect of a radio interview but actually it was fine. Ep has the better radio voice. When I heard myself speak I was horrified! It was broadcast the next day at 1.20 pm. According to Gerard and other listeners we performed well. We kept a low profile, careful not to say too much. When we got back from the studio, we had another telephone call, this time from The Mercury, the paper that previously had printed the bit about our call on the premier. They rang to arrange for an interview. Off we went to Hobart. The next day our photographs adorned the paper together with our story about the Dutch builders who are expected to arrive in August. Herewith the evidence! Through all this publicity we're just about famous and everybody knows who we are. It's a bit embarrassing. We will need to prove that we can do more than talk. We now urgently need the quotes for the prefabs!

Following the publicity we had a visit from a certain Mr Barnett, who was interested in four hundred prefabs. He had bought a subdivision and wanted to do business with us. We had to put this on the back burner, as there is nothing we can do about this now. A visit to our solicitor, Mitchell, brought us the news that the purchase of the block in Kingston still needs to be confirmed in writing by the lady in England and that would take at least ten more days.

On Wednesday we started building for Archie and continued that on Thursday. This resulted in black finger nails, holes in our hands, stiff muscles... but satisfied faces because it's going fine. You can't imagine how hard it is to put a nail through that hardwood, even our skilled carpenters will need to learn how to do that, so in this regard we are now one step ahead! Also, not a single plank or beam is straight, everything is twisted but you soon learn how to deal with it. However, there is more to write about, so I'll let go of reporting on our progress in building for now.

Thursday we received your telegram, of which we did not understood a thing, so we put it aside for a while. We would try later to relate it to our previous correspondence.

On Friday morning Gerard brought us, at work, an urgent telegram from the Post Office, asking us to receive a telephone call from London on Saturday morning. We replied immediately that we would be available at eight o'clock on telephone number 3 in Kingston, which is the telephone number of the Australasian Hotel. We thought that perhaps a shipping company in London might be ringing about freighting prefabs or something like that. It was not until much later that we realised it might be one of you. And so we sat there on Saturday morning, ready for the call. At half past ten the telephonist rang to say that it would come through at one o'clock. Then it became four o'clock, five o'clock and ten o'clock. After eleven o'clock Ep and I were installed in the sitting room of the family Lucas. At four on Sunday morning I'd had enough. We tried to contact the trunk line but everyone there must have been asleep. The whole of Sunday we sat by the phone. By then the whole of Kingston and Kingston Beach knew that the Dutchmen were waiting for a call from Holland. If one of us slipped outside, who ever we came across would ask, 'Have you had your call yet?' Alas, on Monday morning the telephonist told us that the call had been cancelled. Well, that was that.

In the meantime, on Friday afternoon we contacted the Customs Office. The Chief told us that on both new and used machinery there is an import duty of 47½ per cent. We told him that that would be out of the question and that it would be impossible for us to pay such a price. He suggested we write a letter explaining why we needed to import these machines, that the import was a key part of our immigration project and that the machines were vital to the enterprise we proposed to start. He would pass this letter on to the authorities in Canberra and he gave us a fair chance that we would be able to import our machines without import duty. Because of that, we now need a list of the machinery to be imported and its value. About other import duties, enclosed is an official statement by the Customs Department that prefabs are exempted and that all related goods and equipment can be imported free. Only boilers and refrigerators are not exempted but these are in plentiful supply here.

On Friday night, we met a lawyer who, we were told, has considerable influence around the place. We came across him in the bar and he was in a rather jolly state. We later learned that he is quite a man. He is a director of the largest cement factory here. You meet all sorts of people in the bar who are swilling beer and have all sorts of tales to tell. Like everyone else, our new acquaintance is crazy about the prefabs. Speaking of accommodation, on Friday we chased up two flats but we were just too late.

Because we waited for the call until half past ten on Saturday morning, we could only get blue bruises for a few hours. In the afternoon we were going to go on a drive along the Channel and then to the carbide works. That didn't happen. Instead we looked at a beautiful block of land in Batemans Bay, an ideal spot to which we'll come back to later.

In the afternoon, like everybody else in Kingston, we went to the local football match. They play *Australian Rules*. There are eighteen players on each side. The game is somewhere between normal football, called *soccer* here, and rugby. The players attack a weirdly shaped ball and each other, with their hands as well as their feet, and score an incredible number of points. The score was 61-10 in favour of Kingston, which was the cause of great celebration in the bar that night. We were shouted three free drinks!

The next morning we went with Mrs Geard to St John's in Hobart, a beautiful service that we certainly appreciated. As at the Presbyterian service in Taroona there was a separate talk for the children, who sang afterwards and then disappeared to attend Sunday school. Not a bad idea. After the service we shook a lot of hands with all sorts of people and then back in Mrs Geard's car.

She invited us for supper and it was not until half past ten that Mr Geard took us back to the hotel. Mr Geard is not Presbyterian but a Freemason. Apparently just about everybody is. During the afternoon Geard took us to a farm of about twenty acres that was about ten minutes drive from his farm. It belongs to his brother who may be selling it but if that does not go ahead we could rent the house and three acres for £5 per week. The house is being renovated and has a living room, three bedrooms, a kitchen, bathroom and laundry. There is also a big veranda, which could be turned into two bedrooms. As it lies high in the hills you look across Kingston to the bay. It's a nice spot. If we get the chance we will rent it and immediately let you know that we have accommodation for two families. There are also three sheds. We could use the large shed as a workshop and the other two could be used as dormitories. There is lots of space for growing vegetables and having chickens and a few cows. We hope to hear soon whether or not we can get the house.

Since Monday morning we have done nothing but carpentry work. We are making good progress and if we are not held up by the shortage of roofing sheets the house will be ready when Klara and Toni arrive. Our friend Archie is fantastic. We lunch with him at work and can he cook! It's always a feast. Meanwhile, we are given all kinds of tips on how things are done in Australia. He is a priceless teacher. It turns out that his son-in-law is Mr Roy Fagan, the Tasmanian Attorney General. He would like to talk to us about prefabs. If we can get his support we might get large orders. Right now they need four thousand prefabs! We will meet him this coming Sunday, when we will visit him at his weekend place to talk about our plans.

We definitely are very lucky with the contacts that we have able to make. From the one thing we roll into the next. For instance, Mr Geard knows Mr Rex Townley, who is the Leader of the Opposition in Tasmania. Townley is Liberal, Cosgrove and Fagan are Labour. Geard will introduce us to Mr Townley as soon as he is back from holidays. But do not be too impressed by all these Very Important Persons because Tasmania is only a small state, where a lot of people know each other. At the same time, they are a part of the system of State Government and as the State is involved in very many matters it is important to get on with them. As we have received lots of publicity they know about us and are interested in our venture. All of them are curious about how much our prefabs will cost and what they look like. Now to business.

The problem is that we cannot as yet say anything specific. To help us get over this situation I will turn to some technical aspects, including replies to your questions. Prefabs must meet local regulations and functional requirements. It does not necessarily matter if a specific prefab model varies from what is customary here. It was in fact suggested that we enter the market with an original, contemporary concept. What is the response in Zaandam? Have you taken up contact with them? We think that in order to compete successfully, their price for a prefab should be around £1,000 by which we mean the prefab delivered to the wharf in Hobart. After that we can take care of transport, footings, sub-structures and erection. Please make sure that the drawings that come with their prices are unambiguous and that the specification is in English.

Geert rightly pointed out that for tile roofs you need a higher pitch in order to provide a weatherproof roof, in Tasmania just as much as in Holland. That is correct but tile roofs are used only for more expensive houses such as those of Jan Boot and Gerard Rhee. These are not standard but are custom designed and built. By contrast the prefabs would have corrugated zinc roofs, as they would be aimed at the low-cost market.

The supply of sawn timber is not a problem, sawmills supply it in all sorts of sizes. However, all the wood is *green*, dried wood is simply not available. For building timber frames, the green wood is useable. Concerning fixings, wood screws are just as scarce as nails so if you can bring screws that would be great. Door and window furniture here does not differ much from ours; there is a wide range of types and models.

We need a bricklayer as matter of priority, especially for building the fireplaces and chimneys, that's a job for professionals. Bring all you need in the way of tools. For painting, please bring large brushes as a great deal of painting is required, not only for the external walls of the timber houses but also for the inside walls. Wallpaper is almost unknown here. Interior walls are painted so there is no need to bring wallpaper.

Concerning waste disposal, in the city there are sewers and in the countryside waterborne waste is discharged through pipes into a septic tank which is buried in the garden.

In making concrete, *gravel* is used instead of the river pebbles that we are used to in Holland. Gravel is crushed from large pieces of bluestone or other kinds of rock. However, the transport of gravel and sand is a big problem, like all transport here.

As for your own means of transport, the best thing would be to bring a car but if this not feasible then a motorbike would be great. An international driver's licence is not valid on the road but is accepted when applying for an Australian driving licence. Bicycles are not really useful. You would need to be very strong and a kind of magician to be able to use a pushbike here. The gravel roads are not suitable for bikes and are often too steep for the purpose of daily transport.

You can leave the Netherlands on the basis of a declaration that you are prepared to stay initially in the immigration camp in Melbourne. However, there is in fact no need to do so as you can fly straight through to Hobart. You can make bookings for this at Kruizinga on the Vismarkt in Groningen. In Tasmania we will look for a roof over your head; as soon as we have this organised we will send you a telegram.

As far as we can see we have now dealt with all the questions that were asked. We imagine that you all must be terribly busy. We went through it ourselves in the weeks before leaving. Life here is probably less hectic. Sometimes, when we walk along the beach at night, we regard this as a holiday, although we are worried about the international situation.

We don't like what's going on in Korea. The political situation is dangerous. This could lead to a real war between America and Russia. If the Russians play the game in Germany, I mean that they use East Germany to 'liberate' West Germany, then Holland will be in deep trouble. Ep and I will only be at ease when all of you are here. We are inclined to say that if you are delayed by not being able to book a passage, then come by air. The Australians are rather pessimistic concerning the chances of war. Seen from an Australian perspective, Australian pilots are fighting in the Korean war and it is understandable that this topic is the centre of attention. After all, it is on this side of the globe.

Anyway, we count on getting tradesman here sooner rather than later. We must be able to make a start as a building company as there's plenty of work. Even if the ABC was short of jobs we would still be able to find work for both skilled and unskilled people. The fact that Piet is not selling beer anymore does not matter. There are rivers of beer to be sold here, and if he would not be a successful carpenter or baker, we can always get him a job at the Cascade Brewery. We already know the manager there.

We were very happy with Tetje's letter, and recommend this good example to all our girlfriends! We bachelors can do with a bit of support and look forward to your next letters, especially the quotes for the prefabs as this could develop into a good line of business. Did you manage to speak to the Port Line? The freight costs, Antwerp to Hobart, given to us looked good. Shipping would take two months. For large volumes they may be prepared to look at their rates and offer a lower cost. Perhaps you could also have a talk with the people at the Australia Line to see at what volume it would be feasible to ship directly to Hobart. This would avoid the loss of time and the cost of having it lying around on the wharf in Melbourne. Another option might be to ship to Burnie, which is only fourteen hours sailing from Melbourne. Sometimes ships have to wait for weeks in the port of Melbourne. Tomorrow we hope to hear what the score is on shipping it to Burnie. It all takes an awful lot of time.

Mr Geard is still looking for a farm hand from Holland. He would prefer somebody who is married, as bachelors tend to be here today and gone tomorrow. We asked him what kind of employment conditions he is offering. He will provide a new house. It's presently under construction. Wages are about £5 to £6 per week, plus free housing, firewood and a piece of land for vegetables and potatoes. Milk and other farm products will be available on a cost-only basis. Work consists of the daily milking of eight to ten cows and helping Geard with growing oats, potatoes and so-called *small fruit*, which means gooseberries and the like. These are mainly sold to a jam factory. We would like to help Geard but we must remember that our reputation is staked on the person we recommend. Geard is a nice fellow who is able to turn his hand to just about anything and whoever gets the job will be able to learn a lot. However, he should not be a clock-watcher but somebody who has his heart in the work. Geard would like to find a man by December as the fruit harvest starts in that month. If you know of the right man would you let us know? Geard will look after things from there, including his accommodation papers.

We are sending an article on poultry farming with this. It will no doubt be of interest to Mr Muhlschslegel. Please hand it to him with our warm greetings.

Our Jeep is now in Melbourne and tomorrow we will hear how it is going to be sent to Burnie. It sure takes a long time...

Our heart-felt thanks for taking care of our straw widows. This brings us to the end of our story for today. Tomorrow we go to Hobart with a long list of things to do. Although the nights are nippy, the days are full of sunshine and each day we like the Tasmania landscape more and more. Kingston is truly beautiful.

This will probably be the last letter Toni and Klara will read before their departure. Our best wishes accompany them on their long voyage and with longing we look forward to their safe arrival at the airport in Hobart. We'll make sure there's a worthy reception.

The very best and warm greetings.

14 July 1950

Yesterday we received Tom's letter with joy and also your telegram. Today we have been working on the documents you need. More about this later. I will first continue with our serial story.

We spent Thursday 6 July in the city scratching together essential papers for the Jeep, which cost us a great deal of money, about £20. We registered and insured the vehicle at the same time, and we obtained a bank guarantee from the Commonwealth Bank for £113. The customs officer was very helpful in calculating the import duty, so when Ep collects it in Burnie he will not have to waste time on that. We knew the Jeep was coming because we arranged for a telephone call to Stephens in Melbourne in the morning and that same day we received a telegram that the boat would leave for Burnie this Saturday. At long last! The registration number of the Jeep is IN 4281. Make a note of it so you can find us immediately when you come. Apart from the fact that we went to have our hair cut for a second time, nothing important has happened.

On Friday we did carpentry work, and also on Saturday. On Sunday we went again with Mrs Geard to St John's in Hobart. However, we were unable to accept her invitation to lunch because our friend Archie was going to collect us at two o'clock to meet his son-in-law Roy Fagan, the Attorney General, who at the moment is also acting premier. We were well received by him and treated to a very nice afternoon tea. We talked about all sorts of things. We learned that the government is genuine in its interest in prefabs. If we are able to come up with an attractive price we have a good chance of receiving a large order. Almost daily, articles appear in various papers about the development and future role of prefabrication. The members of a study commission for the building industry, the Australian Commission on Domestic Construction, who visited the Netherlands, have also been to other European countries and to the USA to report on housing developments there. The commission has now returned and the various state governments will shortly study their report. Fagan expects the report this week and after they have studied it government will decide on the matter. As far as manpower is concerned, we only need to prepare a list of people and their particulars. Fagan will then raise the matter of their immigration with the Australian Embassy in The Hague. Accordingly, we sent you a telegram Tuesday requesting a list of the names and occupations of those who are ready to move. He agreed with us that for a given number of tradesmen a reasonable number of unskilled workers could come too. So, that means we are all organised for Tom, Piet, Jan and Frank.

Fagan also discussed the issue of immigration hostels with us. We put it to him that to provide, in essence, accommodation for men only was not sufficient and that there was a real need for hostels to provide proper temporary accommodation for families. We said that married men would hesitate to leave their families behind and that if government wanted to be assured that a good number of tradesmen would come, they should be assured initial accommodation for their families. He agreed with us entirely and will take the matter up within government. It would, of course, take time before this would be reflected in the situation on the ground. No matter, we now have in Mr Fagan a wonderful contact of which we can make modest use should the need arise.

Monday, more building work. That night, frozen stiff, we taught the barman in the Australasian how to make good rum toddy. Did that taste good!

Tuesday morning we went to Archie again but at twelve Ep left for Taroona to get a lift with Rhee to Launceston, where he would take the bus to Burnie to take delivery of the Jeep.

Wednesday I spent working in solitude, anticipating Ep's return. The intention was that Ep would return the next day. Late on Wednesday night, as I was deep in the arms of Morpheus, I was suddenly woken by the noise of someone turning the doorknob. Lo and behold, there was our globetrotter, wrapped in two coats, generously interleaved with pages of a copy of *Elsevier*. He was chilled to the bones because he had driven in one go from Burnie to Kingston Beach, more than 350 kilometres, in the open Jeep. The Jeep, so long expected had arrived! Ep could not take the crate with our things as it had been too big to take in the Jeep. It has been sent by train to Hobart and was supposed to arrive this morning. This was, of course, not so because all the wheels turned slower than expected.

The canvas top of the Jeep had been stolen therefore we will have to make do with an open vehicle, mighty cold at this time of the year! The battery had been empty, so Ep had to buy a new one. In addition there were some lesser matters, like the leaking radiator but this can be easily fixed. The main thing is it drives and we are now mobile! This morning we went to Hobart under our own steam. The temperature was around freezing, nice and fresh. Nevertheless, she takes the innumerable bends and heights with surprising ease. The shipment of the Jeep, wonderful that you have been able to fix it!

Yesterday we received bad news. We were disappointed to hear that Mr Geard's brother had decided to sell his property, so unfortunately we will not be able to rent the house. We will have to look for something else. That upset the applecart because we had really counted on the fact that this would go ahead. Never mind.

Now about Tom's letter. Ep and I had to spend some time figuring out how to respond concerning the matter of reimbursement of Geert's expenses, but here we go. Of course we agree to it and also to the reimbursement of the cost of the use of his car. We have to see this as a collective enterprise. If somebody makes his time available for the benefit of the ABC he is entitled to earn a living. Please look at these things in a larger context. The Dutch phase of our lives is now finished. We start a new phase in Australia. Here, our agreement provides a new basis for the governance of relationships between us. In this new phase we need not get upset about a few guilders here or there. We are starting life anew here and everything that can help needs to be done.

We are sorry that Frank has still not managed to get over his deadlock. We had the impression that the whole group was more or less ready to depart. Perhaps we live a little too fast but that, after all, is our nature. As far as we are concerned we cannot turn back now. That was already the case in Holland. We thought that the present political circumstances might be a stimulant for a speedy departure, Frank's included. We don't see a rosy international situation. Now is the time for America to intervene because in a year or so Russia will be ready, and most probably cannot be turned back. This is a personal opinion, but it colours ones behaviour. We are of the opinion that everyone should leave with haste, otherwise it might be too late. In this context perhaps Frank might consider putting some money into our Australian enterprise, his investment would be safe here.

On the matter of loans, we want to have as many assets here as possible. The idea of borrowing money from people who want to move here is not at all discreditable. Hidde is a good possibility and if you can do business with him, then please do so. We have no other opinion other than not wanting to be dependent on strangers.

Concerning the prefabs, your present approach looks fine to us. If we can get ten houses together with the necessary machinery we are on our way. We will proceed here on the basis that the ten houses will come as samples and that, on this basis, the sample orders can be placed. Once we have the ten houses we'll have made real progress.

The registration of the ABC is not yet completed but Mr Mitchell has promised that he will speak to the authorities and that, if all goes well, we'd be able to collect the papers at half past four today. If that actually happens we'll be very happy. If not, there will be no option but to wait till Monday.

Concerning personal transport, a motorised bicycle would be too light. You will need a motorbike for climbing the steep slopes. Ordinary bikes are only useful to men and women with very strong legs. Wicky, for instance, would be able to use one, but most of us would soon tire from hill climbs that are like those in the Tour de France!

You will remember that the night before leaving Schiphol we had a discussion with the director of a firm in Nieuw Vennep. They were considering a deal whereby they would send big machines and equipment for large construction projects to Australia, together with the people who would operate the machines. This would be undertaken on the same lines as the Dutch companies that are involved in dredging in Melbourne. They are working on a very large project and it is now almost certain that most of the machines and many of the operators will remain here on a permanent basis.

The director of the firm in Nieuw Vennep was going to take the matter up with the government in The Hague to see what the possibilities would be for exporting machinery for rental purposes. Here in Australia, the machines would be made available for renting by construction companies, thus ensuring a flow of the so much needed foreign exchange back to Holland. Could you get in touch with the director and enquire to see if progress was made in the matter and, if so, what he might be able to supply in terms of men and equipment? Now that we will soon have a registered company we might be able to organise something that would enable us, as the ABC, to profit from a role in a venture of that kind. We have been told by government that large projects such as the construction of schools cannot be implemented due to lack of manpower and equipment, so we might be able to make a contribution there. The school building programme will also be of interest to us as soon as we have people, but at the moment we are not yet ready.

You will remember that Ep and I spoke with a representative of an engineering company in The Hague. At that time we did not really have enough information about Tasmania, so we let it go. However, if for some reason you cannot now organise quotations for prefabs, it could be useful to take up contact with them again. At that time, they were setting up an organisation for implementing complete housing projects. It would be interesting to see if they are succeeding and if so, if we might be able to cooperate. Don't look at these things in too small a way; we know that Tasmania is interested in 4,000 prefabs right now. Such numbers involve very large sums of money and even if we take on only a limited role that would earn us only a small percentage, it would still run into many thousands of pounds. Even in Holland you'd be pushed to find a single firm that could tackle a project of this size on its own.

Today, Ep and I are going to Hobart to collect our crate, then to Mitchell for the tail end of our registration, and then, for a few days, we turn our backs on the tempting city for our retreat in Kingston Beach. If we manage to get the crate today, then tomorrow we will pitch our tent and we will find out how truly warm the sleeping bags that Piet selected for us are. By the way, Ep succeeded in getting the crate through customs unopened, he had no problems at all, isn't that wonderful?

Well, that was a long story. Today I was not comfortable with my type writing. Tomorrow I will have my own little typewriter back and then I'll be able to climb behind it whenever the spirit moves me. I had to type this letter in fits and starts, between all kinds of other things that needed doing, and sitting in a narrow space in the CCC office, where it is always very busy on Fridays. So this brings me to the end of my use of their typewriter.

Now I'm sick of it. So long!
Eric, Ep

***

Meanwhile in Holland

Father was 46, older than the age limit for immigration to Australia. After numerous meetings in The Hague, the Australian authorities made an exception in his case as father was the leader of the group. However his immigration was conditional. The whole family would have to immigrate with him. There was no alternative. No family, no permit.

I was not yet 21 years old. My physiotherapy studies in Groningen came to an end. My brother Wicky relished the thought of being without Latin and Greek in the months ahead.

In preparation for the big migration Wicky was apprenticed to a building contractor working on a housing project. For the females of the group there were courses in animal husbandry and an extensive course in poultry farming, which it was thought might be beneficial in case it became necessary to be self sufficient. Keeping hens, collecting eggs, feed management and how to build a chicken coop, illustrated with detailed working drawings, were part of the course. It was well attended and enjoyed.

The wives and some of the children attended English lessons. I was given the opportunity to practise my English on the Irish ambassador who visited Groningen for a bakers' conference. I had to offer her coffee and a slice of *koek*, our typical cake from Groningen. For this special occasion I was dressed in a traditional Gronings costume. It was my first chance to speak English to a real foreigner. I was of course quite nervous, but it went well.

It was a confusing time. On the one hand the thrill of the coming adventure, on the other hand the threat of the unknown, and the loss of friends and family. There were emotional visits to friends and relatives to say goodbye. For my mother the departure was fulfilment of a prophesy. As a youngster she often visited her grandmother who was thought to have the gift of second sight.

Kusha serving tea and 'koek' to the Irish ambassador

Tijdens de officiële ontvangst der buitenlandse gasten bood een „Grunneger wicht" de Ierse gezante, mevr. J. McNeill bij de koffie een plakje echte Groninger koek aan

She had told mother that she would move to a land far, far away. And so, in the spring of 1950 we visited our grandparents in Germany for the last time.

There was packing and selling furniture, choosing what had to be left and what should come. Each family could only take one small wooden crate on the boat and one suitcase per person. The sorting was a difficult task. The small crate was packed with the most necessary items needed in the first months of settling in. Clothes, bed linen and blankets were the most important items. At the last moment, mother was able to sell father's shares with a twenty per cent profit. There was enough money to buy father the latest radio set complete with a record player and some classical records and there was just enough space to pack these in the small crate that went with us on board. When father received those in Tasmania he was over the moon. He was very proud of her.

Larger items like the beds, sideboards and furniture were taken apart to go into the big furniture crates that would be sent later. Choosing the non-essential items was a difficult task. Mother packed the old coffee grinder that father had used to grind wheat for bread during the war. It was hard work and the sweat dripped from his forehead! She packed a delft blue pot like the one the ration coupons had been kept in. The round-bellied pewter coffee pot was also to come. It had a little tap at the bottom instead of a spout at the top. The pot was handmade by Groningen's pewter smith and was typical of the province of Groningen. It had a matching pewter tea set, which was also packed. And of course, mother's precious china cups that she loved so much were wrapped up carefully. A painting of the Dutch countryside and a Persian carpet for the coffee table were considered essential items. There were photos in frames, photo albums and father's books. These had been stolen during the war but some had been returned afterwards, often by strangers who had found his name and address on the inside cover. The silver Marine fork and spoon that father had brought back with him from Germany were wrapped in the small red, white and blue flag and were also put in the crate.

The postcard of the Cap Arcona

Mother slipped the postcard of the Cap Arcona inside the atlas. At the last minute she was able to pack the Hammond's New World Atlas that father received as a farewell present, in appreciation of his work as the treasurer of the Anti-Revolutionary Council in Groningen. He was most impressed when he received it! It was beautifully inscribed on the front leaf and said:

To E.J. van der Laan,

Treasurer of the Association of the Anti-Revolutionary Electors

The Council of the Association of Anti-Revolutionary Electors 'Netherlands and the House of Orange', Groningen, presents this book as a token of the grateful memory of the many labours which, under God's guidance, you were able to perform for this association. The Council expresses the wish that you, in your new abode, may faithfully continue to serve the Lord in his Kingdom.
Groningen, July 1950.
For the Council
J. Abels, President, C. Muntingh, Secretary, B. Boersma, Treasurer

Farewell at Rotterdam, 18 July 1950

18 July - 23 August 1950
Aboard the Sibajak, Rotterdam to Melbourne

On Tuesday 18 July 1950, we were the first of the Groningen group to leave by boat. There we were at the quay in Rotterdam about to board the Sibajak for Australia: mother, Wicky 16, Nicky 3 and I 19, and Klara with Ina 14 and Sietske 11.

For all of us leaving family, friends and all that was familiar behind, was a heart wrenching experience. Nearly everyone of the Groningen group was at the quay to wave us farewell. There were Bart and Douwien Folkerts, Jan and Tinie de Vries, Frank Haan, Tjetje de Haan, Piet Laning, Tom and Els Steen, all waving us off on our way to the new country and a new future. The national anthem was played. Paper streamers were thrown from the boat to the people below. After three deafening hoots, the boat eased away from the quay. We were teary eyed and choking on lumps in our throats. Everyone was waving, sadness and happiness rolled into one. I stood on the top of the lifeboat, with Nicky's bear for company and watched as the pier drew away. The streamers broke. The ties were broken. We were feeling really disconnected with everything that had been home and homeland. The boat made its way slowly down the river.

It was very momentous, to sail away and to never come back!

It was also exciting though. Sailing on a boat for six weeks! Like going on a holiday, so different from the holidays we had been used to, which after the war were mainly day trips or short stays on the islands to the north of Holland.

The Sibajak, in the 1930s, was one of the great luxury liners connecting Holland with the former Dutch East Indies, Indonesia. During the war it had been rebuilt into a troop-ship. Now she had been refitted to become a one-class charter ship for taking Dutch nationals from Indonesia back to Holland and migrants from Holland to the New World.

Dormitories had row upon row of bunk beds. There were partitions, but with so many other people around, one was never alone. Despite the various conversions the boat still had some of its old grandeur left: the old wood panelling in the reception and dining rooms, and the lovely stairs!

Men and women were segregated. That was a bit hard on married couples, especially those with small children. The women had to look after them alone. Wicky was in the men's section of course.

There were several bars on board. There was a live band with dancing and there was entertainment every night. Every day there were organised activities for young and old. There was a library and lots of recreational facilities... table tennis, quoits, shuttlecock, board games like chess, backgammon and all kinds of other games. There was even a swimming pool. There was no reason to be bored.

Letter from Klara Pinkster written on board the Sibajak.

Dear Im,
Wednesday 19.
What a strange feeling to be on a boat and to leave your homeland behind in this manner. When the men and women stayed behind on the quay and the boat slipped further and further away, phew, what a horrible feeling! My heart burnt. I almost wished I wasn't on it.

The first meal on board was at seven. It was a small plate of soup, potatoes, filet steak, endive and melon for dessert. You can have more than one piece of meat; that would be something for Tom Steen! The dining rooms are enormous, with round tables set with impeccable table linen and tableware. There are even daily menus. The waiters are from Madura, an island near Java. They stand behind your chair to serve you. They all wear a colourful, neatly folded form of headdress, a strange sight, these dark faces with a cloth round their heads.

The dormitories are sort of alright. A cabin would have been preferable, but so much more expensive. In the dormitories the beds are stacked on top of each other, something to get used to.

Thursday morning.
Slept well, although the boat lay still several times because of fog. And then that foghorn! But, I thought to myself that they are good navigators and that they will certainly take good care of us. The second mate is a nice man who keeps us informed and explains a lot. At the moment we are laying still again. There is a boat close by. They blow the foghorn and they can check where the other boat is with the radar. The fog is so thick that visibility is not even 20 metres.

The children eat at seven now and we eat at a quarter to eight. And do we have an appetite! We eat and eat and eat!

Friday.
There is not much to see. Our boat is halfway down the Bay of Biscay. There is a stiff breeze. Many people are seasick; at least 30 per cent. Wicky as well.

There are many women with children on board. There are two decks for children, one for babies and one for children between 4 and 12.

Toni and I are now used to sleeping with so many people in one dormitory. It's not too bad.

Sometimes ships pass us, a nice sight. Last night there was a large troop ship, completely illuminated.

There is also music on board.

You don't need to take cigarettes with you. As soon as the boat is out of the harbour, you can get all the good English cigarettes you want, only two Dutch guilders for a tin of 50. A real financial blow for Jan de Vries! Try to take some Dutch money with you. In Port Said and Port Aden you can get the same cigarettes for one guilder! You cannot get that with the money used on board, only with real Dutch money. On board we bought chips for our money.

Piet, can you let us know how the photos turned out? We are really curious.

Saturday afternoon.
The beer on board is bad, much too weak. But the meals are excellent. This lunchtime we had kale and sausage, which was very, very nice and big pieces of sausage at that. We each had two, delicious!

We are nearly out of the Bay of Biscay and we can see rocks rising from the sea in the distance, a lovely sight.

The weather is brilliant and we all have a suntan. Of course, I look like a blackamoor.

Sunday night.
This afternoon we passed through the Strait of Gibraltar, with its rock jutting out. It was a fantastic sight. We also saw a school of dolphins playing, lovely to see. And now, we are in the Mediterranean.

Monday afternoon.
It is hot here. Fortunately they have put cool boxes everywhere so you can buy cool drinks. We passed by Tunis and Algeria, a wonderful view.

Tuesday, 12 o'clock.
We are in the middle of the Mediterranean, on our right Africa with its coastline and in the distance its dark mountains, to the left nothing but sea. The boat sways quite a lot and many passengers are seasick again, Poor Wicky as well, again.

Will you please show this letter to Ellie and Gerrit first, also Joop, Ans and Hidde? I cannot write to everyone; that can come later.

Dear All, I hope you can decipher this, the boat sways so much, and I have to write with the paper on my knees, which really is not easy!

We dine so well here every day, it really couldn't be better, as you will find out!

Piet and Dineke, you can also take a playpen when you come by boat and they do all the washing for you on board!

So long, lots of love, especially to Ellie and Gerrit,
Klara

The worst part of the passage had been the notorious Bay of Biscay with a persistent, slow swell that made many people seasick, and the oppressive heat in the Middle East. Apart from these experiences the passage was enjoyable and life on board was fun, with days of many new impressions at ports of call.

The first port was Port Said, at the start of the Suez Canal. Small boats with black men and boys came alongside the ship, clung to the sides of it and tried to sell their wares. On shore it was teeming with people. After that came the Suez Canal and Aden, where it was terribly hot.

The next port was Colombo, a speck in the vastness of the Indian Ocean. We spent the whole day in this strange city and had time to be real tourists. We took a taxi to Mount Lavinia, a mountain near Colombo, where it was cool and there were beautiful gardens with plants that we had never imagined existed.

When the Sibajak was south of Colombo she crossed the line all know so well from maps, the equator. There was even a special pair of binoculars through which you could see it! To celebrate crossing the equator a party was organised at the swimming pool. In the traditional sailor's way, the crew had buckets at the ready that were full to the brim with oatmeal porridge. Everyone who participated had ladles of this poured all over them, after which nobody other than King Neptune himself threw them into the pool. What a mess! Very official looking certificates we awarded to those who were initiated.

From the equator onwards the long haul to Australia started in earnest. Wicky continued to be seasick. When we finally docked in Freemantle, the port of Perth, the capital city of Western Australia, it was a warm day even though it was supposed to be the middle of winter. The port was dusty and dull. There was not much to see. We spent the whole day there and everybody was relieved when the boat was on its way again, this time to Melbourne.

During the last leg of the passage Nicky became ill. She had double pneumonia and was in the ship's hospital. A radio message was sent to Melbourne. When we arrived there was an ambulance ready to take her to the children's hospital. Mother went with her. The immigration officials in Melbourne were very helpful and arranged for mother to stay in Melbourne with a Dutch family named De Vries. After a sad departure, the rest of us carried on. We flew to Tasmania. Pleased to arrive in Hobart, our journey to our uncertain future had ended.

***

Letters from Tasmania

20 July 1950

Dear friends,
First thing this morning we received your telegram about the departure of the Sibajak. At the same time we received Bart's letter of 7 July. I will try to respond to your letter as efficiently as possible. Now that we are in Kingston we are out of the centre of things. Communications arrive later because they are still addressed to us in Hobart. From now on address all letters and telegrams to: Hutchins Street, Kingston, Tasmania!

We are finally getting somewhere but we will not feel secure about our future until all of you are on your way. We shall do whatever we can to receive you as well as possible but be prepared. Initially you'll be pioneering! Don't worry about us signing up for large contracts. We are only developing contacts for further discussions. We did promise Fred Mitchell we'd build a house for him but first we shall need to build houses on the block that we bought. We consider that building our own accommodation and arranging housing for those who work for us is our first and foremost priority.

We're sure that you are working hard to get the quotations for the prefabs and we appreciate that difficulties do arise. The reason why we asked for designs with minimal hall and corridor space is that the cost of prefabs basically relates to their floor area and that it is necessary to be able to offer the maximum amount of useable space within a house of a given size. As the discussion of prefabs in Tasmania focussed on the release of the report of the Australian Commission on Domestic Construction, we had to press for results as otherwise we might fish behind the net. Now that building costs as estimated by the commission are higher than expected our chances even improve. We will certainly be in the picture, provided we can deliver good quantities of prefabs within a reasonable time frame. Everybody is curious to see what we will come up with.

Concerning the prefabs for our own use, floors of Tasmanian hardwood are much superior to the pine floors used in prefabs. If the houses were to be sold to others, hardwood floors would be preferred. So, if instead of flooring you could bring other things that we can use here to build up assets for credit, we suggest that we provide the timber floors and corresponding sub-floor construction here. So we would build the platforms locally, and on these we would erect the walls etc. of the prefab houses. You asked about heating the houses. Anthracite or coal is not used here. Instead, people use large blocks of wood or even big slices of tree trunk. They love their open fires even though these make you feel excessively hot on one side and very cold on the other. So for heating you have to rely on wood, for which very few of the fuel burners that are used in Holland are suitable. Like washing machines and kitchen stoves, you could consider importing electric heaters. Hydro-electricity is plentiful, available everywhere and at a cost that is amazingly low.

You also asked about the place of settlement. We thought that by far the best option would be to settle in Kingston or near it. It's a nice location and land is actually available. We have been given some useful ideas such as buying a number of acres which are then subdivided into blocks that are suitable for building houses on. There is a problem with financing this but we think that we have found a way of getting round it.

There is a school in Kingston about 400 metres from here, right in the street where we are building. For those who would temporarily live in Howden, more about this later. The children could get a lift when we collect the men to go to work. Between Kingston and Hobart is a regular bus service. At weekends there are fewer buses than during the week. In the longer term this will improve because Kingston and other places in the vicinity are expanding rapidly. There is even talk of a trolleybus connection between Kingston and Hobart! For our own day-to-day transport we will need to rely on our Jeep. If it were feasible at all to bring another vehicle we would strongly recommend doing so. We mentioned that the motorised bikes that are available in Holland are not suitable here because of the hills. As in our previous letters, you may have noted that bicycles are only for strong men and boys. This is unlikely to change as the hills, you could call them mountains, are hardly going to be levelled.

We leave the question of raising credit in the Netherlands entirely to you, as it is not possible to see that through from this end. Capital goods that come here provide a useful basis for credit. However, if you find yourselves short of cash for buying capital goods you would need to find the money in the Netherlands. As far as this is concerned we do not understand that Frank cannot help solve this.

Immediately after we received this morning's telegram we went hunting for accommodation. The family Geard has a number of huts that are used for fruit and hop-pickers. These huts provide temporary accommodation for seasonal workers during fruit and hop harvesting times. We can rent six of them through to February. Don't build them up in your imagination, the huts are only primitive summer quarters, but they do have electric light and cooking facilities. Furthermore, as you already know, Archie has a weekend batch overlooking North West Bay in Howden, which is about three miles from here. Next door to him is another batch, which belongs to a friend of his. Archie will ring him tonight but thinks that we might be able to have the use of that too. This would provide temporary accommodation for the families Laning, Steen, De Vries, Deurlo and Schuringa.

This afternoon we collected the accommodation forms from Mr Mellor. We will return these documents signed by the various persons we will be renting accommodation from by tomorrow. Mellor will then cable the Australian Embassy in The Hague via Canberra, to make sure that all is in order. We are very happy that we succeeded in getting it organised so quickly, especially Archie Smith and the family Geard were really very helpful.

Archie, Ep and I are now finishing Miss Freeman's house. If all goes according to plan it will be ready by the time Toni and Klara arrive. We also have our tent, for two people, plus Archie's shed that we can use. At least four men can sleep here. It's not so nice but it has all conveniences, electric light, oven, heater, cutlery, everything is there. Ep and I stayed there and we were very satisfied. Everyone will have to come here with the idea that, for the time being, they will have to camp and make the most of it. We will be deprived of some comfort, but if the spirit to do so is there, then it won't be so bad.

It's a pity that Bart and Geert cannot yet come, we badly need our professionals, but we understand that there are good reasons. In the meantime we are pleased that Wim Sikkema and his younger brother Henk will accompany our tradesmen Schuth and Doedens. Especially in our start-up phase bachelors are useful to us because they need less accommodation!

It is really very fortunate that we found these tradesmen via Henk, who with other friends of Kusha often visited our home in Groningen. I am glad that, before Ep and I left, I was able to talk to Henk's father because emigration is, for these young people, a very big step. As soon as Henk, his brother Wim, Jetze Schuth and Reinder Doedens arrive we can put them up either in the house we are building for Miss Freeman, or in Archie's shed. With the help of the four we will then build on our own plot of land two temporary quarters, shacks, for which we will soon start buying the materials.

Before we can start we need to enclose the block with a timber paling-fence. If possible Ep and I will do this; at least we will make a start. We have applied for electricity and expect to be provided with a provisional connection within a matter of days. The same goes for water, so that is also in order. Normally people build toilets in separate structures outside temporary shacks. We will do that too and at the same time combine these with temporary showers and a laundry.

Next we will need to clear the land. Ep and I will also start on this as soon as possible. However, there are many other things that need to be done right away and these can only get done by doing a lot of running around. So, we are not always able to get our scheduled work done.

You asked if there would be things to do before the prefabs would have arrived. Yes, there will be plenty of work. The four new arrivals will have their hands full! We are still waiting for some of the formalities concerning the subdivision and the transfer of the land to be completed. We can now see our way clear to build three houses after the completion of the shacks and laundry, but to build the third house we need the agreement for the sale of an adjacent, smaller piece of land. In contrast to the shacks these houses will be permanent, for which we can get advance credits amounting to 60 per cent of the future sales value of the properties. So if this were estimated at say £2,000, we would get an advance of £1,200, from which we can pay materials and labour. If we build efficiently, the advance will take us a long way. It may need some additional capital from our own resources but we can assess this only when we have a detailed estimate. The three houses will give us lots of work and if for some unforeseen reason there would be delays we could always turn to our work-in-reserve, the house for Mitchell.

The current plan is that by building the shacks we can accommodate Geert and Bart and their families. As these are large families the accommodation will be a bit tight but never mind, we'll get there. In the meantime, we may have found another possibility. Geard's father is, on his own, building a house for himself, which would take him rather a long time. So we propose to discuss with him if we can complete it for him in the same way that we are helping Archie to complete the house for Miss Freeman. If we succeed we would have access to a further house that could temporarily accommodate two families. As you can see, there are several options and in the meantime we hope for a bit of good luck. Perhaps a little hole will appear that we can crawl into. With hope, we look forward to the arrival of everyone. Once you are all here we'll be able to make a lot of progress.

Please make sure that you take as many blankets as possible with your own luggage. Do not put them in you crates but take them personally. These are necessary to make sure everyone can sleep. The problem with the shacks for the fruit pickers is that they have no furniture and no furnishings, so we will need to improvise there. At any rate Ep and I don't have to look for our hats. Luckily we have a roof over our heads. Many of the problems we now have to face will be dealt with later. We have managed so far and we're not afraid of the future. We are very happy with this morning's telegram because things are moving now. Our hearts will only have peace when you are all on your way. We will do all we can to receive you as well as possible. But stand firm! First it will be pioneering.

The very best boys, warm greetings to all.

24 July 1950

Yesterday we received a letter from Tinie, for which there are many thanks. We will return later to the many questions that were asked. First, some things about the extraordinary happenings of the last few days.

Last Saturday there was an article in the newspaper that implied that if we were to come up with an acceptable offer, there would be orders for as many as a thousand dwellings. The market is clearly there. As we had expected, the report of the Australian Commission on Domestic Construction was only partly relevant to the situation in Tasmania and now hopes are fixed on the builders from Holland and that's us! See the enclosed article.

You will understand that we really look forward to receiving those quotations from the prefab manufacturers in the Netherlands. Even if the firm in Zaandam has decided against becoming involved in prefabrication, we still have not finished with them because we also discussed the possibility of setting up a factory for doors and windows in Tasmania. Did you hear anything further about that? We could write to them directly but it would appear to be better if one of you, together with Bob Houwen, pays them a visit.

The position is that Mr Mellor, the immigration officer, asked us if we had contacts with firms in the Netherlands who not only might be prepared to establish industries here but also would come in with the required work force. He mentioned this to Jan Boot as well. The financing of such a venture would not be a problem. If we were able to come up with the know-how plus the skilled labour, the money would be arranged with government help.

The fact that transport here is a difficult issue needs to be taken on board too. To illustrate this, assume that a firm is producing concrete blocks or roof tiles. Not only would they need to bring in cement and aggregates but they would also need to deliver the goods to a geographically widely distributed market. This brings me to the next point. Even a start-up business like our own would soon have permanent work for a truck. In that context we thought about Ep's brother, Jan, who was also considering migration. Before he took on his present job he had a transport business. He could earn a good living here in transport if he could arrange to bring one or two trucks as capital, which would provide him with security for credit facilities with the bank. Do you think you could have a talk to him about it? You'd be welcome to come up with other ideas to help us solve the transport problem.

Just now we heard that the state government purchased 2,500 cubic metres of pine from Scandinavia. It is amazing that Tasmania, a state with so much timber, needs to import wood but there is not enough labour available to cut Tasmanian wood and to process it. So, apart from doors and windows, if the firm in Zaandam is able to deliver substantial quantities of wood, we may be able to obtain an order. Please speak to them about this. It is important for us to be able to respond to opportunities as they arise.

Now follows a comment on the question of cost of living in Tasmania. In general, prices are a bit lower than they are in Holland. However, that does not say much. The comparison stops as soon as you are here. Then you'll earn Australian pounds and you will think in pounds and shillings. A pound is called a *quid* and a shilling a *bob*. In general, you can say that a labourer is better off here than in Holland. He can easily manage on his earnings and often he has his own house.

There are people who have chickens. There are a lot of chicken farms, although they are not as modern as in Holland. Eggs cost £0.3.10 a dozen. We can try to get small plots so that we can have our own chicken runs.

So far for now, next time when the spirit moves me I'll give a report about the trip we made yesterday in the Jeep from Kingston to Gordon and back. I'm still freezing, brrr!

Bye, bye everyone. Warm greetings.

2 August 1950

Ep and I are as busy as a wigmaker with only one customer, as they say in Groningen. That's why for more than a week we haven't found time to sketch a picture of our adventures. At the end of my last letter I promised you a report of our trip to Gordon, inspired through the spirit of the Muse but the spirit was then not willing anymore.

That Sunday afternoon at half past three we started to drive along what they here call the Channel Highway. Driving along we discovered on the map that if we would drive all the way south we would be able to take another road back. For our adventurous spirits that was too good an opportunity to miss!

The road went hill up and hill down with the necessary bends to scale the heights. When we got closer to Gordon it started to get dark and we had to slow down to struggle through a gang of turkeys. We laughed ourselves sick! Ep hooted and at each hoot the whole gang clucked as loud as they could.

From Gordon we drove along the water's edge through the bush. It started to be pitch dark and cold, cold in the open Jeep. And on and on we drove. It seemed endless. At long last we reached Cygnet, a small harbour town and from there Huonville, a place in the Huon Valley famous for its apple orchards, on the way back. From this valley one has to pass high over the hillcrest. Because one of the headlights had given up the ghost, for Ep it was a devil of a job to negotiate the bends. Going up is not too bad because you can control the car, but if you go down in neutral you go faster and faster and you hurtle very nicely through the hairpin bends: for nervous people it's better to stay at home. A metre off course and you fall down metres to tumble into some other valley. But we took the hills beautifully until we suddenly discovered that the motor had started to overheat. Looked, and yes the radiator was completely dry and there we stood in the dark.

We could see some houses but they were far away. I walked on a bit and saw a light and sure enough there in the back of beyond was a hotel, with a petrol pump, our petrol was also just about finished. After some talk with the rather tipsy locals who were celebrating their Sunday off, we managed to tank petrol and get water and so we tootled along with one light. Next, over a side road to Margate, which should take us back to the main road. This side road is what they call here a *rough road* and can be compared to a solid sand track full of bumps over which we cheerfully trundled along in our Jeep. There are no sign posts and very many side tracks, so you have a constant problem of which road to take. Only once did we choose the wrong turning where we drove rather fast uphill, the wheel kept turning on pine needles and the track petered out. We had to turn on a small kind of plateau of a few square metres, with deep precipices on both sides. Ep with his unsurpassed steering skills managed it beautifully. I entrust my life to him because he always likes to save his own skin first, so there is not much risk for me. Anyway, with our one eyed Jeep and frozen to the bones we reached our tent in Kingston safe and well where we enjoyed our cups of tea more than ever. We had discovered Gordon and that was worth a lot. After so many weeks it was our first pleasure trip and we felt we had earned it.

It is time for business, especially after Bart's letters of 15 and 25 July, which we received respectively yesterday and today. I will come back to those letters because I first have to say that last Saturday we made our first business purchases.

On Saturday afternoon we set off to find fencing materials. We drove to Neika, that's about five miles from here, to visit a guy who was going to get us the timber for building our shack. We had heard nothing from him again and wanted to know how matters stood. We called in at the place where he lives and yes, Mr Webster was at home.

'Hello, how are you ...,' and more of that.

'We got you the list of timber we needed but we have not yet had a call from you.'

'No, because I am going to sell the sawmill.'

'Well... but you will still be able to get us our wood?'

'That'll be at least three weeks.'

'We can't wait that long, we need it next week.'

'Hmm... what do you need first, the long pieces?'

'Er... would you have some fencing rails?'

'Yes, but we'd have to find them in the heap.'

'We'd very much like to have them right now.'

'No... not now.'

'Why don't you get into our Jeep, we'll take a look at the sawmill and then take you back home again.'

'All right then, I'll just get my coat.'

He comes back with his coat and four boys, all climb in the Jeep and off we go to the sawmill. It's in the bush and not much to look at. At the mill we selected fifty long pieces that we could cut in halves, which would give us the hundred rails we needed. 'How much does that cost?' 'Eight bob,' which is terribly cheap because even firewood will cost you more. 'Just wait,' Mr Webster said. He disappeared uphill but was back within five minutes. He said nothing on the way to his home but as he got out he said, 'I'll cut the wood for you.' Only an hour ago it was going to take three weeks but now he will deliver it next week, a perfect example of how things go in Australia. On the way back he must have decided that he liked us and that's how business is done.

A week later we were back at the sawmill, where we loaded the timber for the house across the width of the Jeep. Just imagine, the pieces were more than ten feet long, we just about occupied the whole of the width of the road. Fortunately we did not meet a single soul on the way back so that we arrived at our site without any incidents. We quickly unloaded, drank some lemonade because it was a hot day, and were off to fetch our next load of timber. We had to pick up more fencing material but this time from Howden, on the other side of Blackmans Bay, where we could get the fencing posts. These are heavy, square pieces of timber: they weigh easily 25 kg each and we needed fifty. He said that he did not have them right now but perhaps he could help us with enough posts to make a start. Price: £0.2.6 each. 'Drive over to my dad's place, he's probably got some lying around.' Father Hazel had about fifteen but would have the balance for us on Tuesday. Fifteen on the Jeep and off again we went with the load of poles. We could make a start. We thought it an event and were really proud that we, with our own transport and reasonably cheaply, had got hold of the stuff.

On Monday Ep went with Archie Smith to Hobart, where Ep bought nails. He was able to get three hundred pounds as well as drain pipes, tools and explosives. He was well received in the various stores. The publicity must have helped, in fact they were very generous because nails are almost impossible to get.

Some details about explosives. When you make a hole in the ground or dig up a tree stump, and you don't want to dig because you're too lazy, you use explosives. You make a small hole in the ground half a metre deep. Then you attach a detonator and a fuse to the gelignite. The whole thing is set just above the bottom of the hole. To the top of the fuse you attach a small piece of gelignite and you put your match to that. After a few seconds the fuse starts to sizzle and after a few minutes the explosion follows. They call it a *blow*. We blew to our hearts content and apart from a sporting pleasure, it is very effective. The thickest stumps are loosened and with the aid of an axe and spade are easily removed. Tree branches and leaves are immediately burned, so this is an eldorado for boys because they can light fires to their heart's content. Now finally back to business, I've been too long winded.

Ep has just gone to Geard for more signatures on housing declarations, and will then cable you. When we received Bart's letter yesterday we did not then have time to study it in depth because we had to go to Hobart for our piece of land.

We used the occasion to call on Mr Fagan and we showed him the drawing that Bart had sent, without mentioning a price. He rather liked the design and thought that a house-type like that would be suitable. He did not like the corrugated fibre-cement board roof covering as it is unknown here and people might not feel confident about it. Nevertheless he asked, 'When do you think you can deliver the first hundred units?' We said we thought that that might be possible within about five months. We had to take a risk, as we had no indications from you about production capacity and rate of delivery. For instance, how many every two months? So this is what we asked in our telegram. We made a rough estimate of what we thought a house like that would cost here and came to £1,750, excluding the land and the cost of equipping the laundry because we had no figures for that. The laundry is fitted out with two troughs, mainly for depositing the washing, a copper for boiling the washing and a boiler for providing hot water to the house. As an alternative to the troughs and the copper, an automatic washing machine could be installed. We do not yet have prices for these but we'll find out.

It is very important that the drawings you send are as detailed as possible. Don't forget that this is all we know about the products and that we need to rely entirely on this information. Ep and I are no experts in this although we are learning. The last two months we have picked up a lot. The drawings need to be sufficiently detailed so we can explain to the potential client just what they represent. It is more work for you people but remember that we are talking about big investments and people here are entitled to fully understand what it is that they would be buying. Furthermore, the people who are assessing the proposals include very capable professionals. The prefabs they are making at the Agricultural Bank are first class and the chief architect of the bank would need to approve our drawings. We also need samples of the lining of interior and exterior walls and roofing.

We have a query about painting. 250 hours per house seems a hell of lot! Bart knows this much better than we do but we calculated that even if you work fifty hours a week that's five weeks worth of work. How on earth could we ever deliver a quantity of homes? We must think in lots of at least fifty, so we must find non-conventional ways of speeding up delivery. Could the separate parts of the prefabs not be spray-painted in Holland so that over here we would only need to assemble the pre-finished elements? Also, please give thought to the interior lining. The Agricultural Bank now uses self-coloured hardboard so that the walls need not be painted. This means of course that the quality of finishing should be high, because you cannot make good. However, this should be possible in off-site manufacturing. Both speed and quality are important. The fact that we would erect the homes ourselves makes what we have to offer more attractive.

The design by De Groot, with the amendments that Bart had already included in the drawing he sent, could be submitted for consideration but as a submission it is incomplete; we also need a detailed specification. In the meantime we will not make commitments of any kind unless we receive proper quotations. Please don't be too scared of the sums of money involved, what is important is that the designs must meet the requirements. Especially delivery times are crucial. The housing problem is an urgent one. We heard, and this we were told in confidence, that last week there was a representative in Tasmania of a French prefab manufacturer. In addition, there was a prefab supplier from Austria, who was also prepared to send people for local assembly. However, we were at the same time assured that the market potential is such that there is room for all of us. Please take a fresh look at the matter as a whole, take our comments into account and send us detailed drawings and specifications. Again, payment for the prefabs is not a problem, this will be organised at this end. In the meantime, many thanks for your hard work; we think that Bart and Geert came up with a good design. It was well received by those who saw it.

Yesterday Ep and I dropped in at Mitchell's but he was not in. That was a pity, because we needed to have certainty about Hutchins Street. We have a large block there that will hold two houses but we are also counting on being able to buy a smaller block next to it, which would enable us to build the three houses that the architect is designing. However, Mitchell's secretary, Miss Woods, came out and told us that the transfer of the block and the additional piece of land in Hutchins Street is now in order and that we only need to pay £360 in total. That is not expensive so we are very pleased. It's a beautiful site and this morning we had the verbal agreement of the town clerk to building three temporary dwellings there, in anticipation of the permanent houses to follow. We also saw the architect, Mr Wilson, who will be here on Saturday morning to look at the land. He will then prepare sketch plans for the three permanent homes. He will design these so that they are suitable for selling on at a later time. However, initially we shall need them ourselves, but we consider that in due course they would be sold because we have a new plan to build later on a much larger piece of land, and that's what we bought this morning!

On the hill across the valley of Browns River, straight opposite Hutchins Street and about a quarter of mile from the main road, we have been able to buy from Geard about five acres for £500. The terrain is well situated and in a sheltered location. As it is at a height of about three to four hundred feet above sea level, there is a view across Kingston and along the course of the Browns River towards Kingston Beach and the sea beyond. Here we will build the settlement that Geard has already named 'Little Groningen'.

The site is large enough for twenty building blocks of 60 x 150 feet. At 9,000 square feet each, the blocks are quite spacious. Ten of the blocks will be along an existing public road. After five blocks there will be a new access road to a new parallel road. Along this the other ten blocks are placed. In order to take the trees off the land and to level it we will hire a 20ton bulldozer, which will cost around £50. We will need to supply our own water, for this we get a strip of land that gives access to the Browns River which runs through the valley on the other side of the existing road. For installing an automatic pump, for supplying the houses with water under pressure, we will need to budget £200 but this is less than it would cost to extend the municipal water supply to our site. Electricity is on-site, 1100 volt! This will need a transformer but we will do this together with Geard, in this way it will cost us only £20. We will all be able to live on this site, which also has space for our workshop and stores.

It was a big step, but we took it. Our financial reserves are now largely depleted. At the same time we thought that owning the site solves so many problems and offers such positive perspectives that we felt that we should take the chance that was offered to us. We also have an option on an adjacent piece of land so that, in the future, we can extend if we want to. We thought that the whole situation was so much in the spirit of what, as a group, we had dreamt of that we went ahead. Now we will be able to focus on developing a wonderful community here, and to enjoy its benefits and the possibilities it will offer. The site is as yet somewhat isolated but if you consider that a single block on the main road in Kingston costs £200, you can see the economic advantage of this course of action. When I say isolated, I mean to say that the public road leading to the site is rough and it is located on the edge of the bush. At the same time the location is beautiful and the local climate is the best to be found in Kingston, very sunny and out of the so-called *sea breeze*. You look right across Kingston to Kingston Beach, a beautiful panorama. Ep and I are very pleased with it and have good hopes that, when you are here, you will like it too.

There is a lot to do now; we hardly know what to do first and last. We have to finish the house but can't get the roofing. The whole world has been set in motion to try and find some for us. Then we urgently need to start on more clearing and building the shack for Jetze Schuth and his family. They will be here in ten days time! For the time being we will need to improvise but we'll get through it. There is also a great deal of administration connected with the purchase of the sites, the designing of the houses in Hutchins Street and putting in applications for approval. It just goes on and on.

We're also giving constant attention to the processing of the accommodation papers that you people so urgently need. For Toni and Klara this is now in order. Miss Freeman has now confirmed in writing that she agrees to the use of her house and is in the process of signing the relevant declaration for the accommodation. We have arranged with Mr Mellor that we will coordinate with him one week before the arrival of the Sibajak in Melbourne, and that, if the accommodation is all in order, he will arrange for the families to be taken directly to the airport and for the seats for the flight to be available. So that will all be attended to at this end.

Ep is presently on the war path to get things done for Bart and Geert and we expect to be able to clear the relevant paper work with Mellor tomorrow or the day after. We first thought that once you had signed a paper that you agreed to be accommodated in the camp for immigrants, no further housing declarations would be required. That turned out not to be the case. We're now fixing it and you will have the papers before 2 September. We also need to fix this for Ellie Schuth and Corrie Doedens. As yet I've got no idea how this can be done. The answer to that problem will surely land on its feet too.

Concerning money matters, we hope that you'll be able to bring a number of prefabs and machines. We cabled you asking for the amounts involved as we need this information in connection with the new credit for buying wood and other materials for the shacks. We're through our pounds for the time being. For our credit application, I need to know how far we can jump. Hopefully I will soon get encouraging information.

Ep came back just now. He has managed to get housing declarations for Doedens and Schuth! He's negotiated this on a swap-basis. He has offered that Doedens will help Geard's brother with the electrical installation in his house. First Ep thought that there would be a problem with this because Doedens does not as yet have an Australian licence but for Geard that was no problem. You never guess why. He holds a licence! It is a miracle that we ran into this family. Boys, I can jump for joy.

As we now understand it, all of you, except Frank, will leave with the boat of 2 September and, God willing, you'll be here by the middle of October. If we are counting noses correctly we now need to find accommodation for a further forty seven people. No mean task, but time will solve this puzzle too.

We hope Frank will soon know more and that he can come. Hope also that Bart doesn't get bogged down because of his business.

In our business there has been major development. We have people and equipment coming and the ABC is now a big property owner. Everything is going fine! Importantly, we seem to have an unusual flair for getting on with the Australians. Yesterday when Ep and I dropped in at Mitchell's his secretary, Miss Woods, came out and told us, 'All's in order, you'll get both blocks for £360. First you were to get only one but after Miss Liptrot met you it suddenly became two blocks. Do you know why? Because you have such charming faces, nobody can resist you!' Well, what do you make of that! We were flabbergasted. We don't hear that very often! So, after having tickled ourselves, we will close for today. I could tell you more stories but I am afraid you will get reading indigestion.

Good luck boys and girls, till we meet again. Warmest greetings.

3 August 1950

Much to our surprise a long letter from Tom, which we speedily devoured and which gave us cause to immediately pencil a telegram, which we hope will bring courage to your tired souls.

For a start the situation concerning Hidde is not as gloomy as you think. In that respect we are not worried. He will always get a job here. We made up an employer's certificate with the ABC as right now we have no time to go to the Ministry. That will come at a more opportune time. Mitchell is not here this week, so we have no chance to ask for an explanation from him about Hidde's law degree. It'll be alright. We consider it most important that he comes and trust you will do the upmost to make it possible that he can leave by boat on 8 September. We will look after the necessary papers.

Hidde is able to help us out with the 20,000. We need it as credit for the development of our plans and therefore the machines and prefabs must come. Arrange it with Hidde. Although your sombre suspicions may come true, which we don't believe will happen, he can survive on 20,000. Just imagine he would not accept a job but goes to study, then he can get his degree again in three years time and practise as a lawyer. For a clever guy like him, this would not be a problem. But, we will find him a job that suits him, don't worry about it. We are full of hope. Hidde with his knowledge can fulfil a superb role in our community and his wife is one out of a thousand. So far enough about this, I think we are sufficiently clear about it and so we count on Hidde arriving soon.

We trust that, before you read this, the telegram we sent will have given you new heart in dealing with the problems of emigrating. We were sorry to read that Frank, Bart and now also Jan are still having problems in disposing of their businesses. We hope that all will turn out well in the end and that there will be more optimistic news about them in the next letter. Concerning Tom, Piet and Geert, we agree that you bring the proposed machines with you and as soon as we have the complete list we will try to get an exemption from import duties. So, over to you. We very much hope that your efforts in obtaining an export permit from the Nederlandse Bank will be successful.

This afternoon at three, we observed a moment of silence as we thought that at the time, six o'clock in Holland, our first brothers-in-arms would take off with the KLM. We will follow them from day to day on their travels and hope to meet them in good health in a few days time at Hobart's airport.

Ep is already on the move again to get an accommodation permit.

Henk Sikkema, Jetze Schuth, Wim Sikkema, Reinder Doedens leave for Australia

Concerning the matters you raised, yes, it is important that after all of us have left the Netherlands that there is someone there we can trust and who is prepared to act on our behalf. In that regard we have full confidence in Jan van Oosten and if he, in consultation with Gerrit Zuidland or Bob Houwen, would be prepared to represent us on a longer-term basis then that would be appreciated.

You don't need to worry about the financing of the prefabs. We'll be able to meet the manufacturer's requirements once we have received a fully specified and priced offer that is acceptable. Crucial factors in the assessment of offers will be the delivery time and general reliability. We need assurances that quality standards will be maintained throughout. We continue to look forward to receiving the much-needed quotations. I know that you will need to persist and that these things are not easy but it is very important to our venture because there is good money to be made.

The up and coming construction technician that you were writing about appears to us to be quite suitable but you know more about his capabilities than we do, so it's up to you. To start off with, he will need to work with his hands. Please make this very clear to him, as initially there will be no need for designs and drawings. This might change later. His experience in road design could possibly be useful at some time in the future.

Like us, you are by now receiving many questions from people in Holland who are thinking about emigrating and looking for general information. However, I suggest we confine ourselves to attending to matters that are essential to our own migration. Being a building company, the ABC is not really equipped and does not have time to act as an information desk for migration to Australia. So people with requests for information that do not relate to the development of our own business might be referred to the proper channels. That's what they are there for and what they get paid for. As a group, we are busy enough as it is and there is no need for building up other peoples' expectations and having to worry about meeting them. We do realise that these last months are very busy for you and that you are continuously on tender hooks. Take it easy boys and don't get nervous.

Would you please ask Jan Niemeyer to print business cards with our names on it? The cards should show the ABC logo and there should be separate ones for E.J. van der Laan and E. Pinkster. We need the cards urgently because people here always stumble on our unfamiliar names. Sometimes rather funny, but always inconvenient. PINKSTER is not too bad but VAN DER LAAN, that's difficult. Would you also ask Jan to give you the printing plates of the logo for our letterheads? Please give him my best regards and tell him that I am so busy that my private correspondence comes to nothing.

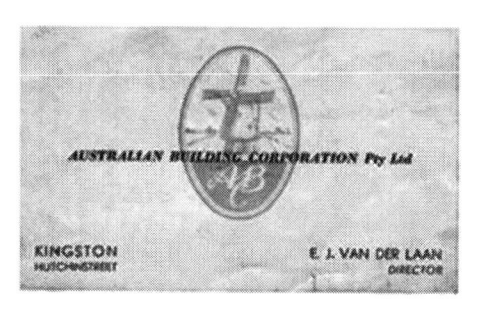

And now, last but not least, the letter from Els. Warm thanks for your encouraging words. We note that you keep up the good spirit but you should not have too high hopes about the accommodation here. Yet, everything will be alright in the end. You will need warm clothes, especially at night it can be bitterly cold. During the day it is mostly sunny. The last two days we have had rain and experienced an Australian downpour, just like Dutch thunderstorms, the water rushes from the hills downwards. In a second you are soaked through. August is the rainy month, so we can expect a little water. When it rains it is impossible to work outside.

Els, when you wrote about a borreltje, we started to drool. Boys, I would give anything for a real Dutch gin. The weak concoction that they serve here is nothing! Sometimes Ep and I warm ourselves with stories about earlier extravagances. We will have to celebrate the reunion in old style. Els, once again a big thank you and we'll see you soon. In the meantime we have become such confirmed bachelors that we only know women as a concept. Soon we hope that concept will become reality.

Boys, keep your spirits up! Don't lose courage and look on the bright side, like the Australians do. Do not see too many bears on the road, keep steadfast. Once we are all together as planned, everything will be alright. We so much look forward to you all arriving here that I have no words to describe it. We will take this letter to Hobart to post, so that not an hour will be wasted.

Warm greetings.

Ep has just returned from his wanderings and so I start again because he has fixed a lot of things.

We now have all the certificates of accommodation and tomorrow the papers can go to Mr Mellor, who at the same time can stamp our employment guarantees. It may take a few more days but you can count on it all being in order. In case there are delays with the mail, we will make sure that the emigration authorities in Melbourne are advised of your accommodation. We'll arrange this through Mr Mellor, who really looks after us well.

Attention! Under all circumstances make sure to freight the luggage to Hobart otherwise we'll be in deep trouble. We enclose a copy of the letter that was sent to the Dutch emigration department. The last sentence will surely butter them up!

It is already late and now hurry to Hobart and visa versa. Bye.

3 August 1950

Council for Emigrants
Lange Voorhout 20
Den Haag
The Netherlands

Dear Sirs,
As in the coming weeks and probably also in the future you will have to assist many emigrants to Tasmania, of which many will belong to our group, we take the liberty to inform you about the various travel possibilities to Hobart, Tasmania.

It is very much desired that you allow these people to travel by air from Melbourne and that the airfares be paid in Holland. We understand that from your point of view there have been objections and we fail to understand the reasons for these. Passengers to Hobart can travel by boat from Melbourne to one of the places on the north coast of Tasmania, either Burnie, Launceston or Devonport. This trip lasts 14 to 16 hours and is very uncomfortable. The Bass Strait is often very rough and many passengers become seasick. From any of these places the train journey to Hobart takes 8 to 12 hours. As the boat only sails twice a week, last month there was only one sailing a week as one of the boats had to be repaired, it will be necessary to pay accommodation costs for several days. In addition, one has to eat and drink during the sailing time and the train journey, resulting in more expenditure. All these costs together add up to more than the airfare. The flight from Melbourne to Hobart takes only 2 ¾ hours and only costs £6.

We take it that these facts are unknown to you and trust that after this explanation there is no reason for any objection to giving your consent to prepay the airfares, from Melbourne to Hobart, in Holland. You will save your compatriots much trouble and inconvenience. When one arrives in a foreign country and is immediately confronted with the worst travel connections and the troubles associated with them, then courage is really put to the test, and we think that that is unnecessary. You will please us and many others to give your assistance in this matter in order to avoid the unnecessary troubles and we thank you already in advance.

> It is very much our pleasure to report to you that our business here
> is developing well. We have been able to set up our company and have
> received every possible support from individuals as well as the authorities.
> We are in a position to offer employment to many Dutchmen and if
> international circumstances don't change we will undoubtedly be in a
> position to receive many more compatriots here.
> Yours faithfully,
> E J van der Laan
> E Pinkster

In Holland, the remaining members of the group were unaware of progress and the rapid developments that were taking place in Tasmania. Towards the end of July, the mood amongst them was sombre. Three of them had yet to dispose of their businesses. This was not easy. All of them had difficulty in keeping up with Eric's requests for prefab related quotations and the other tasks they were asked to fulfil. Each bit of information in Eric's letters raised new questions and they found it difficult to gain a full understanding of the circumstances. Above all, there was the time lag. In 1950 it still took weeks to get a reply by airmail.

At the time, wartime friends of Ep and Klara, Hidde and his wife Ans, had asked members of the group in Groningen about employment opportunities for Hidde. As their response had not very been positive, Hidde had written directly to his friend. Ep replied.

5 August 1950

Dear Ans and Hidde,
This letter is written by Ep.
Yesterday we received your letter and the one from Tom Steen that concerns you. We immediately sent our friends in Holland a telegram saying that you should not be losing any more time in making a decision. I assume you have already heard about it.

We don't understand why our friends are so pessimistic. We surmise it is due to being so far away and having little idea about the situation here, although we do try to explain it in our letters. How we would love to be in Holland, just for a few days, to answer all the questions that come up! Letters can sometimes be vague.

We don't think that Hidde will have any difficulty finding a job here. We've talked this through with the Secretary General of the Department of Education, and other authorities, and we know that anyone with Hidde's education can be assured of employment, provided he or she has sufficient command of English. I have no doubt about that in Hidde's case. Hidde, you probably look at this more critically, but I know how you are. Be assured, it is not too bad. We also asked a friend, who is the father-in-law of the Acting Premier, about Hidde's case. He discussed this with the Acting Premier last night and this morning we heard from him that the case is viewed favourably. His advice was that we take the case directly to Mr Cosgrove, the Premier, as well as to the Minister of Education whom we have met already. We have as yet not broached Hidde's subject as we think it is better to tackle this when you are actually here, then we can get down to business. We hope that this puts your minds at rest.

We have been able to get all the necessary immigration papers. Employer and accommodation declarations are ready for you. They will be sent to our friends on Monday. As far as that is concerned you can proceed with the business of leaving as soon as possible.

It won't all be roses here, and Hidde, you will have to get used to the fact that ordinary teaching will be difficult, especially in the beginning. You will have to get used to the work first. With your education and, besides that, your extensive general knowledge, according to us, you will be able to teach the Tasmanians quite a lot. Education is at a good level here, but there is an acute shortage of teachers. We do not know the exact figures but the lowest salary is a bit more than £420 a year. This amount is sufficient to lead a normal life. We think that you will be able to earn more than that when you start.

We are, and were, aware that in the beginning circumstances would be less favourable than at home and we took that into account, just like you will have to. For sure, there is no need for you to spend your precious pounds in a luxury hotel Ans! Accommodation is extremely difficult but we'll do our best to find something. That 'something' won't be luxurious. It will be more or less like a poor summer holiday cottage rather than a house. But, better times are in sight. The most important thing is to get everyone here, out of Europe. That is our aim.

And, if Hidde stays healthy, there is no reason why you Ans should have to get a job yourself. I think you are needed in your family more.

This letter is rather dull. The true writing spirit is not moving me. That can happen, even if there is no reason for it. Our building venture will be successful without a doubt and it will bring in money.

We have every reason to be grateful and we are very happy with the way things have developed. We have been able to get good contacts, we are healthy and our families are already nearing Colombo. What more do we want? On top of it all, the work is fantastic, to give everything to build up something new – even though it is totally different from what you would ever have dreamt of doing. You should see us during the day! Carpentry, sawing, digging, and working with a pickaxe! It does give us big blisters, sore muscles and stiff backs, but it is lovely work! We feel we're getting stronger every day and we are now able to do heavy work for a whole day. Apart from that, as you already know, we visit many people to spread our tales in such a way that they remember us and hope that they may be able to help us if necessary. This way we get more contacts too. This is really enjoyable and satisfying work.

Further details about Tasmania, I needn't write about now. In case you have questions, don't hesitate to write. We'll be happy to answer.

Dear people, I must stop now as it's become a long story. I really hope that everything will run smoothly for you and that we will see you here in the near future. Will you please give our greetings to our mutual friends? Ask them to send me a letter and I'll try to find time to answer. Letters are always welcome in a foreign land.
Greetings to you both and the children.
Keep your spirits up! Ep

Ep and Eric's bewilderment about the apparent reticence of the group in Holland was realised Monday evening, well after Ep's letter had been posted. A telephone call brought news of the cause of the gloom. Eric responded to this the next day by writing a letter and, for once, he was indeed upset.

7 August 1950

To the ABC Club,
Yesterday was a day of very high ups and very low downs.

The immigration official in Hobart, Mr Mellor, came here to see for himself and liked what he saw. He gave us the vital letter that all is in order. We were overjoyed that we passed the test and that everything was all right. You should have seen us after he left. We sat sort of dancing in our Jeep as we raced to Hobart for the second time today to send you that precious letter.

It was already seven before we were back and burst into Mrs Geard's home. She had almost given up on us, but she was happy that she could offer us her delicacies. And there was a telegram for us. They had rung her from Hobart. We rang of course immediately. Number 4001, extension 262.

To the right of me a radio jingles, Ep on my left and dear me, this is where the telephone was answered. Why in the world did you telegraph in b..... Dutch? Sorry! After much humming and hawing we deciphered the exact meaning of the words. Ep and I looked at each other. What in the world was wrong? Especially the first menacing words, 'NO BANK AGREEMENT STOP AWAITING MITCHELL PAPERS STOP'

Well boys, those papers of Mitchell are no help to us at all. Mitchell had already told us that the heavy envelope had been sent by surface mail by mistake, but that we should not have any worries because the Certificate of Registration would be more than sufficient.

Our Certificate of Registration proves that the company exists. The letter from the Commonwealth Bank confirms that they will make credit available to the company. The letter from the Tasmanian Government, signed by Mr Fagan, states that the company will be considered for the supply and erection of prefabs. What else could the bank ask for?

The statutes that were sent by sea mail are in draft form only. The statutes have nothing to do with the registration. They set out countless regulations concerning the conduct of the affairs of the company, some of which we do not yet fully understand. We had arranged for a meeting with Mitchell to further discuss these. However, as the crucial thing was to get the company registered, also for the purposes of the Bank, we said to Mitchell to do so on the basis of provisional, more or less standard, statutes that later would be amended to suit our particular requirements. Mitchell had assured us that we would be able to do this without any problems at all.

We thought that the evidence of registration would be the document that the bank in Holland would require but if, instead, they want to become involved in the nitty-gritty of the statutes... As Ep and I stared at the words of your message we wondered what was behind it. Perhaps nothing. But why do they refuse to cooperate and not issue the export licence? Why such special attention by the Bank. Surely they have other things to do? Well anyway we slept on it.

Today we have been digging until our backs are bent down with hard work. Now we sit here in the tent by our electric radiator and Piet's kerosene lamp that cannot be praised enough and we are pondering it all. We have concluded that the best thing is to write a formal letter to you, in which we will set out some arguments that may be useful to you in dealing with the Nederlandse Bank. This epistle is closed. It is put very simply but perhaps it will do the job. Don't forget in this case we are in the dark and we are only guessing, we don't know for sure. Perhaps we are barking up the wrong tree but take the will for the deed. Give it all you've got and we hope that this letter can be of service in this matter.

We had prepared afternoon tea for Mr Mellor in our best Australian manner, which may have impressed him more than anything else! Anyway, he was pleased. We get on well with him.

He will send the papers for Toni and Klara to Melbourne and he will make sure that an immigration officer gets these and also their flight tickets before they get off the boat. I have asked Toni to help Klara a bit to get over her fear of flying. The flight takes only two and a half hours. It is so much better that way than the awful and tortuous trip by ferry and train. It is not at all tiring and you can see a great deal of Tasmania from the air. You will all enjoy it greatly. I have asked Toni and Klara to pack blankets in the suitcases that they take with them on the flight. Their packing cases will be cleared by Stephens & Co in Melbourne and sent with the first available boat to one of the ports on the north coast, Burnie, Devonport or Launceston. These ports have better connections with Melbourne than Hobart.

Finally, we understand that De Groot's estimate of the cost of the prefabs came out 1,500 guilders higher than the price calculated by Bart but that is all we know. On the basis of such summary information it is not yet possible for us to submit a quotation. There may be nothing wrong with that price but we need the technical drawings of De Groot as well as a complete specification of what is on offer. Please be generous with the information you provide because we are asked about the prefabs in great detail. It's also important to know the manufacturer's performance capacity and his delivery times. For instance, how soon can they complete the first fifty units? Come on boys, come up with the goods! Because of our nerves on how you are faring, we light one cigarette after the other these days, at your expense of course! You are making our life expensive!

And now, good night, sleep well. We hope that in the future we will save you from further heartaches. Our poor hearts have already had to suffer so much from the absence of our wifely support and inspiration. In addition we sometimes have to pull so hard on tree trunks while clearing the site that we fear they may break! We hope you will share the experience with us soon. After all, shared sorrow is half the sorrow and shared joy is doubled.

We will all have a good time together, no matter the problems you may encounter in the preparation. So long, see you soon.

Hutchins Street,
Kingston,
Tasmania

7 August

Messrs B.J. Folkerts, F. Haan, G. de Haan, P. Laning, J.Th. Steen and J. de Vries, the remaining participants of the ABC in Holland.

Dear friends,

We were very surprised this morning to receive your telegram with the announcement that no decision had been obtained from the Nederlandse Bank for the export of a number of machines and prefabs and that the decision could only be made after receipt of the Articles of Association of our business.

By mistake Mr Mitchell sent the Articles by ordinary mail and to save time we sent a copy by airmail this morning.

In our opinion the Articles cannot explain the picture the Nederlandse Bank apparently has of our situation here. We assume the letters we sent of the Commonwealth Bank and the Tasmanian Government, as well as the official Certificate of Registration of our business, more than clearly show that we have a realistic chance of success.

The Articles however show only our two names as founders of the Association according to the present rules. The agreement we made remains in force so that after your arrival here you will have the same rights.

The capital of the ABC partnership is £10,000. This will be reached once the travel subsidies under the Australian Government's Ex-servicemen Scheme are deposited into our account plus the amounts that the foreign exchange control will allow us to take out of Holland. The amount of £10,000 does not seem much but it will be enough to enable us to float the business. Once we have a contract, the Tasmanian government provides company loans of up to 90 per cent of the contract sum for building houses and this will be put into our current account with the Commonwealth Bank. It is therefore possible to contract work with very little capital.

However for the execution of the work we need several machines that we cannot purchase here with our capital. The machines have to be imported from Holland. We cannot image that the Nederlandse Bank raises objections that not only affect our eight families but also the skilled and unskilled labour force that we will attract from Holland

and for whose upkeep we are responsible. Besides, if we get an order for Dutch prefabs, and the chance for this is great considering the highly competitive prices, we will have to erect these prefabs with our own labour force. This will need to be done quickly and first class equipment is a necessity.

We hope, for goodness sake, you will be able to convince the Nederlandse Bank that it is not done to send a number of enterprising compatriots, naked and healthy, to a far and foreign country without giving them a chance to build a new future with their own possessions.

Here we are able to create a good opportunity for a large number of compatriots. This is not idle talk. Yesterday we had a visit from the chief of immigration office, Mr Mellor, who would be jubilant if we would bring more Dutchmen to Tasmania. Amongst other things he spoke to us about various industrial possibilities, on which we hope to comment later. For the time being we will concentrate on our own business and the speedy development, the machines and prefabs are vital to it.

Consider it: in a few months time we will have to support fifteen families and also we have to create accommodation for them. This last issue has been dealt with temporarily, but it has to be improved as soon as possible. We will be pleased to receive your telegram regarding the positive reaction of the Nederlandse Bank as this is of the upmost importance to us in order to secure more credit for the purchase of basic materials. The latter are scarce here and it is necessary to order these early to enable a steady continuation of the business.

We are also anxiously awaiting the definite quotations of the prefabs. We are being questioned about it continuously.

In definite hope of good tidings, with warm greetings,
 E.J. van der Laan
 E. Pinkster
 Australian Building Corporation

14 August 1950

Oh, how pleasantly life flows on. It is already a week ago that I climbed behind my beloved typewriter and although I would rather lie on my back and sleep, I know that on the other side of the ocean a number of comrades are waiting for our news and so here we go again.

We have had a very busy week, slaving away on the first shack. I refrain from a chronological account because it would become a too monotonous story of much sweat, tired backs and broken fingers. Yet... building is a beautiful profession, because as you see it rise before your eyes, even if you are creating a simple thing as a shack, you cannot escape feeling something like pride rising in your chest.

But, let me tell you about the arrival of Schuth, Doedens, Sikkema and Sikkemas! We had figured out that if they left on 3 August, they would arrive in Sydney on 9 August and be here the next day. We listened to every radio broadcast if there was news about a KLM flight with migrants but no, not a single word. On 9 August we sent a telegram for Schuth to Sydney, requesting that they cable us about the arrival in Hobart. No answer. On the tenth we cabled to the consulate in Sydney to ask them to give them all possible assistance in the transfer, but no word.

It was in the evening, when we received a telephone call from Mitchell to ring him. Just as we came back from the milkman, where we had used the telephone, a car came racing up the hill. It was the postmaster who came to tell us that four of our friends were waiting in the waiting room of the ANA, Australian National Airline. I still had my work clothes on, so at top speed washing, dressing and with the rate of an express train to Hobart.

And lo and behold, there they were, our boys! Tired and sleepy because they had flown in one go from Singapore to Sydney. They were able to get a direct flight and so arrived in Hobart at half past four. They had sent us a telegram but that arrived the next day together with a reply from the consulate in Sydney. So they managed to escape us.

We had intended to make it a big show, with the press etc, but that did not happen. At any rate we are very pleased to have the boys here. First we accommodated them in the Australasian Hotel.

First thing Friday they went with Ep to Hobart but on Saturday they started work immediately. They did not want to lose one moment. So Schuth, Doedens, Archie and I are now doing carpentry work and Ep and the Sikkema are digging foundations for the second shack. We worked that Saturday until darkness fell.

On Sunday, with six of us, in the Jeep we went to St John's in Hobart. After the service the minister told us what he had in mind. When our whole group was in Kingston, there could be services there in the Church of England in the afternoon at half past two. That seemed a good idea to us. In another village the Presbyterians lent their church to the Church of England and he thought they would agree to the swap.

St John's Presbyterian Church, Hobart

In the afternoon we went with the boys for a small outing and we climbed Mount Wellington. At a height of 1,200 metres we had a snowball-fight with some Australians, and of course we won gloriously. It was freezing so we soon went down to

181

Kingston again to huddle over the electric radiator and Piet's wonder lamp to keep our feet warm.

That evening we went to visit the family Geard where we ended the evening by singing the *Wilhemus* and *Grönnens Laid*. It was a lovely Sunday.

So that was it. And now some answers to your letters which we received in the meantime.

First of all, Dineke, many thanks for your encouraging note. We hope to see you soon with your Piet. Yesterday when we were at Geards, Ep said, 'We really do miss Piet here.' You know we are all such dry guys, and we need Piet's juicy sense of humour. When the boys told us that Tom and Piet would not be leaving until the business with the prefabs was cleared up, we said immediately that that was not a good idea.

We think it's important that all of you come as soon as possible and get out of Europe. We are rather pessimistic regarding the chance of war. Maybe we are too pessimistic but we would rather be on the safe side.

We received good news from our wives about their journey. They like it very much on board, the food is good and the service is excellent. That really put our mind at rest as they did not have very high expectations of the accommodation on board but it does not seem to be so bad. At any rate their news is encouraging and should be a relief for those who are to follow.

Concerning Piet's letter, we like his idea of bringing some films about life in the Netherlands and his idea to include one about a model milk farm is good. In taking the film, please give extra attention to the winter stables for the cattle as these are not used here but could be of interest to milk farmers. Please also bring a film about the city of Groningen, something that makes an interesting show, especially the markets on Tuesdays and the historic buildings. This talk of films suddenly reminds me about the government information service. I think they have short films on a range of topics and I remember that there is one on housing. Do you think you could try to get hold of that? If necessary, you could argue that this would help to promote the export of prefabs, so it is in the national interest.

People here know very little about the Netherlands, The only thing that everybody knows about Holland is that the country grows tulips.

It was very good to read that you have managed to find good tradesmen. When will they be able to come? In view of the accommodation papers I need their details as soon as possible. Please also send other relevant details, so we don't grope in the dark. Are they married? If so, tell us the number of people in their families.

Piet remarks several times that the pace at which things are happening in Tasmania is difficult to keep up with... and we thought he would be just the man who would have a bit of speed and stamina! Don't forget that Ep and I find the thrill of the experience as good as the gift of second youth and this rejuvenation awaits all of you! So come as quickly as possible, so we can all go through it together.

By the way, now that the four young men are here things go even faster than before. Compared to a few weeks back it is like a witches' cauldron. Building... making tea for the builders... buying materials...

thinking about prefabs... estimating... dealing with correspondence... chasing up suppliers... filling in forms for every imaginable purpose... discussions with authorities, should I carry on? Hurry, hurry!

Bart asked what would happen if the Nederlandse Bank does not approve the export of our own prefabs. Our suggestion is to not worry about it and to take the second best option, Plan B, which is to spend the available money on machines. In case of Plan B, please do as much as you can to get the machines here as quickly as possible. On the basis of these we'd be able to get credit and they can be used to help us with the construction of our temporary houses.

Prefab quotations are a headache by now; frankly we've lost track. On 2 August we commented on the first quotation based on Bart and Geert's design. We then heard nothing until your telegram, from which we gathered that the design by De Groot would be 1,500 guilders dearer. Next, we received drawings of three designs by Herder but no corresponding quotations.

The Herder designs have the problem that they show internal toilets located away from external walls. They should have external windows for natural light and ventilation, as required by the building regulations. One house, at the back, has an internal height of seven and a half feet; this should be at least eight feet. The designs are only relevant if they can be approved under the building regulations. In all, we are still not in a position to give either prices or delivery times. We can therefore make no offers and we cannot receive orders. To avoid misunderstanding all-round, we need detailed and complete cost estimates and complete specifications of all items that are included in the offer. For instance, in the case of freight we need to know if the cost of insurance is included.

We have heard that government will be proceeding with negotiations with French and Austrian companies. Two French manufacturers have been here, they have offered to build houses with the help of three hundred Italians. Our guess is that the French and Austrian prefabs would be entirely in pine, so we better quote on that basis and then state that hardwood floors would be available as an extra. The timber floors would be right through, including the bathroom, toilet, laundry and kitchen. Again, concrete floors can be offered as an extra. We have found that building the basic floor in local timber is not feasible as dried wooden flooring boards are simply not available. Therefore we now ask for the timber floor construction to be included in the basic price of the prefabs. To make an offer we need detailed drawings and specifications, schedules of fittings and equipment, shipping costs and, for our own use, fully priced quantities of materials and labour, rates of production and delivery, and conditions of payment. As soon as we have these we will be able to discuss the matter with government.

We are now building the shack. Apart from the cost of the land we calculated it will cost £300 per shack. If we had to build twenty of them it would cost £6,000. Say we get 50 per cent credit for it, we still have to fork up £3,000. Even then, we don't have a penny of working capital. This problem is therefore most urgent.

We invested £1,000 in land. Besides that there are living expenses and the purchase of various essential materials that have cost us quite a few pounds. That is why we are perhaps keener than you to get Hidde here. I see him as being a positive element in our community. No way a pioneer, like Bart, but he could be invaluable to us because of his other qualities. Being here we see things in a different light. We see our money shrink from day to day, but the work goes on. So consider it.

Wicky and Henk sawing the wood for the 'stamper'

Jetze and Eric prepare the ground with the 'stamper'

Left: Henk on the frame of the shack

Below: Wim at work on his wedding day

The first cottage in Hutchins Street was completed on 4 September 1950

Midnight is approaching and the boys have just left. We had quite a discussion about building in Australia. Schuth's joiner's heart has been painfully affected by the rather rough and ready way in which the houses are put together, although he agrees that it is difficult to think of how else the very green and twisty hardwood could be used.

During the discussion I tried to get on with typing this letter. Ep is now checking to see if we have covered everything, whilst I take a minute for quiet reflection. It is fun to have the young people here. We form a real community and work as a real team. Ep and I concluded that we needed to do some stocktaking and that that might be just the right kind of job for Henk, who matriculated only a few weeks ago and did well in his book keeping exams. So I mentioned it to him and his reply came back in a flash, 'As long as it won't be my regular job.'

So there we are, straight from a life of study into carpentry and he has no desire at all to change his hammer back into a pen. What is the reason for that? Is it a reaction against life as we know it in the highly civilised but over-organised Netherlands? Is it a kind of cultural tiredness, or the opposite, a kind of cultural frenzy fuelled by the desire to win a place in this new land and then to be part of the process of developing a new culture? It's natural to say that we, as immigrants, just want to build a new existence for us and our children but putting it that way is perhaps too easy. There is always something of a climber in me, not in the sense of making money, but in terms of contributing one's mite and that very small stone to the further development of God's creation. In this respect Australia offers vast perspectives. And, as immigrants, we can see these and respond to them. That is why I love being here. I'm sure Ep agrees but he is still busy flushing out errors and omissions in the letter. I see here a big task ahead and therefore, to all of you, get here as fast as you can. Finish off your business there as quickly as possible and don't hesitate to catch the first available boat. We need you here, in the first place to help us with the very concrete task of building roofs over our heads. Secondly, to graft a bud of our so varied and rich European culture onto this young tree, that one day will be the mighty tree Australia.

Right now Ep calls me back to reality, so I turn my attention to the missing points that he has identified. It is now after midnight and we have decided that it is time for a glass of Australian cognac, as a symbolic break from the treadmill of building and business.

Ep reminds me that this Wednesday we have a discussion with Mellor about strategic imports and the financing of projects that are potentially of interest to government. Possible projects include the manufacture of prefabricated concrete elements, which are widely used in Holland but which we have not seen here. As it contributes to fast and efficient building it may be something to think about. With a team of good workers, this being a form of capital, we can produce something. It will be appreciated in Australia. We can build on that appreciation and that can be our profit.

Lastly, on a different topic, please bring with you all kinds of stamps from Holland and other European countries. We have found that many people, old and young, love collecting stamps. We're always asked for them.

If we have our pockets full of stamps we can use them as small goodwill gestures.

That brings us to the end of his letter. The very shape of the tent is now suggesting an attitude of sleep. A rooster is starting to crow. That is the sign for bedtime. In Holland the rooster crows when you turn in your bed for a last time before falling asleep, here the rooster calls you to bed. That's not different. I should add that, here too, roosters do not lay eggs. That's also the same as it is in Groningen. So not everything is different, even here you have to go to bed to sleep. This in my opinion should be abolished for the simple reason that it's too hard to get out of bed in the morning. Our new arrivals complain about that too!

Blankets! To our horror the gentlemen did not bring any. The whole Australian army is now being raided for blankets for our team. Don't forget we have nothing here. Nothing, and again, nothing.

And now, good night and sleep well. 'Happy drooling!' as Piet would say to the boys when he was in a good mood, and it is only seldom that he's not. Bye boys and girls, yours.

16 August 1950

This afternoon we had a very lengthy discussion with Mr Mitchell about the formation of our company. More about that later.

The most important item of our discussion was that Mitchell has offered us a machine that he designed for pressing concrete blocks. We thought that we should let you know about this right away as it may affect Bart who was thinking of buying a mechanical press that is available in Holland. Some time ago an initial version of the machine designed by Mitchell was made. The manufacturer did so free of charge provided it would be available cost free for the construction of a house. Mitchell now wants to have a second machine made, which he estimates will cost £200. We would be able to pay for this in kind by providing labour for the construction of his house. Operating the machine requires a minimum of three operators but production improves with four. The press is now under construction and he will be able to tell us over the weekend when it can be expected to be ready. If this goes ahead we would not need to bring a concrete block press from Holland, so the money could be used to buy other machines. If Mitchell's machine is a success we would almost certainly be able to raise credit for its full commercial exploitation, which may involve say £1,000. Ep and I think that there would be money in this and that we have a generous offer from Mitchell. We would need to have a concrete mixer, but as Geert is bringing one with his household goods, that aspect is covered. So when we have heard from Mitchell we will write about this again.

Last night, I went through the draft statutes in detail and this morning discussed some points for further clarification. I now think I understand most of the ramifications. We talked with Mitchell for more than two hours. For us it was an excellent introduction to Australian company law. Mitchell is actually a very nice person, every inch a gentleman. We think he takes a special interest in our venture. He certainly advises us well.

We explained our financial position to him and he is very understanding. For instance, registering a company with the authorities costs £50 but he said that we could reimburse his office later so we could now use our money for other things. So it was with a bit more confidence that we, today, signed the contract for buying the five acres from Geard, which means that ten per cent of the purchase price is now payable. 'Don't worry, I will fix that,' Mitchell said. 'But you can get a cheque from us now,' we said. 'No, there is no need; that can come later.' We even have the impression that, in case of emergency, he would help out. We have set out for him what we think the shacks will cost and we asked him if he knew of people who, as an investment, might be interested in having houses built on adjacent sites. The reason is that if our development were to be surrounded by others the real estate value of our houses would go up and therefore our credit with the bank would increase. He will see what he can do. He also said that he thought that the land we bought from Geard was very good value for money.

Another matter we discussed with him concerned our organisation, especially options concerning the relationship between the company and its employees. We are worried about how to tie our employees to us. The problem is that wages must be paid in cash. We are not allowed to open accounts for the employees as this is being regarded as banking activity and a Company Limited as ours would not get approval. One possibility is to deposit that part of the wages that is not paid in cash into an account as an instalment on a future house. We also considered giving the employees one or more shares in the company. The company has a capital of ten thousand shares of £1. These could be given away for free, they could be partly paid, or several persons could jointly own them. Last night I sat up until midnight to study these matters and today we have sought council about those aspects of the statutes that we were not certain about. Now we seem to be reasonably well informed.

Mitchell would love to have a jacket like Ep and I have. At the last meeting he asked for it. Would you please buy one for him? It is of thin material, you know what I mean. You buy them in the Pelsterstraat, I've forgotten the name of the shop. Mitchell has about the same figure as Tom; his size would fit. Buy such a coat and send it with the first person who comes this way. Don't forget it. We'd love to please him with this because he is most helpful to us.

The first shack is now finished, apart from the roof and the floor. We think it looks beautiful, at least to our eyes, but perhaps these have integrated more than we realise. Jetze Schuth thinks that the construction is too heavy and according to his Dutch carpenter's opinion not well enough finished. However, those in the know here argued that this would be pointless as the green wood has already shrunk. Don't think about the gum wood being green as a small matter. If you put a nail in the timber the sap spatters in your face.

Oh well, we could write a lot about it but you'll be able to see for yourselves when you are here. If only we had about twenty of those humble shacks! Tomorrow we start on the second. The timber poles for supporting the bearers already stand in the ground. At one corner they stand quite tall as there is a diagonal fall in the ground below the shack of more than six feet. This means that entry is at ground level but the floor of the bedroom is six feet above the ground.

Today we received the plans for the three houses that we hope to build in Hutchins Street. Today and tomorrow we will study the proposal and on Friday we'll decide. The plans need to be approved by the council before we can access credit that the bank is making available against the security of the land and the approved plans for its development.

The news that reaches us from Toni and Klara continues to be favourable. They wrote that it had been hot in the Red Sea and there had been some seasickness in the vicinity of Port Said. Only a week to go and we will be reunited! Just where everyone will find a place to sleep and how we are going to store all the things are still open questions but we have found that time solves many problems.

I forgot to mention that we talked to Mitchell about Hidde. According to him he could surely find a place in a lawyer's office as an assistant. How much he would earn could only be decided after Mitchell would have talked to him. So, there is a chance. In a lawyer's office he would be able to start studying straight away for his qualifications as a public notary. We do not have to worry too much about this.

Enclosed is a letter from Ep and a copy of a letter he wrote and sent to Ottevanger of the newspaper Trouw with the request to publish it. This is the most important item for today.

Boys, till next time. We are sure you people do not have to look for work, neither do we and so we wish you strength with your labours. So long, warm greetings to all.

Eric   Ep

> Dear friends,
> I wanted you to see the scribble I sent to Huib Ottevanger with the request for it to be published in Trouw. Eric was going to send you a very short note, but he was suddenly inspired and now, as usual, it turns out to be a long story. I was waiting anxiously to use the typewriter because I felt that I wanted to write to you myself for a change.
>
> > Boys, I so long for your arrival here. What a wonderful time we will have together.
>
> It's a pity that your efforts with the Dutch authorities have not been so effective so far. A bit more capital would smooth the path for our start. If it doesn't succeed, it won't be your fault. We know that neither time nor effort have been spared and that you have not left one stone unturned. Be comforted that we will manage even with less.

I'm sure there are wells here we can dig! When we know how we stand with our own funds, even if we have to come up with something else, Eric and I will do what we can. We already have vital capital with our new workforce. The first four newcomers are doing very well. We work together with pleasure, and we work hard. If this is the standard then we will really be able to shift some work!

We use the boys as advertising by showing them off and introducing them here and there. People regard them as being admirable and plucky. Our image has already risen through their appearance and behaviour. In selecting manpower in Holland characters are as important as craftsmanship.

Eric and I are getting more and more work with the administration and the organisation with the result that we sometimes have to stop our building activities, which we find very annoying. It is very satisfying to be able to help with your own hands. Nevertheless, that which weighs heaviest tips the scales.

There is one thing I want to emphasise. Don't worry about our leaps and bounds. We don't. Talk here with the authorities is about big things, for instance a thousand prefabs. But we don't give any commitment. As far as that is concerned, although our letters may not always give that impression, we are cool and down to earth, just like businessmen from Groningen. We'll not hastily commit ourselves. We proceed slowly and carefully with the important things, all the time keeping our fingers on the pulse of your progress in Holland.

So that was it. My warmest greetings and see you soon.
Your Ep

19 August 1950

To the ABC club,
It is Saturday night. Today we worked like navvies to finish the first cottage. Yesterday we had a lesson in the King's English...our friend Mellor told us that we should call our creation a cottage, not a shack. It would sound more positive and improve our chances to get credit. Now there's a friend! So a cottage it is! In our mind we can picture a score of them peopled by all our friends, in Little Groningen.

We were pleased to receive a letter from Frank, who asked what people here think of the chance that there will be another war. There is no simple answer. There are optimists who predict at least a few years of peace but most people probably expect that fairly soon there will be war again. Things are not going well in Korea, China is threatening to invade Tibet, China could attack Formosa any time and with American attention spread over so many fronts, and American forces dispersed, Russia will have the chance to invade Western Europe and secure its ports. It is probably true to say that Europe is not capable of defending itself now and could not stop Russia if it chose to attack.

Ep and I feel that, if Frank cannot dispose of his business now, a solution for him could be to take up as much credit as he can obtain on the basis of his business, put a manager in charge of the business and come here with his family. Frank, in Australia they would tell you, 'Don't sit on the fence any longer.' In our opinion there is room for a commercial laundry but you will have to attract personnel from Holland. Here, girls are not to be found for the job. We suggest you cut the knot, be prepared to lose some guilders, come over here and earn some pounds. It is, as the French say, 'As simple as saying, 'Good morning'.' Frank, there's work ahead for many years to come and this is not an incidental view.

Mr Fagan, the Minister, said that government was interested in building four thousand houses and when these are ready the next four thousand will be needed. For a building company of a reasonable size there is work ahead for a long time. Even schools and hospitals cannot be built because there are not enough builders.

When we saw Mr Cosgrove he said to us, '... you'll be able to build schools for me, I can't find builders for these now!' If we had a sizeable team with a core of good tradesmen, we'd be 'on the ground floor', as they say here. It took me a while to figure out what it meant!

Those who have no special training will also make it, there are so many things they can do. Earlier this week I asked Archie how we compared to the average Australian carpenter: did we do less work? 'No!' he said, 'you're pulling your weight.' And that after only two months of training! Of course we are not yet experienced craftsmen. We also cannot do the more complicated tasks that, for instance, Jetze Schuth can do. That's exactly why we need the tradesmen. Actually, we need people with a range of skills to meet a range of needs. Already, Ep and I have noticed that it is not possible for both of us to hammer away all day. There are too many other things to do, like getting building materials. We almost need somebody full-time to do just that.

Concerning your question about ceramics and starting a pottery, there are certainly opportunities here, in luxury stoneware as well as crockery. However, Jan Boot is looking into this and that being the case it will not be expedient for us to operate in the same branch. For the foreseeable future we would do better to focus on the building industry. This is an area of proven demand and readily available funding, where our contribution is welcomed with open arms. Let's make a success of it. Concerning Swedish prefabs, a ship arrived only this week with sawn and dressed pine from Sweden. We even managed to get a small part of it. A catch is that the wood is dearer than comparable local products. However, we do think it is a very good idea to get prices for prefabs from Sweden. It is very important for us to have the widest possible base for our information. I keep hoping that we will be able to develop our activities in this area. I believe the future of building lies in off-site manufacture.

Although the future belongs to prefabs, just now we are doing other things. For machining hardwood we use the same machines and tools as for softwood, only heavier. Your question as to whether or not we should consider starting a sawmill I find difficult to answer. There are a great many mills but they have insufficient capital and have no modern equipment. As yet, I have seen too little of the industry to be able to form an opinion.

However, I have the impression that starting a brick factory, a joinery/carpentry workshop or plant for kiln-drying hardwood offers more interesting perspectives.

Concerning your hobbies, hunting and fishing are widely practised here. Hunting is free. A lot of people hunt kangaroos. Guns and ammunition are readily available, both shot and bullets are used. For fishing you need a licence, just now the salmon-fishing season started. People fish in lakes, rivers and the sea, mostly with rods with reels. Fishing gear is excellent but very expensive. At sea people fish with loose lines, usually a long line with a piece of lead at the bottom and one or more hooks. You haul in the line, and feel if the fish are biting. People catch red fish, black fish, barracuda and other kinds of fish that are all new to us but that are very good to eat!

Well, that probably answers the questions that Frank asked. Thank you very much for the opportunity to share, once again, at least some of the knowledge and insight that we are gathering, at times with difficulty, about this new country Australia, which is now our home.

Now, some practical hints for those who soon will be departing. Please make sure that, apart from the all-important blankets and bed linen, you also bring things for daily use such as pots, pans and electrical hotplates. But please pack them in the small packing cases that will arrive here before the big ones do.

We do not know what Toni and Klara have in the cases that they are bringing with them in the Sibajak but we have arranged for these to go with them on the plane to Hobart as part of their luggage, so we have access to whatever they have packed right away. Don't forget that all we produce here are empty houses; there is nothing in them! To avoid high costs it would be good if those who come with the other ship, the Johan Van Oldenbarnevelt, bring a special urgent suitcase with their bedclothes and essential household goods which they can take on the plane so it arrives here at the same time.

Also, please pack some Douwe Egberts or another good Dutch coffee in the same suitcase. We have not yet been able to find a coffee here that is to our liking.

We think it would be useful if Bart and Geert took basic builder's equipment with them. I am thinking of a circular saw in particular. At the moment we saw until our arm drops off.

Concerning Tom's comment that the Australian Embassy in The Hague still had not received the accommodation certificates for Tom, Jan, Piet, Deurlo and Schuringa, we again spoke to Mellor about this. He had written to the Immigration Department in Canberra. Their response was that they had cabled their approval to the embassy in The Hague but that they had replied that they had not received any relevant applications. We have said that this had to be a mistake because these had been submitted some time ago. We hope that in the meantime the matter was sorted out.

Now, it's time to think of Christmas! We need something that we can offer to our business relations. Would you have a hunt around for suitable business gifts for the ABC? We were thinking of Delft blue items like a miniature windmills or decorated clogs or the Delft blue ashtrays that people have in Holland. There are firms that supply goodwill gifts. The presents should be recognisably from Holland and no rubbish, the quality must be good. It's very important for building goodwill.

It's gone past midnight, but there are a few more things that should be mentioned.

We had a visit from our four young men and talked to them about business matters. We have agreed that they will work for forty hours a week, earn normal salaries, and in case of overtime will be paid proportionately and not at a higher rate. Instead, they will get a share of the profits that is in proportion to their salary. We have also said that we would like to consider giving them a share in the business but that this could not be decided until after you had arrived. They would take up as much of their salaries as they would need to live on and pay the balance as instalments towards the cost of a house that the ABC would build for them. They thought all that was fine and said that they had come to Tasmania on the basis of their confidence in us and that this would continue to be the basis of their relationship with us. We were all pleased. Ep and I think they are great guys.

Later, we talked about the drainage from our cottages and Schuth proposed that we dig a pit from which the water would soak into the ground. I mentioned that if you hit a layer of clay the water would not be able to drain away. Ep, who is very familiar with what is at the bottom of the many holes he has dug, commented that the clay is more than half a metre in depth and that you'd have to get through the clay. In my innocence, I then asked what would be below it. The answer was sand. Our plumber Doedens, who knows all about the behaviour of water, then noted that if water would get into the pit it would rain in Groningen! So boys, take care with the first rainfall... it may be dishwater from Hutchins Street!

We sorted out where everybody will sleep once Toni, Klara and the children have arrived. The current plan is that Doedens and Schuth will sleep in the tent. The brothers Sikkema and Wicky can sleep in a room in the house that Archie is building. Kusha, her small sister Nicky and Ep's daughters, Ina and Sietske, in the one bedroom of the cottage, Toni and I in the other, and Klara and Ep sleep in the living room.

We need to go hunting for beds and blankets, because at the moment we only have enough for five persons. We are still juggling, but we'll manage. We are making good progress and within a few weeks we should have more space at our disposal.

The Sibajak arrived in Freemantle and left from there that same day, exactly on schedule. If everything goes according to plan it will arrive in Melbourne early on Tuesday 23 August. We have booked seats on the plane that leaves Melbourne Airport at 2 pm. ANA will collect the baggage from the ship, so on paper all is in order. A week from today we hope to be together with our families again. Together we will be like a big extended family, all thirteen of us!

Now that the light from our kerosene lamp has been reduced to a weak shimmer, I believe I have more or less said everything that is important. Ep is exhausted and he cannot keep his eyes open. I am therefore obliged to join him and we wish you, from a dark night in Kingston, the very best. Goodnight, and see you soon.

25 August 1950

This afternoon we received Tom's letter dated 9 August, but stamped in Groningen on 17 August! Whether Tom made a mistake or whether he kept the letter in his pocket, our love for him assumed the first. Ep thanks him for the compliments in honour of his birthday, we hope to celebrate all our birthdays together when the whole club is here and then as Piet would say, 'We'll have a party to be remembered.'

We were very pleased with the enclosed drawings and look forward to the list of the machines to be sent so that we can prepare the necessary documents for duty free import. This will help greatly with further development of matters here.

We were more or less hoping for something after repeated questioning by Geard as to whether we had heard anything from Holland. Well, we have now!

Furthermore, we were very pleased with your telegram that arrived yesterday and from which we concluded that there is nothing to stop the export of machinery and also that houses can be exported. Only on the 22nd of this month, we received a letter from Ep's brother who told us that export of houses has been approved as long as the building cost would not be higher than 5,000 guilders. We had the impression from his letter that this had already been the case for some time and are therefore surprised that you were somewhat muddled over this matter. No matter now, the telegram threw some light onto our gloomy feelings and we now eagerly wait to hear more from you.

And now about the arrival of our families last Wednesday night. There is a saying '...don't worry, it won't be the same...'. Well, it certainly was not the same. Just listen. On the strength of the report that the 'Sibajak' would arrive on the 23rd in Melbourne, Ep and I had taken all sorts of measures to arrange a worthy reception. We had our more or less crumpled suits pressed and put on fresh shirts after having taken baths in the Australasian Hotel. In short, we looked our Sunday best on Wednesday afternoon.

We had arranged for the plane tickets with ANA and also that the cases should be sent by plane, through a migration officer in Melbourne. In the morning we had a phone call from Mellor that the families would not arrive at half past four, as we had arranged, but at half past seven. Archie, together with his wife, was keen to welcome the ladies and they would bring some flowers.

At half past six Ep and I set off with the boys' best wishes. We were running a bit late but at five past seven we were in a village called Cambridge near the Hobart airport, which is 13 miles on the other side of

Hobart. Suddenly our lights started to play up. They went out, on again, out again. We had never been in Cambridge before and of course lost the way. We had no choice but to stop to see what was the matter with the lights because without them it is irresponsible to drive around those sharp bends. That took ten minutes. It seemed impossible to get to the airport on time but Ep did his level best and we sped like crazy, along the right road, to the airport. He took the bends like a racing driver and, thank goodness, we saw the landing lights. Beautiful, by the way.

Just before the airport we passed a car. The driver hooted his horn loudly. We stopped. Friend Gerard Rhee: 'Your wives are not there, the plane was almost empty. I've not seen anyone!' A little further on, Archie was in his car with his wife and a whole load of flowers. He had just come from the ANA office where there had been a phone call that the families would arrive the next day at half past four. Surprise and disappointment all round.

We slunk off, had a glass of port at Rhee's to ward off the cold and drown our disappointment, and then went off to Kingston Beach. Because we still needed to finish our cottage, we had made reservations for everyone at the Australasian. On our way we met Schuth and the others who were going there for the official reception. So they retraced their steps and we returned instead to Archie's shack for a cup of tea. We were only just seated when we heard a noise. 'Are there Dutch people here?' someone called. The door opened and there was Rhee. Again, surprise all round. He said, 'I have good news and bad news. Ep's wife and children have arrived and Van der Laan's children too, but Toni and Nicky had to stay behind in Melbourne.' We raced outside, and believe it or not, there were Kusha and Wicky, and Klara and the kids still in the car. They had arrived at the airport at a quarter to eight with TAA instead. They had gone to Hobart by bus and there Kusha had rung Rhee. He had immediately jumped in the car and had collected them all. Joy mixed with sadness, the normal earthly game in which no pleasure is ever pure.

In the meantime the family here has grown very big. Today the last work is being done on the cottage. While I am typing the boys have just come in for a cup of coffee. The last few days they have worked till twelve at night and even longer, and tonight it will be until midnight again. They are such a nice lot of boys, working like donkeys without even prompting.

It is really *gezellig* and cosy. Klara cooked a real Dutch meal today and you should see how they tucked in, eleven people in a space of 3 x 4 metres. Mountains of bread and potatoes disappeared like snow in the sun! Accordingly the capital of the ABC diminishes, but this will grow with all the work that gets done.

Today it resembled a gypsy camp here. Klara and Kusha did the washing outside, boiling the linen in an empty drum on a fire. Ep has been busy all day gathering enough beds and blankets from here and there and just now it looks like he's managed it. Please remember to have blankets with you, they are needed like bread.

And now down to business. Of course it would be marvellous if we could get a few prefabs here as demonstration models. Surely you can arrange this one way or another. An initial production and a possible delivery time of six months is very attractive and certainly not to be dismissed. It speaks for itself that the import, subject to an attractive price, will give us better chances to increase our capital than by any other means. If at all possible we should not let this go. We will not profit from importing houses using money from outside the firm. We will only have profit by transferring our own capital. We are both inspired by a spirit of independence and share the opinion that ours does not deviate from yours. If we borrow money from others, they must also have a say in the business and frankly we do not want that. Just now we started to do our sums again and we think that with the money we have here now, with machines and discounts, we'll come a long way with the cottages that we are building. We now build our small houses better in order to increase the chance of getting credit and we can again get credit on the land that we have bought. In connection with this, we like the idea of Hidde's coming and we wait with interest what Bart will have to write about that.

Of course there is a chance that we get an order for a model house, if only we have an accurate quotation, which we have already asked for several times. It has to be completely worked out; a fact we assume that you are well aware of by now. We have explained this repeatedly. We can only come with an offer that is complete, with all the details, price, description, delivery terms, and so on. Consider this properly. In case we cannot take any houses, it may be possible to do it this way. We will discuss the question of the purchase of a truck when all of you are here. We are not able to consider this now.

About the labour force which is coming: Kars Slot and family, and batchelors Wierenga, A.W. van Rij and Jan Dijkenga. We will wait for the precise information before we send work declarations, because we are able to fix these any day.

As far as Mr de Vries is concerned, whom Tom mentioned, we do not know anything about him. Toni wrote about him when on the boat but we have not done anything about it, as we did not hear any more from you. In the meantime Mr de Vries has apparently continued to Sydney without further ado. We have not heard anything from Koster either. Most probably he is not in Tasmania otherwise Mellor would surely have told us.

We are still sad about Frank who is in two minds about coming. In our last letter we expressed our opinion and we really hope he will change his mind.

4 September 1950

This is the first letter from the house that we built with our own hands!
When this epistle reaches you we assume that Bart and Geert and their wives and children are already well and truly on their way. According to our information the Johan van Oldenbarnevelt leaves tomorrow. Our thoughts are with you when you take your leave. Tonight we'll celebrate your departure, and, bursting with anticipation, we wait to celebrate your arrival.

We received Bart's letter a few days ago and also the letter from Piet, which made our day. I hope to return to the business side of things a little later. First, to continue my chronological report. Our lives of digging and hammering do have their highlights!

On Saturday 26 August we did not raise the flag but we did celebrate that night when we moved into our first cottage. The large front room looks like a communal living room with a long table made of hardwood, a radio and a bottle of brandy that cheered our souls.

On Tuesday we had a visit from a member of the Kingborough Council, Mr Shoobridge. We had run into him before and he had invited us to come along but we had no idea that he was someone of significance. He told us that on Monday 11 September 1950 our plans for Little Groningen would come before the council and he would like to keep us informed about developments. After talking to him for a couple of hours, it became apparent what this was all about. For one thing, we are required by law to construct a proper, sealed road within our subdivision... to cut a long story short that would cost £3,000. We would not need to do that right away, but if that was the case the council would require a bank guarantee for the project. I will not expand on it otherwise it will become a sob story.

Shoobridge also gave us the address of a large timber merchant in Ellendale, with whom we are probably going to get in touch. Last but not least he invited us to come and defend our plans at the council meeting on 11 September. The council was very interested to make our acquaintance. So we shall be present at the hearing and we shall do our level best to see what we can achieve.

The next day Ep and I went into Hobart as fast as the Jeep could carry us to discuss the matter with the relevant authorities. The result was that we decided to build along the existing road. As that would limit us to ten blocks, we might buy some adjacent land that also has frontage onto the existing road. The negotiations have started and, who knows, some surprises may as yet pop up. You should be here to appreciate all our adventures.

That evening we went to the farewell party for the owners of the Australasian Hotel, the family Lucas. There was free food and lots to drink. Everybody had a grand time and we came home in a happier mood.

In Holland, Corrie Doedens with Jo on her wedding day

Friday was a very special day. Wim was getting married, albeit... without his bride! In anticipation we waited for the big moment at half past eleven at night. To relax us a bit the proxy bridegroom treated us to port... with the idea of having a toast, but at half past eleven we only had a little left, so we toasted the bridegroom with half empty glasses. After the toast followed a speech by his brother Henk, who tried to switch Wim's ring from the left hand to the right hand, to turn the engagement ring into a wedding ring. Henk tried hard but our friend Wim had been hammering since he arrived here and that makes your fingers hard and thick. After a few abortive attempts and a lot of advice, it finally worked and it was time for another toast. Kusha then conjured from her suitcase half a litre of real old genever gin. You should have seen us! A sudden glow transformed our faces, like the morning sun kissing our Tasmanian hills. That real Dutch borreltje, did it ever taste good! Especially after all those weak Australian drinks. It seemed like new blood was flowing through our veins, so with great enthusiasm we toasted the young couple once again and wished them the very best on the new road before them. Half past eleven was really a very moving moment. We were all impressed and of course are all anxious to know how it went in Groningen.

And today, again, we have another party! It is Kusha's twentieth birthday. That is why I will not make this letter too long.
So now to business.

About the letters from Bart and Piet. We look forward to the list of machinery for the workshop. Piet wrote that they are already busy packing and crating the items, but he did not say which items they are. Bart also referred to it. In various letters reference is made to Tom's letters to come, but alas we have not received them as yet. Young men, please do give us the information otherwise we will end up in a mess. We assume the requested items are included and hope for the best.

And now, about Hidde. After the outpourings of Hidde and Piet, we have reached the conclusion that this is turning into a somewhat sordid affair. We are of the opinion that you should not be responsible for Hidde and his family. He will be able to get a job. In case he would not, he would surely be able to stretch his twenty thousand for three years and that will be the end of our agreement. As far as we can surmise from this complicated business, we conclude that Hidde has sold his business on the strength of discussions with you? You can hardly leave him in the lurch. His disposition may not be to your liking, but we think it will turn out to be fine. We are of the opinion that the twenty grand can be invested in prefab exports. No more be said, no trouble with Hidde please and if possible see him through. You need not give him priority.

We can understand the views of Piet and Bart. Maybe we have gone too far in connection with the finances. No doubt we have felt the need for capital here more than you know. I must say it's a real nuisance to be so far apart and not be able to discuss events together. It is really true what Bart says, '... if only we could talk, the matter would be settled in no time.' First and foremost we do not want this to become a bone of contention and we submit to the decision you make about this.

So far, no man has fallen overboard and no doubt things will straighten themselves out. We cannot assess if tempers flared so much that there is hardly any hope of a peaceful coexistence. And so, we leave it you, we cannot say anymore.

That's it for today. We'll send a copy to Bart and Geert on the boat, so that on their journey they can still share developments with us.

Especially to them, 'A good journey and safe sailing!' We wish you not too much seasickness and a minimum of being bored. The very best and see you soon.

In anticipation of hopefully early news of the machinery, greetings to all.

18 September 1950

Dear brothers-in-arms,
Last Wednesday was a happy day because letters arrived from Tom, Els, Bart and Piet. The contents also pleased us and we immediately started with the various tasks that were set out in the letter.

First of all I want to tell you that Toni and Nicky arrived here last Friday. Toni is in very good health, Nicky not so. Sure enough on Saturday it turned out she had chicken pox. She's much better now and we hope to have her healthy again in a few days. From now on we don't need to be so worried anymore. Nicky survived the pneumonia, it did look very bleak at one stage, but thank God we could keep her.

A copy of this letter will be sent to one of the ports so that our brothers and sisters who are now on the high seas will also be informed on what is happening here.

My small typewriter is not in the best condition so I ask all readers to excuse the miserable print.

Since the forth of September, we have made good progress and the Van der Laan family now lives in the second cottage. Toni thought it was much better than what she had dared to expect. By furnishing it with various items from the small crates that have arrived in the meantime, ours and Ep's house look much more attractive. It's been arranged that Doedens and Schuth will board with Klara and Ep and the brothers Sikkema will stay with us. So far we have not paid any wages and for the time being we have arranged that the ABC pays for all household costs. We will settle this later.

At Hutchins Street, Kusha, Henk and Wicky going to a party

A complete account of our adventures would take too much time, but the most important event was our visit to the Kingborough Council, where the decision on our subdivision was to be made. The gentlemen were all very friendly and we had to endure a number of encouraging speeches. We thanked them profusely for the honour shown and in the end our plans were entirely approved. A reporter from the Mercury who attended the meeting took the opportunity to interview us. You can read the result in the enclosed paper cutting.

In order to avoid the immediate investment of a lot of money we have been able to get an agreement that we first build the ten homes that have access to the existing road and that we initially use the land at the back for our workshops only. For these we will need separate approval but this is not expected to lead to any problems.

Tonight we will have a meeting with the municipal building inspector. The council is prepared to supply water to us, but cannot promise this because it is not getting enough water from the Hobart reservoir. The problem is that Kingston is expanding so rapidly and there is not enough water to meet the demand. However, we have been assured that water pipes will be laid as soon as possible. We will now have to install an electric pump to pump our water up from the Browns River. One of these days, we will have a meeting with an engineer. The firm of Webster & Co. are specialists in this field. As you can see, we're never short of problems: there are plenty to be solved.

One question to solve is how we can build houses for our people in the most economical way. The cottages now under construction cost about £500 in materials and labour. Although they are not unattractive they are only temporary structures and therefore we still need to build the permanent houses. We are now thinking of building these houses in phases. The first phase would be tight but liveable and would be extended to become a complete house as soon as possible. The problem with doing it this way is that building the first phase of a house takes more time than is needed to build a cottage and we are short of time. When the families arrive we have to be ready.

For the arrival of Bart and Geert and their families we'll be able to manage because by that time we'll have three cottages as well as the temporary use of Archie Smith's house. One of us can live there. We hope you bring sufficient bedding and blankets with you because that continues to be a real headache.

Our crates arrived last Monday at six in the evening. When we finally managed to unload these hulking big things, every now and again threatening some lives, we started to unpack right away, a job that kept us busy until midnight. It was like a Saint Nicolas's night. Alas, the contents brought more disappointment than joy. What we had hoped for had not arrived. We didn't find electrical hotplates or the beds that we need so badly. What we did find were ornate Dutch sideboards that we could really do without and various odd items, but nothing was complete. Not a bed could be assembled. For instance Toni and I were so pleased to see the headboards and foot-end of our bed emerge from the crate and so sad when the connecting side pieces were missing. Ep and Klara's joy and sorrow was in reverse, they found their side pieces but that was all. With spit and string we managed to assemble a bed but it took us a great deal of our precious time. To be honest, it must be said that the cases were very unprofessionally packed. The wrapping was good and nothing was broken but how in the world is it possible to pack only parts of some items? This should not have happened at all. It's a mystery to us.

Oh well, we won't complain, despite the makeshift arrangements our little box houses are very cosy. As part of emigration, we have to put up with some degree of discomfort. Having learned from the experience let me stress that the beds and blankets are amongst the first priorities. You must make sure that you have these at hand as soon as possible. If feasible, those catching the boat in October would be wise to send beds and bedclothes in advance.

We would never have been able to get through all the work here without our all purpose, nearly always overloaded, beloved Jeep. We are able to get people and materials to the right place at the right time as both Wicky and Henk are licensed to drive the vehicle. Wicky had asked Henk to go with him to the police station to act as an interpreter so Wicky could apply for a driving licence. Wicky obtained his licence without any problem. Then the desk sergeant asked Henk if he wanted one too, since he was doing the paperwork anyway. 'Do you have ten shillings?' As it happened, Henk did, so he put them on the counter and his licence was completed. As the sergeant handed it to Henk he said, 'I take it you can drive.' Indeed, that was the case. In Groningen Henk had had driving lessons but these came to an abrupt end when he crumpled a bicycle. So, just as well there are no bicycles here!

Wicky and Henk on the back of the jumping beans jeep

I will now deal with matters arising from Tom's letter. The list of machines is fine and we immediately contacted the Collector of Customs for an exemption from import duties. The formal application has been submitted. Keep your fingers crossed. If it were to be rejected we would turn to more heavyweight support but for now we have to wait. We will need to get further technical information as soon as possible. For instance, we need the electrical requirements of the motors so we can complete the applications for electrical supplies. We also need their dimensions and working space requirements as these are needed for the design of the workshops. The freighter Port Brisbane is expected to arrive around mid November, which is about the same time that we expect the remainder of the group to arrive.

Our own packing cases, which we assume also contain tools and equipment, are expected to arrive 2 October. Could you let us know what, apart from household goods, is in them? So far, Customs have been very good and have not bothered us and we hope that will continue to be so.

Concerning the use of concrete vibrators in Tasmania, we have not been able to get information about these. In mixing concrete builders use a broken aggregate called *bluestone* instead of the river gravel that we are familiar with. This is comparable to the road metal that was used on roads before the introduction of bitumen, the rubble that was so disliked by the tyres of our bicycles!

That at least five prefabs will be sent is very important to meeting our housing needs. We hope you'll be able to arrange for early shipment. We agree that is a good idea to have several types of houses. That gives us more experience in their assembly and we'll be able to invite authorities to come and see our range of houses. In the meantime it will be necessary for us to buy and store good quantities of timber. If we want to be able to do something with our machines we will need to have stocks of dry timber. At the moment this is impossible to get hold of. So we plan to buy green wood and to stack it so that the wind can get through it and dry it in the open air. Here they call this *season-drying*.

The problem is that this needs more capital. It's difficult to know how to make the pennies stretch. When we have twenty people at work we need to have materials to keep them going and cannot afford loss of time due to delays in the delivery of materials. All this requires a great deal of organisation. We will also need to look again at the transport of goods and people. The Jeep can handle a lot but not enough. One of these days we will need to consider the purchase of a lorry. We're pleased that Geert and Bart will shortly be here, so they can help us in making big decisions of this kind.

As requested we have inquired after a non-functioning brick factory but there are not any. We also think that, at the moment, we should not become too involved in this because it would take a lot of organising and we understand that some of the raw materials are not so easy to find. If there were skilled workers in Holland who are willing to migrate, it would not be difficult to find work for them. The building materials firm Kemp & Denning have a brick factory and are short of trained personnel. So we propose to make a deal with them. We would find a number of skilled brick makers and, in exchange, they would give us preferential treatment in the supply of bricks and timber. We'll talk to them about this on Wednesday. At the same time, we should not bite off more than we can chew. The development of our building venture places many demands on our capabilities and capacity. For the time-being there will not be a great deal of time for other matters. It is not that you just pick up the telephone and place your order with one of your suppliers. You have to go there and fight for it in order to get it at all!

Attached please find the accommodation guarantees for Kars Slot, Gerrit Slot, De Vries, Van der Niet, Van Rij and Rieks Wierenga, as well as the guarantee for Wim Sikkema's wife, Jo. As you may have noticed we can issue the certificates ourselves! Mellor trusts us one hundred per cent. This is great but it means that we cannot afford to slip up. And now off again to our building venture!

Finally, it is the turn for all the other letters. The letter from Piet managed to make us laugh again. We need that every now and again. Our worries make our faces look like those of undertakers, so it really is mandatory for Piet to write to us at least once a week. Since he is busy getting ready to leave, it would be unfair to expect that. He'll have to make up for it once he is here. We are very pleased that he managed to get hold of some films about Holland. These will be very useful for promotional purposes.

Good news too that Gerrit and Ellie Zuidland have, after all, nearly decided to come too. This is great; Klara especially was thrilled. But, as the saying goes in Groningen, 'Nearly is not good enough.' We hope you will be able to push them in the right direction.

As in all the letters from the ladies, Els' unburdening has lightened our days. When this letter reaches you, her problems will have reached their peak but after 15 October she will have five weeks holiday and perhaps be served her favourites, pork chops and a borreltje.

Last but not least, Bart's letter written just before leaving. We will send you news while on board. Bart and Geert, with all our hearts we hope that you will have just as good a time as our wives did. They were full of praise about the good service. We advise you to continue by plane. Toni thought it ideal. Geert will be surprised by the pleasant experience. You will pay a few pounds more than the boat fare that is already paid. Please send us a telegram when we can expect all of you to arrive. You can be sure of a joyous reception.

Herewith I am at the end of my epistle. If I have forgotten something, please forgive me. Warmest greetings from the whole colony here, and especially from yours.

25 September 1950

To the ABC Club on land and on the seas,
Over the past week we had no reason to complain as we received five letters, from Frank, Piet, Tinie, Tom and also from Tetje, written from the hospital bed on the Johan van Oldenbarnevelt. To start with the last one. We wish you a speedy recovery and hope that you are back to health when you come ashore in our new homeland.

As Frank requested, we attach an accommodation guarantee for him and his family plus his employment certificate. We hope he'll be able to dispose of his business in a profitable way and we're sorry that his last letters are again not very optimistic in this respect. Mellor has authorised his papers as well as those of Vogd and the painter Groothuis, who will work with Bart. With so many people coming we almost lose track of the arrival dates of all the workers and their families. For instance, what is the position with the families of Deurlo and Schuringa? Do they also arrive with the boat of 15 October?

Piet's idea of becoming a photographer is better deferred. It's true that there is no shop for developing and printing photos in Kingston but Hobart has plenty of these. I can't assess whether or not there is room for more. But don't cry Piet! I am of the opinion that this work is far too light for an athlete. We need your muscles, man!

Piet, the ladies have asked me to ask you to select and bring some nicely designed lampshades, and also handcraft materials so they can make their own. Right now we are still enjoying the glare of bare light globes with bayonet fittings. Later under your good guidance when the parties start again we will need soft lighting. You know what I mean. The ladies depend on you. When more people are here the ladies will want to visit each other and they would like to be able to receive visitors in attractive interiors, so they really rely on you!

Some more items that have to be brought: seeds, beans without strings, runner beans and peas, a couple of mops, scrubbing brushes, for Toni a coffee filter pot and ten metres of white cotton. Take as many cigarettes as you are allowed as they are expensive here and the quality is poor. Furthermore, we urgently need some good hammers, a heavier type than the ones that arrived in the crates. You really have to strike hard to drive the nails through the hardwood.

Tinie asked if a medical practitioner from Groningen would be able to practise here. I'm afraid that the opportunities for professional people do not look good. Just lately legislation was passed that allows a very limited number of foreign doctors to practise here. For the whole of 1950 the number will be four. The ones who get through first have to work for a full year in a hospital, and then have to be prepared to be posted to a location where a practitioner is needed, and which is selected by government. If your contact is still interested, the best thing for him to do is to write directly to the responsible minister, Dr F. Turnbull, Department of Health, Hobart.

Wim is a little worried concerning the woman he married. Will she arrive with the October boat? So we ask you take extra care of the beautiful lady. Send her at the first opportunity otherwise Wim will die of longing for her.

We'll need a bit of time to study the designs for the prefabs that Tom sent but our first impression was that they look good. Ep and I have just now discussed this and we think that, since the arrival of Geert and Bart is not far away, it is better that we wait so they can help us decide. If all goes according to plan they will be here in a fortnight. We look forward to hearing from them about the many things we do not yet know. There is also the problem of being short of time. The completion of the cottages is taking longer than we had allowed for. We have decided that, if only five prefabs are coming, we will need to build the other five houses at Little Groningen ourselves, initially with the minimum allowable floor area for permanent dwellings, which is 659 square feet. They will have a combined living room and kitchen, three bedrooms and a bathroom. The houses are not large but designed so that they can later be extended as needed. As they will be permanent homes we first need to pour the concrete foundations. This will take time. Until the concrete mixer arrives from Holland we will need to make do with a small mixer that is turned by hand. Furthermore, digging for the foundations, drain pipes and septic tanks also takes a great deal of time due to the rock-hard soil.

We have made good progress with the purchase of wood and other materials. On the other hand, we have to deal with delays in getting the site ready for building, the installation of the pump for the water supply and other things that we need before we can really start. We do the best we can and will fight hard to get the entire accommodation ready in time.

Boys, please try your hardest in getting the prefabs on the ship as soon as possible. We will run into trouble if we have too many delays. We'll be relieved when Bart and Geert are able to share responsibility with us. If you still see a chance to send a number of competent tradesmen, please do so. That would greatly benefit our progress. Don't spend too much time on pondering about it, just go ahead and do it.

We are receiving letters from various places from people who are totally unknown to us asking for information. It would be good to have a couple of private secretaries to answer them all.

And now to finish. We have so many things to think of and discuss that there is little time to sit quietly and write you a decent letter. By now the letters are no longer proper accounts but rather check lists of the most important things. It is about time the whole club is here and that we are spared the task of having to write, although I must say, I have done so with great joy and pleasure.

Boys, see you later, which would be half November. Greetings from all, tall and small, and especially from your Eric and Ep.

***

On 6 September 1950, the MS Johan van Oldenbarnevelt left Amsterdam on her first migrant voyage to Australia. The ship was named after the executed Dutch statesman who supported Willem I of Orange in his struggle for independence against the Spanish during the 80 Year War. She had once been a luxury ship that carried passengers to and from the Dutch East Indies. The interior had marble, stone carved hippopotami with electric light bulbs in their mouths, teak panelling carved with exotic insects and gold embossed wallpaper.

JVO in Aden

The JVO arrived in Port Said a week later, sailed through the Suez Canal onto Aden. From Aden the trip to Perth took two weeks and on 9 October 1950 the JVO arrived in Melbourne with 770 passengers hoping to begin a new way of life in a new country. Bart and Douwien with their children Henk 13, Sita 11, Tineke 9, Jeltje 6 and Wim 3 and Geert with his wife Tetje and their boys Geert 13, Douwe 11, Willem 9 and Anno 6 were amongst them.

206

After two voyages the Johan van Oldenbarnevelt was refitted to carry double the number of passengers. She plied the seas between Holland and the Antipodes, carrying migrants bound for Australia and New Zealand, for the next 12 years.

As the families Folkerts and de Haan were settling in Tasmania, the families De Vries, Steen and Laning were preparing for their departure from Rotterdam, scheduled to leave 17 October 1950. They were booked on the SS Volendam, a one class ship carrying 1,682 passengers. During the war she was converted to carry troops. The bunks were three deep and the segregated dormitories were overcrowded. The ship was old and as it turned out, this would be her last voyage to Australia.

Autumn storms in the Bay of Biscay rocked the boat, making many ill. Clothes had to be washed by hand with saltwater soap and guarded while they dried on deck, so they wouldn't be stolen. There were no special facilities for babies or children; a far cry from what Klara had said about the Sibajak.

They docked in Port Said. Many young children were afraid of the traders and sellers in their long robes and their fezzes and hid in the folds of their mother's skirts. On the next leg of the journey the weather became hotter. Scores of children came down with measles and had to share 3 to a bed in the overcrowded ship's hospital. The trip was stressful. Tempers flared. Finally six weeks later, on 20 November, after a long and tiresome journey, they arrived in Australia, docking at Freemantle. They could leave the boat for a few hours. The feeling of their feet on terra firma was wonderful. It was spring. The air was clear, the sky blue and the temperature agreeable. The flowering plants were lovely and quite different from those in Holland.

Last trip for the SS Volendam, 17 October 1950

The Volendam docked in Melbourne on 26 November 1950. Piet and Dineke and their children Bart 3, Klaas 2 and baby Cathy, then Jan and Tinie and their children Koos 10, Aafje 7 and Roelof 3, followed by Tom and Els and their children Thomas 7, Frederika 6 and Johan 4 waited in line. The immigration papers were completed:

> Port of Disembarkation – ~~SYDNEY; NSW~~ *Melbourne*
> Proposed Length of Stay in Australia – PERMANENT
> Purpose of Stay – PERMANENT RESIDENT
> Does Passenger Hold Authority to Enter Australia for an Unlimited Period of Residence (Yes or No) – *Yes C 54199*

Intended Address in Australia – ~~RECEPT. CENTRE, BATHURST, NSW~~
Hutchins Street, Kingston, Tasmania

They transferred to the airport and flew straight to Hobart, where the rest of the ABC club and their families were waiting to welcome them.

The seven families crowded into their accommodation and a week later together celebrated Saint Nicolas, *Sinterklaas,* the patron saint of children and sailors, the only way we knew how, the Dutch way. The night before Saint Nicolas Day, shoes of all different shapes and sizes were placed by the chimneys or the back door. By morning these had been miraculously filled with King peppermints, double salted liquorice and other goodies. To the great relief of the children, there wasn't a bit of salt to be found in any of the shoes as they had all been so good. That day, 5 December, the traditional Dutch party started. Sinterklaas, regally dressed in a red, bishop outfit, came to Kingston for the first time in his life! He was assisted by his devoted helpmate *Zwarte Piet,* Black Peter, who was clothed from head to toe in black and carried a heavy jute bag. Since Sinterklaas had left his good horse behind in Holland, he and Zwarte Piet had to walk to the hall where an official welcome had been arranged. On route, Zwarte Piet scattered all sorts of sweets around for the children to pick up. At the hall, seated on his throne, Sinterklaas welcomed the children one by one, asking them if they'd been good. As that was usually the case, they were all given a small present and told to always be good! Naturally, they all promised that. We sang our repertoire of Sinterklaas songs and the younger children were each treated with a balloon. Of course, Piet was Sinterklaas. I acted as Zwarte Piet. It was great fun and enjoyed by all, young and old.

Afterwards to celebrate the feast, father invited the Sinterklaas team for a drink in the pub in Kingston, but I was not allowed in the bar. Females were allowed to sit in the snug and were served through a small hatch from the bar. Father was cross and said that if I was not allowed in he and his party would go and drink elsewhere. But that was the custom in Australia; no women in the bar.

A few weeks later we were celebrating our first Tasmanian Christmas with roast pork, potatoes and apple sauce. It was sunny and the weather was hot. So strange. Hot weather at Christmas! It was not many years later that a lot of us abandoned the pork and potatoes and adopted the better alternative, a barbeque on the beach.

***

1951, Kusha looking at Kingston Beach and the Brown's River

The directors of the ABC dressed for an outing to the beach, 1951

Family Van der Laan
Wicky, Toni with Nicky, Eric, Kusha

Family Steen
Frederika, Els, Thomas, Tom, Johan

Family Pinkster
In Holland with Oma Pinkster, Sietske, Ep, Ina, Klara

Family De Vries
Above: Children Aafje, Roelof, Koos

Below later in Tasmania: Aafje, Koos, Tinie, Roelof

214

Family Laning
Above in Tasmania: Piet, Cathy, Bart, Klaas, Dineke

Below in 1957: Klaas, Dineke, Jenny, Cathy with Herman, Piet, Bart

Family Folkerts
Above soon after arrival:
Douwien, Henk, Wim, Bart, Sita,
Tineke, Jeltje

Below in their prefab in Little
Groningen: Douwien, Jeltje, Sita,
Bart with Wim, Tineke, Henk

Family De Haan
Above at the Hutchins Street cottage: Tetje, Henk Folkerts, Geert, Anno, Nicky with doll

Below at Auburn Road: Willem, Geert, Douwe, Anno; in front Geert, George, Tetje

The crates have arrived

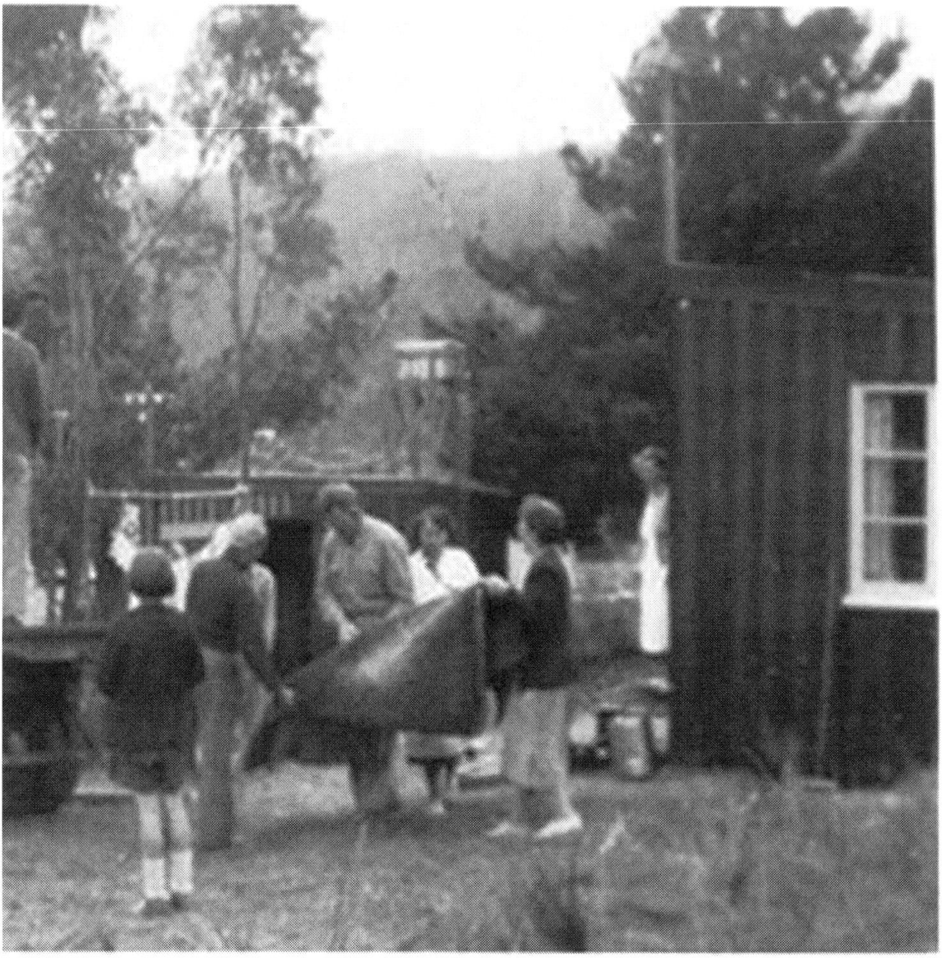

Emptying the crates

"Disappointment mixed with joy"

Little Groningen

The ABC office (above) and the workshops

1 November 1952

Dear Frank,
Spring is flooding Tasmania and with a new spring, a new sound. So we will try to find the right tone to entice you to set aside your objections and to lure you out of the tent of silence in which you have been hiding. Today it is four months and a day since we last composed a letter. Alas to this day we are still in suspense about the fate of our composition.

How are things, old man? Is there nothing new to relate from Groningen? A bit of our hearts still remain there. We miss the much needed contact and we would so appreciate to hear a heartening word from you every now and then.

A few days ago, we had our second annual general meeting where the balance and the profit and loss accounts were approved and we thought that you would be interested in the state of affairs, so we are sending you a copy.

As for us, we are very pleased with the results and our bank manager thought it a much improved position compared with last year's. Apart from our debt to the bank, we still have a debt of £800, the rest is within our own club. We are very happy that we will be free of that debt soon, after all the trouble it has caused. We have met our commitments towards it one hundred per cent.

The last couple of months we have not had a favourable economic situation but things are starting to improve. In July we started the project in Dover, a school for the Tasmanian Education Department. At first it did not look as if we would be getting any of that work but after several meetings with the big bosses we have been allotted £18,000. This is big backing.

We are now in the last stages of two other jobs that we are doing. They will be finished this year and so we have to get something else soon. Geert is busy right now working on various specifications and if we are not altogether unfortunate some jobs will come from that, amongst others, a school for £20,000. It is a rainy year this year. There is more rain than has been the case in years and that is only extra expense for us.

The migration to Kingston keeps on going. There are now some 125 Dutchies here. The families Klap and Mus have arrived, as have the couple Storm. The Storms were blown in by Jetze Schuth and the Muses and Klaps live together in a house we were able to rent for them. We are still waiting for a plumber and his family, related to Doedens, who will board a boat at the end of November. Herewith we come to an end of the families we have been able to attract. Considering the economic development we feel that we have to stop here for the time being.

Piet is still in the sanatorium, with TBC, and is on the waiting list for an operation on his left lung. He has written to you and would very much appreciate if you would answer him one day.

Geert was unlucky because about ten days ago he got the mumps, but he's getting better right now.

Jan de Vries broke a rib a fortnight ago and is also on the sick list.

Another of our group has to follow a cure of six weeks rest as an x-ray they took showed shadows. How this will turn out we do not know.

So you see that even here we have calamities. Apart from the seemingly necessary colds and sniffles, everyone is otherwise in good health.

After the birth of seven baby girls since we arrived, several mothers are expecting new offspring and we hope for a strengthening of the male gender!

We have had a lot of bad luck with the various goods that Mrs Balkema brought with her. She had hinges and locks in her crate that was shipped via Melbourne and this has been kept by Customs together with Geert's leather coat and all the handles for the spades. She was penalised for violating the customs act and about three weeks ago I had to appear on her behalf before a commission that is investigating this whole business. I do not know how it will turn out. At any rate a lot of bother and costs. These hinges and locks certainly bring no luck.

I would love to continue my story but just now Wicky and April are coming in. They are giving me the choice between the typewriter or a present that they have brought with them for my birthday yesterday. And it is... a stone bottle with real Dutch genever gin! I hope you will not think ill of me for opening the latter and closing herewith.

Dear Frank, we do hope to hear from you soon. Please do not forget our Piet who can do with a cheerful boost. Greetings to Tjits and to both of you warm greetings from your old friends.
 On behalf of us all,
 Eric

***

In the end, three families of the original group of resistance fighters were unable to come to Tasmania.

Bob Houwen hoped to migrate but the decision was not an easy one to take. Bob's wife Annie felt she could not leave Groningen, so they decided to stay. It was Bob who would lay the foundations for the archives of the Resistance in Groningen. He understood what had motivated the resistance fighters and what had made them take such horrific risks during the war. He was a source of knowledge of what exactly had happened for many years during the war.

Gerrit Zuidland, although he did not sign the agreement, seriously considered migrating. Gerrit and Ellie had always participated in the group meetings in Groningen. As late as September 1950, the Zuidlands still intended to join the others in Tasmania but Gerrit finally decided to stay behind and help in the reconstruction of his devastated country.

Frank Haan signed the agreement and paid his share in the full expectation that he and his family would also migrate to Australia. Their migration papers were finalised but circumstances prevented him from joining the group. It was impossible to sell the laundry business.

From emigrant to immigrant

'...this young tree, that one day will be the mighty tree Australia.'
Eric van der Laan in his letter dated 14 August 1950

The Kingston Glee Club provided a valuable source of social contact. Here some of our Australian friends, the pianist and her sisters behind her. Amongst the 'Dutchies': Tom and Els Steen, Wim Sikkema, Tetje de Haan, Toni van der Laan (who loved singing), Tinie de Vries, Corrie Doedens, Jan de Vries and Reinder Doedens.

After our arrival in Kingston, we made friends easily. The Tasmanians welcomed us into their homes and while we had to wait for our household goods to arrive we could borrow whatever we needed from them. They helped us to find our way in a country that was so entirely different from what we had been used to. Once we had settled, we were all very happy. We soon fell into a regular routine and were making new lives for ourselves in our new country.

The men worked as labourers on the building sites six days a week, the women made home as best they could. We soon found out that the intensive course in poultry farming proved to be a red herring. Eggs were much cheaper than in Holland and although keeping *chooks* was fun, any plans for keeping rabbits were soon dashed. Australia had such a problem with rabbits that myxomatosis was introduced that same year in an attempt to control the rabbit population.

Once the Christmas holidays were over, the school age children started at the local schools. For my brother Wicky, a life free from endless homework suited him. He could work with his hands, which he enjoyed, and he could participate in outdoor sports to his heart's content. I was keen to continue my studies, enrolled at the University of Melbourne and it was not long before I was teaching in a primary school in Hobart.

Down Under, we knew nothing of the stir that continued in Groningen. Discussion on the migration of the group first hit the newspaper on 16 June 1950. The protestant leaning Groningen newspaper *Nieuwe Provinciale*, New Provincial, published an article on the positive side of migration, followed the next day by counter arguments.

The first article discussed the group's formation, based on the solidarity and trust between members of the group that had developed during the war. The piece asked what had actually moved the group to emigrate. As far as the paper had been able to establish it was not that the members of the group saw no future in the Netherlands. All of them held good positions and were doing well. One reason might be found in the Cold War, which by 1950 was leading to very frosty relations between the super powers. The paper noted that amongst the emigrants there was a mood of concern about the threat of a war against the same kind of dark force that had overwhelmed the country in the period 1940-1945. They believed that if a new war eventuated, they would feel responsible to fight again. The idea of a new oppressor weighed heavily on them.

During the war, they had fought against injustices. After the war, they were disillusioned with the system and they opposed the political injustices that had become apparent in post-war Holland.

The paper suggested that they had clung to an ideal kind of post-war society, a thought that had sustained them during the years of darkness. Now that post-war Holland had turned out rather differently, deep down they were disappointed. The paper pointed out that the world they were seeking did not exist, not in the Old World and not in the New World. The world would never develop ideally and those who did not accept this would end up disappointed.

The next day, the paper discussed how those who were left behind perceived the emigration. It said that as the ones who were leaving suffered from a misperception, it would be better let them go. However, the paper argued, these ex-resistance fighters would still be amongst the finest of men. They had proven that. The fact that the nation was unable to retain them was a serious problem that the people and the government needed to address. The mood that things were not going well in the Netherlands had to change. The ex-freedom fighters should realize that what they fought for was not a post-war nation where peace and quiet reigned, but a nation assuring freedom. In this, they had succeeded but the post-war path of freedom was determined by democracy and not everybody thought the way the ex-freedom fighters did. Developing a new vision could solve this. It could be possible to stay in the Netherlands and continue the fight for a better world, but, the paper conceded, it would also be possible to do this in the New World.

Discussions in various newspapers continued throughout the summer months. Ep contributed an article to Trouw, the paper that had started during the war as an ink smudged underground broadsheet that was so important in maintaining communication between the resistance fighters. By 1950 it had grown to become a major national daily.

The debate on the departure of so many ex-resistance fighters and their families resurfaced in 1953. By then, 10,488 Dutch emigrants had left for Australia. Over 15 per cent had gone to various destinations in Tasmania. People were noticing.

Some thought that our migration was a good example of the enduring spirit of freedom. Others thought that the best of men should not leave the land they loved and had fought for. The debate was soon in the press again and the New Provincial sent a journalist to Kingston to provide a first-hand account of the ABC group.

By 1953 the ABC was going well. Archie's house was completed. The three cottages in Hutchins Street were always ready to receive new immigrants.

Team of the Dover School project seated for lunch: Geert Mus, Jan de Vries, Mr Klap, Ep Pinkster, Eric van der Laan, Geert de Haan, Wim Sikkema, Rieks Balkema, and hosts standing, who 'cooked to the satisfaction of all', Mr and Mrs Dirk de Vries.

Two workshops, one for joinery and another for electrical work and painting, had been erected in Little Groningen, together with a number of prefabs and several locally designed homes. They had built a house in Blackman's Bay for Mr Matthewsen, a name that forever gave the Dutchmen problems pronouncing. A new wing to the Clarendon Children's Home, a house in Pittwater and more prefabs for Dutch families had been completed. For the local council, the ABC built an extension to the Kingston Primary School.

For the State government they were now building a large school in Dover, some eighty kilometres south of Kingston, at the edge of the inhabited world.

In the beginning cash resources were tight and making ends meet was challenging. Money was short. Wages were credited and withdrawals could only be made if needed. Eric did the administration work, often after a full day of labouring. However, within a few years a fleet of new Holdens had been added to the company assets and finally even the Mayor of Little Groningen had learnt to drive. In spite of owning a large fleet of vehicles that would have justified operating their own bowser, the ABC bought all its petrol from the local garage. When asked about this Eric replied, 'It's a matter of principle to support local business.'

The Jeep that Piet so often referred to as a can of jumping beans, because of the way everybody always jumped in and out of the thing, gradually fell apart and when the art of starting it on a slope without it rolling backwards was no longer possible she was turned into a boat engine. The Jeep was replaced with a big sedan. Finally the company bought a truck to ferry the ABC people to work, to church and to the early meetings of the Abel Tasman Club in Hobart.

Statue of Abel Tasman carved in King Billy pine by Dirk Bolt in 1951

The immigrants did not focus entirely on their own community. The women had weekly visits with their Tasmanian counterparts, the meeting places alternating between Australian and Dutch homes. There was also a social 'Glee Club' with Dutch and Tasmanian members. It was an ideal way of getting to know other people and their way of doing things.

Social outings were a regular occurrence and organised often. There were picnics to Hastings Cave, organised games, competitions on the beach, or boat trips, all with a lot of singing and joviality. Piet with his natural talent usually provided the entertainment. He could play a comb with a cigarette paper, he could sing and he was always ready for a joke. Piet even organised a singing group that became very popular, consisting of middle aged Dutchies dressed as school boys, called the 'Lads'. One very different outing occurred after a tremendous storm, in which the roof of a house in Cambridge had blown off. The directors had read that the house belonged to a Dutch immigrant. Even though he was not known to the group, the ABC arrived at the house the following Saturday with materials and labourers to fix it, all voluntarily. This came as a complete surprise to the grateful owners.

The Dutch in Kingston used their weekends to build their own homes and to tend their gardens. When it came to sport, some of the Dutch children were playing cricket and others football, according to Australian Rules.

It may have been this article that gave rise to further interest from the press. On 20 November 1953 there was another article in Trouw. Eric was again interviewed by a journalist. This time, Eric provided an insight into the excitement and tension that had accompanied the original decision making:

> We did thorough research and came to the conclusion that it would be best if we went to Tasmania. I'll never forget the evening we signed our agreement. It had been stressful... we had talked about migrating for years. The time for the big decision had come and, together with our wives, we took that decision.
>
> Ep Pinkster and I went to Tasmania ahead of the others to get things organised for the arrival of our families. In Holland, we had recruited a number of tradesmen who followed us some weeks later.
>
> Getting started was difficult. The two of us spent a cold Tasmanian winter in a tent. I'll never forget it. We had to work hard. We are all fully-fledged builders now, but we still have to work hard.
>
> In a sense, we were not typical immigrants. We were different in that we had put our money together and had a well-considered plan. We functioned as a magnet, which we still do. We attracted other immigrants and more and more people have joined us. We can receive new immigrants better than otherwise would have been possible. Newcomers who later wished to spread their wings and go their own way had our full support.

The next morning the reporter walked with Eric to church, where Eric was to read the sermon. The young Reformed Church had, for some time, been looking for a minister. As he sat amongst the churchgoers, the visitor reflected on what he had learned about the group. True, they had not been ordinary immigrants, collectively they had a certain amount of capital, they did come with machines and tools and, yes, they came with a good plan. Yet, he realised there had been more. These factors had not been the only ones that had contributed to the success of Little Groningen. Perhaps it was also due to the faith of these people. At a meeting of the Abel Tasman Club in

Hobart, the reporter had spoken to someone who was not associated with the group and who was not a churchgoer. This man had said:

> These people have an unbreakable spine. They form a community and that is important. Some people perhaps don't quite fit the mould but, even for them, the community provides an environment that keeps them up and going.

After arriving in Tasmania we went to the Presbyterian Church in Hobart where the Reverend Reid was the minister. The services were in English of course. We sang the psalms and it was amazing to discover that the tunes, the words, their rhyme and rhythm were very similar to those of the Dutch psalms. This gave a feeling of belonging and the thought that nothing was so different after all. Attending church services in Hobart worked well for the time we were still a small group of people. As more migrants joined in, transport to Hobart became a problem. Reverend Reid agreed to come to

1952, after church at the football club

Kingston Beach to conduct a service there instead. These services had started in a small meeting room of the football club, which we were allowed to use on Sundays, with chairs that were borrowed from the Saturday picture theatre. For those who could not understand English, a Dutch sermon was read out in the evening.

When in 1953 there was a split in the Presbyterian Church, over a matter of conservatism and modernism, the Reformed Church of Hobart and Kingston was founded. It was not a question of who was right or wrong, it was a natural development. As with the arrival of the other settlers in Australia, the Anglican Church came with the English, the Presbyterian Church came with the Scots and the Roman Catholic Church came with the Irish. It was almost inevitable that, with the Dutch immigrants coming in, a Reformed Church would take root.

Money was raised and the Reformed Church in Kingston was built, mostly with voluntary labour, in 1954. At the time, a small group of people, including Eric, were laying the foundations for the Reformed Churches of Australia, now with more than fifty congregations throughout the country. In 1954, they founded the Reformed Theological College, RTC, today affiliated with the Australian College of Theology, in which many churches work together. It is part of the country's higher education system. The prospect of a university might not have daunted the RTC founders. The Free University of Amsterdam was started by Abraham Kuyper as a theological college.

Kuyper had worked for the delivery of education free from domination of the state. This was based on the principles of the 16th century French theologian of the Protestant reformation, Calvin. It was the education issue that gave rise to the rapid growth of the AR party. For years, the education funding controversy in the Netherlands had exercised minds at all national levels. Eric and others believed that equal treatment of private and state education was of the utmost importance. In their point of view, life and education are linked and education is the responsibility of the parents, not of the state.

Eric devoted his attention to parent-controlled education and became founding president of the Christian Schools Association. Ep was vice-president. Together they formed an enthusiastic and propelling force. The first meeting took place on 23 July 1954. Plans were made for a school and a building fund was established. The school was to be named after Calvin.

Eric continued to undertake many tasks that involved a great deal of work. We were surprised how after a day on the building site he would, after dinner, reach for his files and fill the evening working until late at night. Initially stored in the sideboard, later the files were housed on a specially built shelf. Sometimes he took time to play chess. Toni would sit and knit and together they would listen to their much beloved Beethoven.

In November 1954, Toni and Eric celebrated their silver wedding anniversary. Piet Laning was Master of Ceremonies. It was an occasion for a big party and members of the Dutch community cheerfully joined in. Their practice of combining hard work with great feasts was typical. At parties they would drink genever gin and smoke cigars, and sing songs at the top their voices, about the horse-shaped weathervane on top of the Old Grey One, and about sailing from Rotterdam.

The printed 36-page programme of the silver wedding festivities prepared by Piet says it all. First, there was an opening address by the recently appointed minister of the church, who was fresh from his Friesian homeland. The address was not too serious because the programme records the tongue in cheek adage that he contributed to the occasion, 'Intemperance is the pillow of Bacchus.' His address was followed by the singing of Psalm 103, 'Praise to the Lord...' after which the party got under way.

In honour of Toni's interest in singing, Piet presided over an international cocktail of musical presentations. Of course *Grönnens Laid*, the anthem symbolising Groningen and her people that was popular amongst the resistance fighters during the war, was included.

Being who he was, Piet advertised on the last page of the programme for a subscription to his publication, which would be published every twenty-five years. Those who paid in advance, Piet wrote, would receive the next issue free!

The Dutch loved to party. Such parties baffled their fellow Christians in Tasmania, as many of them did not drink or smoke.

The following year, 1955, Eric and Toni received their Certificates of Naturalisation as Australian citizens. The documents, dated 27 July 1955, were followed by a personal note from the Minister of State for Immigration, Harold Holt, who later became Australia's 17th Prime Minister. In his letter of 14 March 1956 Holt asks Eric and Toni to accept it as an expression of his personal goodwill and that of the Commonwealth Government. Holt concluded by congratulating them on the step they had taken and on their membership of the Australian family, wishing them happiness and prosperity for the future. The letter was only a standard letter, but it's been kept amongst prized family possessions to this day.

By 1956, enough funds had been collected to purchase a site for the new Calvin School. My husband, Dirk Bolt, was asked to design the first building. It consisted of three classrooms, each opening out onto its own outdoor space complete with tables and seats for the pupils. The school,

Calvin School designed by Dirk Bolt

paid for entirely with private contributions instead of Government funding, took some years to complete. The first classroom block was finally finished in 1962. Mother laid the foundation stone at the opening of the Calvin

Christian School and a time capsule was incorporated into the brickwork. The school was the first of its kind in Australia. In 1970 three similar classrooms were added. Ten years later secondary education started and by 1990 senior secondary classes had commenced. By 2000, the school had expanded even more. Today, Calvin Christian School is part of Christian Schools of Tasmania, a group of five co-educational schools, open to all families seeking a Christian education for their children. Over the past 50 years, the Calvin Christian School has matured into a vibrant and dynamic community and has earned a reputation for its commitment to excellence in education.

Toni van der Laan lays the time capsule at the opening of the Calvin School, 1962

Amongst old papers I found a copy of the Hobart newspaper, The Mercury, dated 19 September 1968. The headline said that the school built by the settlers showed that their culture had become part of the Kingston community. The article continued:

> Calvin Christian School occupies a proud place in the district education in Kingborough. Established in 1962, the attractive brick school with an enrolment of 146 children is a glowing example of the embodiment of Dutch culture into the community. Initially 77 boys and girls, most of them children of settlers from Holland, began their lessons at the school, with its large windows providing plenty of fresh air, light and sun.

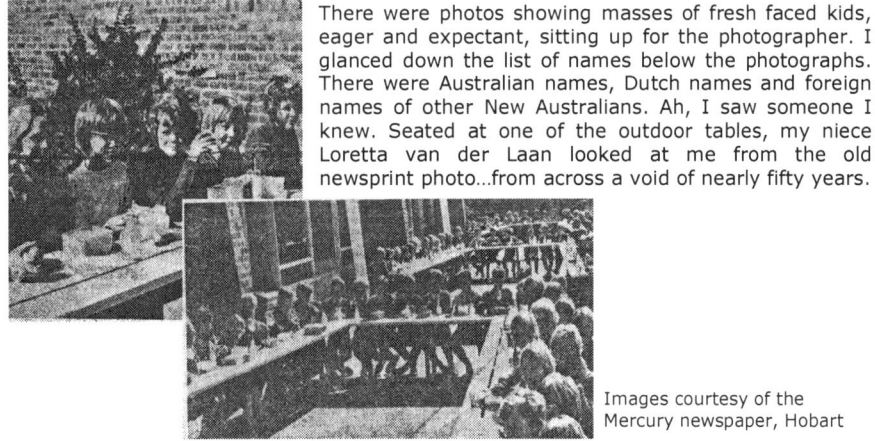

There were photos showing masses of fresh faced kids, eager and expectant, sitting up for the photographer. I glanced down the list of names below the photographs. There were Australian names, Dutch names and foreign names of other New Australians. Ah, I saw someone I knew. Seated at one of the outdoor tables, my niece Loretta van der Laan looked at me from the old newsprint photo...from across a void of nearly fifty years.

Images courtesy of the Mercury newspaper, Hobart

New Australians in Little Groningen

'We, the older ones, still feel a bond with Holland but our children are less aware of it and their children will have forgotten it altogether...'
Eric van der Laan, in his letter dated 14 September 1957

One Sunday on the football grounds after church

An academic from Groningen who was studying group migration asked Eric for information. In his reply of 14 September 1957, Eric tells Dr W. van der Mast what happened after the arrival of the other members of the group.

> In October 1950 the families De Haan and Folkerts arrived and in November also the families Laning, Steen and De Vries. So within six months from the date of our initial arrival, seven members of the group and their families had settled in Kingston. On the site of five and half acres workshops, stores and five prefabs had sprung up, whilst eight other houses had either been completed or were under construction. It became known as Little Groningen, and also as 'the

Dutch Settlement'. On the smaller site in Hutchins Street the three cottages were always ready in time to receive the next batch of arrivals. We were the first Dutchmen south of Hobart and attracted a lot of attention.

Our first building skills were acquired helping Mr Smith to complete a house. When it was ready the first assistants were telegrammed to come. In Holland we had made a list of building workers who we could use at a later stage. Within a few weeks we had completed the first Hutchins Street cottage, ready for the first families. From Hutchins Street the families moved to Little Groningen, one after the other, as fast as the houses became available there. We all had a great time.

Financially, we were able to develop our business independently. We were able to obtain credit and were paid on completion of work enabling us to start the next project. Contract activities started with the building of an extension to the school in Kingston, which was the first government contract that we were awarded. This was later followed by many others. From a business point of view the setup of the Australian Building Corporation Pty Ltd is such that the founders, who are all directors, are the principal shareholders. A lesser number of shares are allocated to the employees. Each of the seven directors receives the same salary. The group has no formal leader and business management of the ABC is in the hands of its directors. Sometimes one or sometimes another director comes forward to deal with a particular matter.

It is a privilege to be able to live here, thanks to group migration. After seven years the core group is still in existence but the boundaries of the larger group have faded. It has never been the idea that the group should form a closed community. Everyone is independent. Amongst the original seven directors there is still a strong feeling of solidarity, although the bonds are weakening.

There is no talk anymore of a group future, nor is there any talk about leaving the group. In the first few years, people came almost exclusively to Kingston for or in connection with the ABC. Now, some of the initial employees of the ABC have started their own businesses, others have changed to another profession. Through links with these people, other immigrants have come to Kingston. Today the ABC still forms a kind of centre of activities for Dutch immigrants but, as a whole, they no longer form a coherent group. About 400 immigrants from 50 families now live in or around Kingston. Their number is increasing steadily, although no longer as quickly as in the early years of rapid growth. In general the immigrants like it here. The best indicator of this is that, from Kingston, practically none of the immigrants have returned.

The Australian Government is happy to have Dutch people here and provides every kind of assistance. We immediately received full support for setting up our business and within a week of our arrival had met the Premier, who was very interested in our prefabs. Our original idea to settle on the north coast was abandoned. To this day we have not regretted it. The degree of cooperation with the local authorities is excellent and the contact with Australians is first class. The fact that there are so many Dutch people here means of course that contact with Australians is not always as intensive as it might be if there were fewer compatriots. Yet we do not form an enclave, we are simply part and parcel of the local community. Most of the marriages are still between Dutch people but several Dutch men and women have married an Australian partner, including my own son.

I look at it in this way. We started as a group but the natural development of population groups is that after a while they become part of the population as a whole. The advantage of group migration is that people support each other and that, especially for the women, is all-important. We, the older ones, still feel a bond with Holland but our children are less aware of it and their children will have forgotten it altogether and will only be Australians. This also applies to the language. Of the older generation, most of the men speak English well, the women much less so. For their children it makes no difference what language is spoken although, some already have difficulty with their Dutch.

The general standard of living is excellent. Every house here has a bath and hot and cold water. Interior design is more modern and more comfortable than in Holland, at least in Holland in the 1950's, why I don't understand. We have an excellent local doctor. Hobart has a symphony orchestra and one can often hear famous musicians who are contracted by the Australian Broadcasting Commission. One can often hear celebrities, you would not even hear in Groningen. We listen to the radio a lot and there are excellent programmes. In most Dutch families though, the organ is still the favourite musical instrument. In general we have adapted to the local customs. We speak the language and eat the food, although the Dutchies still eat more potatoes than the locals. Many Dutch people go swimming at the beach. Kingston has a football club that plays in the first division but ended up in the middle this year. Soccer is really only played by immigrants. Australians prefer Australian Rules, a sort of football which is a mild kind of rugby. And we build the Australian way, although we still lay bricks the Dutch way.

Our children go to state schools. We have formed an association for parent-controlled Christian schools for starting a school locally. The association now owns a site for a school and the design for the school has also been prepared for a building, initially with three classrooms and facilities to match. The main problem is to get the necessary capital for the building costs together and the guaranteed income needed for meeting the running costs. These are high and, for a small community, almost impossible to come up with.

When Ep Pinkster and I arrived here in 1950 we attended church services at St John's Presbyterian Church in Hobart. When others came this initially continued but later the local minister, the Reverend Reid, conducted a service in Kingston every Sunday morning. As he was an orthodox preacher that was fine and the arrangement continued for about a year and a half. Then however, differences developed about modernism within the Presbyterian Church. Those in the community who sought to adhere to more traditional reformation values started their own church, the Reformed Church of Kingston and Hobart. Of the seven initiators of the ABC two, Pinkster and Steen, stayed loyal to the Presbyterian Church. For Dutch families around here and in Hobart the Presbyterian Church has called for a Dutch minister. There are now again Presbyterian services in Kingston, which are also attended by members of the Methodist and Congregational Churches. Ep Pinkster is an elder of the Presbyterian Church. The other members of the ABC and their families who became members of the Reformed Church have in the meantime built their own church and, since 1954, have a Dutch minister. There are youth clubs for boys and girls of different age groups.

When we arrived there was a great demand for prefabs in Tasmania and extensive enquires had been made in Holland about what was available on the market. The plan was to import the prefabs from Holland and erect them in Tasmania. Later this turned out to be more difficult than we had envisaged. However that formed part of our plans. With the money we had left in Holland we decided to buy five prefabs and a complete set of machines for the builders' workshop. For this we needed a special export licence from the Nederlandse Bank. It was not until January 1951 that this finally arrived...

It is said that a disadvantage of group migration is that it gets in the way of integration. I do not agree with this but hold the view that this needs to be seen in the context of time. I don't think that for older people there is any real need to become entirely Australian. What does it matter? Those in the group who wish to do so can adapt at their own pace. Group migration does not obstruct that. Especially the men are, through their work, so continuously in touch with their Australian environment that they soon become part of it. If, in addition to work, people have other interfaces, for instance in politics or sport, their lives become so rapidly absorbed in Australia that an Australian victory at the Olympic Games is perceived as their own. Soon, people support either Prime Minister Menzies or the Leader of the Opposition Evatt, depending on their political choice. Every immigrant sooner or later becomes part of this country. In the rare cases where this is not so they will find their way back to where they came from.

In the early years the group had regular contact with friends in the Netherlands but this has gradually reduced to almost none. We wrote regularly to some people who originally had intended to come with us but could not for various reasons. The ties with them have now grown weaker. We feel less and less need to maintain old bonds.

Our home is now here and we particularly like where we live.

Kingston is a beautifully situated village on the banks of the River Derwent and in the shadow of Mount Wellington. There are beaches, forests and mountains here. The climate is attractive and we have more room to live. In terms of the natural beauty of its landscapes Tasmania is a privileged state. I would recommend that you come here for a holiday... you would then be able to see for yourself if my account is founded on the truth.

My own view of the group migration is that it was successful... However, things always work out differently from what was expected. Our group started with rather idealistic ideas. Our aim was that together we would build up a new life and that others too would profit from this, also socially... For group migration it is of the utmost importance that participants are sought with wisdom, that their cooperation is founded on a principle, that the group adopts a firm outline plan, that this is realised in the way it was delineated, and that one suppresses his egotism... the latter is the most difficult task.

Van der Mast wrote back to Eric thanking him for his '... admirable and extensive letter...' in support of academic research that the Free University of Amsterdam was undertaking. He added, 'It must have been a great deal of work for you.'

Eric at work

'You should see us during the day! Carpentry, sawing, digging, and working with a pickaxe! It does give us big blisters, sore muscles and stiff backs, but it is lovely work!'

Ep Pinkster, 7 August 1950

St. Clements

Thursday 9 April 1959

On Sunday 5 April 1959 Eric read a sermon in the Reformed Church in Kingston. The sermon had been written by a minister in Geelong, Melbourne. By coincidence, his name was Van Groningen. The sermon was about the observance of the Sunday, the Day of Rest. In the best of reformed church tradition the sermon expanded on three aspects: the reasons for the observance, the spiritual nature of the observance and the eschatological significance of it. Eschatology, about the end of things, and so it was...

On Wednesday father went to the summit of Mount Wellington, 1271 metres above the River Derwent below. On the mountain high above Hobart, the Australian Building Corporation was constructing a building that was part of the television and radio transmitter installation scheduled to open in 1960. Father was on an inspection visit to see how work had progressed. The site, accessed via the narrow road known as Pinnacle Drive, was ideal for broadcasting as it provided line of sight transmission to large parts of southern Tasmania. At the summit, icy winds, gusting up to as much as two hundred kilometres per hour, take visitors by surprise. Father went for a short visit only, without even an overcoat and against mother's insistence that he wrap up warmly. He caught a cold that developed rapidly into acute pneumonia.

Father died early the next day.

We buried him in the cemetery of St. Clements. He and Ep had worshipped at the church there on the first Sunday after they arrived in Kingston. The white painted wooden Anglican chapel is near the bottom of Hutchins Street where nine years earlier father and Ep had started out on their venture, camping in a cold and draughty tent.

Ep wrote that Eric would not see the fulfilment of his ideals but with God's help those who remained would complete the tasks. I wondered... what had driven my father to tackle all the things he did. There was the building business, the church, the theological college in Geelong, the Christian school and the many other things that he had fought for. The most dangerous and intense fighting he had undertaken was against oppression during the war. He had fought for and risked his life for freedom and chosen to seek it. In this, much of the courage to fight again and again came from the knowledge that he was in it, not alone but, with his brothers-in-arms. They knew what they were doing. They knew the dangers involved but chose to accept them. There were no regrets afterwards.

Father's belief in God was strong, although he did not impose his view on others. He accepted that many people had different opinions. In the great things he followed his own course, dealing with matters as he came across them, in a way that he would describe in seven words only:

Feet on the ground, heart in heaven.

The last letter from Tasmania

The postman came. There was a letter on the floor of the porch. It was from my old friend Henk Sikkema, who migrated in 1950 to help build the first cottages. Of those he migrated with, Henk was the first to set out on his own. After a few years he decided to pursue a career outside the building and construction industry. In 1959, he and his wife Anne moved from Kingston to Melbourne, where Henk had found a job and at the same time could return to his studies. While on a trip to Tasmania visiting relatives, they had gone back to Kingston to see what it was like.

9 April 2008

Dear Kusha,
It isn't all that long ago that we met up with you again in the city of our birth, good old venerable, staid Groningen, to attend a reunion of ex-students of the Christian High School there, where we first met in 1943 and where we shared a period in our lives of which I have the fondest memories.

We shared another period of our lives in Kingston Tasmania in the early fifties of the last century, doesn't that sound like ancient times! As you may not have been back there recently and as we, my wife Anne and I, recently revisited that pretty place, almost sixty years later, a trip down memory lane is almost irresistible and I fancy you could perhaps be interested in some observations about what the place is like now.

When we arrived there in 1950 we found a wonderfully quiet little seaside village with grand Mount Wellington dominant on the horizon. The mountain as well as the spectacular views across the Derwent towards the Iron Pot lighthouse is, of course, still there. Now there are shopping centres, traffic lights, roundabouts, lots of traffic and sad to say a lot of ugliness. So there is that contrast. Walk for instance along the Esplanade. On the one side the sea and the beach as beautiful as ever but look the other way and, oh boy, much of what you see there isn't all that pretty anymore; many simple old-style houses have been replaced by quite un-pretty structures. You will recall the Australasian Hotel on the corner where the Beach Road meets the Esplanade which was such an impressive, almost majestic, old historic building: gone, replaced by a service station.

It was at that hotel where we, that is the ABC's first four employees Reinder Doedens, Jetze Schuth, my brother Wim and I, were first accommodated, at the ABC's expense!, as it was thought that we needed a rest after our arduous five day KLM flight from Holland. The date of our arrival was 10 August 1950, a date easy to remember, it being the last day of my eighteenth year. Perhaps it was to celebrate my birthday the next day that in the evening we all went to the bar, which was full of men, and only men, letting off steam after a week's work. There was a most convivial atmosphere and plenty of the amber fluid going down thirsty throats. We must have looked like extra-terrestrials to them and I must say we did feel somewhat out of place. It wasn't exactly what we were used to, and Holland seemed a long way away. One chap thought we needed cheering up and showed some lewd pictures for us to admire. It had the opposite effect however and your father made it quite clear to him that we weren't interested. I cannot quite remember how long we stayed at that hotel but I do remember the wonderful meals we enjoyed there. Eggs and bacon for breakfast and sumptuous dinners with copious, delicious desserts and always being asked whether we wanted second helpings. But although this paradisiacal life was all very well, we had come to do some work and were actually quite anxious to start sooner rather than later, instead of lazing around for a week or so, which we were expected to need to get over our supposed travel weariness.

The ABC's two scouts, your dad and Ep Pinkster who were Mister van der Laan and Mister Pinkster to us, after all, they were our employers, had in the meantime acquired the property in Hutchins Street. Therefore, we walked from the hotel for our first day of work along Beach Road, as far as that little church and then up the almost vertical Church Street. We had the urgent task to build ccommodation for the families already underway from Holland, the three shacks, which you of course remember. The one in the middle became very special to me as that was the Van der Laan one, where I lived as one of the family for some time. Kusha, allow me take this opportunity to put on record my profound gratitude to your family for providing me with a home away from home at a time when I, apart from all the ups of the excitement of the new life in Tasmania, I also had the downs of at times feeling lost in such a totally different country. The shacks are no longer there of course and, in fact, I could not recognise the exact location of the site any more. There are now houses all around it. Being high up it still presents the same panoramic view of the mountain. That hasn't changed, but it is now across large built-up areas that in our day were mainly paddocks. Unstoppable progress I suppose but it means a drastically different Kingston.

Going down memory lane also led to a trip to Little Groningen, the other ABC property but even more out in the sticks than the one in Hutchins Street. It was also more difficult to find, again as it has been swallowed by a new suburb of Kingston called Firthside. The road towards it is now officially called Groningen Road. It is a nice gesture of goodwill on the part of the Kingborough Council, reflecting the local community's acceptance and maybe even appreciation of the new Dutch community in its midst. Groningen Road is now a sealed road of course and no longer the goat track it was in our day. A little detail that has stuck in my mind about it is that the telephone wire along it went from tree to tree; rather clever as it saved cutting down trees for making poles and obviated felling even more trees to make room for them. In the end I was able to locate Little Groningen because the old ABC workshop is still there although in a pitiful state. Dilapidated describes it, a sad sight. We were so proud when we built it. My small contribution was helping install the electrical wiring. Apart from the workshop, I could also recognise at least one of the prefabricated houses that the ABC people brought over from Holland, I think the one next to the one of your family, where again I received hospitality for quite some time!

And so, yes many things still look familiar; in fact revisiting Tasmania always has a coming home aspect to it. The nearly ten years I lived there were after all years of going through the migrant experience at a very young age, the age when you think you'll live forever. Other things have disappeared, as has the ABC, as far as I can see, it was never the same again after your father died and thus losing its irreplaceable leader and driving force, but that is another story I suppose. What has certainly survived is the Church. It is clear that the Church and certainly the building of it, and I don't mean just the bricks and mortar, has been a major factor in the success story of the Dutch migration to Kingston. It is sometimes suggested that Kingston provides perhaps the only example of a successful group migration. But I am not too sure that it was really a pre-planned group migration as such. Yes, there was the ABC group but I wonder whether the original seven founders of it thought much beyond the number seven. I am inclined to think that the larger Dutch community in Kingston just happened, snowballing as it was, by the early settlers attracting more of their own kind. Those who came later did not join a group and subject themselves to a regime of rules and mutual obligations. What bound them together was rather, I am inclined to think, a shared outlook on life. This view extends beyond going to church and led also to the establishment of the Calvin School, which nowadays is large beyond recognition. I gather it has an excellent reputation and hopefully is able to pass the convictions of the original founders on to new generations.

When the new highway to Hobart was built, a bridge across it was needed to provide access to Firthside. From this bridge one has a good view of Kingston and one cannot fail to see, in the distance, a substantial building with a cross on top. It is the new Reformed Church, much larger than the original church on Channel highway that Dirk designed. In fact from here and other positions the church is a dominant feature of the landscape. If one were to regard this in a symbolic fashion one would probably exaggerate what the Dutch church oriented migrants have contributed to that wonderfully quiet little seaside village we remember from more than half a century ago. But even if it may not entirely have been the outcome of a planned group migration it is a success story nevertheless and I derive great pleasure and some satisfaction of having played a part in it, however small.

We must keep in touch and I hope to hear again from you one of these days, or better still to meet up again somewhere in the world and if we, unexpectedly, do manage that we will no doubt talk some more about our shared experiences in good old Kingston.

In the meantime however, let's concentrate on the future and hope that our good present life may continue for some time yet.

Your old friend,
Henk Sikkema

***

I folded the letter Henk had sent me, put it with my father's letters from Tasmania and closed the book.

Kingston from Groningen Road, 2008

370 ac
Granted to
Rowlands
100 ac
Grant to
T W
Rowlands
P 46 & 47

100 ac
Grant to
T W Rowlands
P 46

150 ac
Granted
John Lucas
P 47

RIVER

40 ac
Gr[anted]
N
Lucas

J B
Watchorn
Pur
123
22 S S

2 a
188

163½
Gra[nted]
to
John
Lucas
2 a
188

168 · 0 · 0
Granted to
J T Firth
12/37

on of
0 0
ed to
rth
46

390 · 0 · 0
Granted to
J. Folley
2a
46.7 & P 46

234 · 0 · 0
Granted to
W. T. Firth

Church
Site 22

12/34

Granted to
N Turner

Granted
KINGS
John Lucas

100 ac
Grant to
P
Gormley
P 46

Lot 678 152 ac
Daniel O'Connor
Pur

2 a
188

200 · 0 · 0
Granted to Jas Baynton
P 46

150 · 3 · 37

150 ac
Granted to
John Lucas
to
2.0.2 7/10 Gravel Quarry
Held by Minister for Lands and Works under
Thos perpetual licence
Mathieson
P.46
40 ac
Grtd to
N Lucas
163½ ac
Granted to
John Lucas
90 0 0
Granted to
N Lucas
BONN
SANCTUAR
Under the
Protection
57 1 20
Granted to
E P Lucas
& others
Granted to
NGSTON
n Lucas
100 ac
Grant
to C Rawlins
Jetty
39 Surrendere
Beach between L.W.M a
0.1.14 9/10 Surrd t
0.1.1 4/10 Acqd for
0.1.4 6/10 Acqd for K
182 R/15.
317/15.
BORON
300 0 0
Granted to
E. J. Manley
P47
P.859
50 · 3 · 37.
7.0.0

References

Books:
Armed Forces, U.S. (1945). *The Stars and Stripes: Daily Newspaper of the U.S. Armed Forces*, Germany, Edition Volume 1, Nos. 26-35.
Babbington-Smith, C. (1957). *Evidence in Camera: The Story of Photographic Intelligence in World War II.* London, Chatto & Windus.
Banga, F.E. (2005). *Groningen terug in de tijd: Bewogen jaren uit de Groninger historie.* Groningen, Banga Book Productions.
Boekhoven, G and Laning, P. (1980). *Memoirs of Neuengamme Concentration Camp.* Typed publication.
Bolt, Frank (1981). *Old Hobart Town Today.* Kingston, Waratah Publications.
Brooks, Sir Norman (1945) (as released 2006-2008), *Warcabinet minutes, W.M. 45(45) – W.M. 60(45)* also known as 'The cabinet secretaries' notebooks', London, The National Archives.
British Armed Forces, War Crimes Unit, 2nd War Crimes Investigation Team (September, 1945.) As reported by Major Till. London, The National Archives.
De Cock Buning, A., Tom, Den Verheyen, L., ed. (1988) *The Netherlands and Australia: Two hundred years of friendship.* Amsterdam, Otto Cramwinkel.
Department of Works and Housing (1947). *Australian Housing.* Melbourne, Department of Works and Housing.
Dijkstra, K.D. (1945). *Waarom terug uit Neuengamme.* Winsum, FA Mekel.
Downing, T. (2011). *Spies in the Sky: The Secret Battle for Aerial Intelligence during World War II.* London, Little Brown.
Folkerts, B. (1945). *Mobilisatie-Oorlog-Bezetting-Vrijheid.* Gronginger Archieven [462-492].
Gardam, J. (1988) *Brown's River; A history of Kingston and Blackman's Bay.* Kingston, Rotary Club of Kingston.
Geertsma, S.P. (2011). *De Ramp in de Lübecher Bocht.* Stichting Vriendenkring Neuengamme.
Groninger Archieven (2004). *Plaatslijst van de systeemkaarten van verzetsbetrokken.* Groningen (www.archieven.nl).
Houwen, B. (1945). *Verslag over de illegal werkzaamheden tijdens de besetting.* Groninger Archieven [555-582].
Houwen, B. (1981). *Gesprek tussen Jan Thomas Steen en Bob Houwen op 18 mei 1981.* Groninger Archieven.
Jacobs, B. And Pool, E. (2004). *The 100 year secret: Britian's hidden WWII massacre.* Guilford, Connecticut, The Lyons Press.
Kluiters, F. (2008). *Dutch agents 1940-1945.* (www.nisa-intelligence.nl).
Laan, E.J. van der (1945). *Verslagen.* Groninger Archieven (various references).
Laan, E.J. van der (1950). *Brieven aan leden van de Australian Building Corporation.* Family archive.
Laning, P. (1945). *Verslag over de illegal werkzaamheden tijdens de besetting.* Groninger Archieven [208-242].

Mast, W. van der (1963). *Praktijk en patroon van recente groeps emigraties.* Proefschrift, Vrije Universiteit, Amsterdam. Groningen, P. Nordhoff NV.
Niemeyer, J.A. en Tameling, B.P. (1979). *Groningen toen.* Groningen, de Groninger gezinsbode.
NNZ (2002). *Content and packaging: 80 years NNZ.* Groningen, NNZ.
Oosten, F.C. van et al (1970). *Bericht van de tweede wereld oorlog: Austalië. ontzet.* Amsterdam, De Geïllustreerde Pers NV et al.
Pee, R. van (1955). *Ik was zo in 1944: Relaas uit Neuengamme en Blumental.* Antwerpen, EPO.
Pinkster, E. (1945). *The Netherlands Red Cross Team.* Groninger Archieven.
Rolsma, H. Gevangene no. 77431 Torsperre. (ca 1945) *Neuengamme, De ramp in de bocht van Lübeck.* Groningen, H. v.d.Woude, Jr.
Schuyf, Dr. J. (2005). *Nederlanders in Neuengamme.* Kimabo-Zaltbommel, Stichting Vriendenkring Neuengamme.
Veen, J. van der (1988*). Australië: het onbekende Zuidland naderbij.* Groningen, Volkenkundig Museum 'Geradus van der Leeuw'.
Vereniging van Groningse Oud-Illegale Werkers, Redactiecommissie (ca 1949). *Hoe Goningen Streed.* Groningen, J. Niemeyer's Uitgeversmaatschappij.
Wieringa, K. (2005). *Dutch migration to Tasmania in 1950: Motivation, intention and assimilation.* Thesis, Hobart, University of Tasmania.
Williams, A., (2013). *Operation Crossbow: The Untold Story of Photographic Intelligence and the Search for Hitler's V Weapons.* London, Preface Publishing.
Zoetmulder, S.H., red. (ca 1947). *Nederland in den oorlog zoals het werkelijk was: Herinneringen en onthullingen 1940-1945.* Utrecht, Uitgeverij P. den Boer.
Zuidland, G. (1946). *Verzets verklaring.* Groninger Archieven [828-832].

Other:
Supplementary material found in Wikipedia and subject-relevant websites, newspapers and other press material, and personal records.

Photos and pictures:
Australia Post, cover stamps
Dirk Bolt: p87 Sketch of Grote Markt in ruins 1945, p95 Translation Grönnens Laid, p103 Flight map
Eric Bolt, p76 German naval flag
Frank Bolt: p133 View over Kingston Beach, p 209 Kusha overlooking Kingston Beach, p231 Calvin School
Kusha Bolt née van der Laan: p11 German marine fork, p130 View of Mount Wellington from Hutchins Street, p154 Postcard of the Cap Arcona, p184 Wicky van der Laan and Henk Sikkema sawing the tree to make the 'stamper' for the laundry, p184 Jetze Schuth and Eric stamping the laundry floor, p185 Frame of the first shack, p185 Henk on the frame, p185 Wim Sikkema on his wedding day, p185 The completed shack, p211 Eric and Toni, p218-219 The crates from Holland have arrived, p220 Unpacking the crates, p221 The ABC office in Little

Groningen, p221 The ABC workshop, p227 Dirk Bolt carving the bust of Abel Tasman

Canadian Army, Department of National Defence, p64 Map Sketch 47 - The Advance across Germany 23 March – 8 May 1945

Department of Works, Commonwealth Directorate of Housing, Canberra, April 1947, *Australian Housing,* p118 Typical Australian house

Max Dupain, p114 Mr Boot's office in Elisabeth Street

Otto Eerleman, p13 Painting of Grote Markt

Jan Ensing, p14 Goudkantoor

The Examiner Newspaper, Tasmania Archive and Heritage Office, PH30-1-1811, p111 Floating Bridge Hobart

Haughton Forrest, p136 Kingston Beach from the Brown's River

Gemeentearchivaris van Groningen, *Album van Oude Groningen,* Christ Weigelij Senioris Herædes, p12 Map of Groningen number 17 with projected places of resistance fighters

Groninger Archieven: J.G. Kramer, p15 Grote Markt market day ca1895 Photocollection Groninger Archieven, 1785_17572, 'Nieuwsblad van het Noorden', p20 Parade on the Grote Markt 1943

Sita de Haan née Folkerts, private source

Hobart Register of Land Grants, p244-245 Land Grants Map Kingston

Holocaust Education & Archive Research Team, p60 K-Z Neuengamme

Klaas Laning, private source

Piet Laning: p7 Group photo, p23 Koninginnelaan, p94 Memorial in Neustadt, p95 KLM check-in, p95 Ep and Eric on the scales, p96 Greeting the chief steward, p97 Boarding the plane for Australia, p156 Kusha on the Sibajak, p172 First ABC employees leaving, p224 The Kingston Glee Club, p229 After church in the Kingston Beach Hall, p233 The whole group from Holland at Kingston Beach 1951

Sietske MacDonald née Pinkster, private source

Marketing Groningen, p13 Korenbeurs in snow

The Mercury newspaper: p232 Toni laying the cylinder at the opening of the Calvin School, p232 Loretta and friends, p232 Lunch at Calvin School

Military Wireless Museum, Kidminster, UK, p50 A-MkIII suitcase transceiver

Aafje Mol née De Vries, private source

National Archives of Australia: p195 P1185 Van der Laan A. Immigration card, p195 ID photo

National Library of Australia: Frank Hurley: p112 Government State Buildings, p112 Hobart waterfront, p115 Franklin Square, p116 Hobart harbour

The Mercury newspaper, p142news-page 1904706

Nieuwe Provinciale Groninger Courant: p226 The Dover team 1952, p237 Eric van der Laan

Nieuwsblad van het Noorden, p152 Irish delegate offered koek

Oorlog en Verzets Centrum Groningen: P.B. Kramer, p63 Grote Markt in1945; p73 Fré Lode's metal prisoner tag H77394; p73 Torsperre badge

Private sources: p16 Typical street organ, p18 Eric, p31 Tom, p33 Bob, p34 Ep, p35 Gerrit, p36 Frank, p38 Jan, p39 False ID, p40 Piet, p41 Ration Card, p42 Bart, p88 Geert, p91 The signatures, p172 ABC business card, p197 Jo Sikkema on her wedding day with Corrie Doedens, p200 Kusha, Henk and Wicky to a party, p 202 Wicky and Henk on the jeep, p210 Dressed for an outing to the beach, p211 The Van der Laan family, p212 Tom and Els, p212 The Steen family, p213 Ep and Klara, p213 The Pinkster family, p214 Tinie and Jan, p214 The De Vries family, p214 Tinie de Vries and children, p215 Piet and Dineke, p215 The Laning family, p215 Family Laning some years later, p216 Bart and Douwien, p216 The Folkerts family, p216 The Folkerts family in Little Groningen, p217 Geert and Tetje, p217 Tetje, Henk, Geert, Anno, Nicky, p217 The De Haan family, p253 The seven directors of the ABC

Unknown photographer: p21 Swastika, p21 Double sigrune, p28 Star of David, p100-101 Farewell from Schiphol

Royal Air Force, UK, p74 Cap Arcona in flames

Anton Rengers, p13 Noorderhaven

John Rickard, www.historyofwar.org, p66 Typhoon being prepared for attack

André van Schaik, p73 Gerard Boekhoven's prisoner tag H77389

Henk Sikkema: p221 The ABC workshop, p243 The Reformed Church from Groningen Road

Freddie Steen, private source

St.John's Presbyterian, Hobart, p181 St John's Presbyterian Church

Tasmania Archive and Heritage Office, E.R. Pretyman Photographic Collection, NS1013/1/959, p137 The Australasian Hotel

Tasmanian Philatelic Society: front cover 1/- Platypus September 1959, 3d Tasmanian Stamp Centenary November 1953 for 100th Anniversary of Van Dieman's Land 4d Courier stamp, spine 1d carmine Van Dieman's Land 1853, 2d Tasmanian Postage 1887, 1d red Kangaroo and Map January 1913 the first Australian stamp ever issued

Trouw newspaper, p65 News-page Liberation of Groningen

United States Holocaust Memorial Museum, p68 Soldiers on parade at Neuengamme 1942

Fred Vandenbom: p206 The Johan van Oldenbarnevelt at anchor in Aden in April 1951, p207 Volendam 1950

Lee Weller: Front and back cover of Kingston Beach, p134 Greenlands, p140 The thinking rocks at Kingston Beach, p238 St Clements church yard

Jan Wolters, p98-p99 Musical score Grönnens Laid

Zomer & Keuning, Utrecht, p155 Farewell Sibajak Rotterdam 1950

Appendix - The Deed of Contract

Deed of contract

This 16th day of March 1950 the undersigned:
1. Barteld Jan Folkerts, born 8-9-'11, house-painter, resident Dorus Rijkersstraat 1a, Groningen;
2. Fokke Haan, born 5-4-'03, manufacturer, resident Tuinbouwdwarsstraat 22a, Groningen;
3. Eerke Jacob van der Laan, born 31-10-'03, confidential clerk, resident Koninginnelaan 19a, Groningen;
4. Pieter Laning, born 2-2-'14, representative, resident Semarangstraat 20a, Groningen;
5. Egbert Pinkster, born 6-8-'10, managing director of the foundation 1940-1945, resident Paterswoldscheweg 51a, Groningen;
6. Jan Thomas Steen, born 30-8-'12, municipal official, living van Heemskerckstraat 26b, Groningen;
7. Jan de Vries, born 28-12-'10, shopkeeper, living Nieuwe Ebbingestraat 44/I Groningen;
8. Geert de Haan, born 8-10-'11, contractor, resident Wierdaweg, Winsum;

all intending to settle in the Commonwealth of Australia, in a place later to be fixed, testify to found a community of interests.

1. This community of interests make it their object to help each other by all means, material and immaterial, during the timeof preparing the voyage, during the timeof the voyage itself and during the time of arrival and settlement in the Commonwealth of Australia.
Solemnly they declare to be willing to perform this contract in the same sense as they have performed their mutual duties during the occupation of the Netherlands by the German enemy. They look upon this contract as if they have sworn to it.

2. This community of interests shall found a Company at Hobart or elsewhere in the Commonwealth of Australia. This Company shall be named " Australian Building Corporation " , hereafter called A.B.C. Immediately after their arrival in the Commonwealth of Australia two special instructed members of the A.B.C. will register the A.B.C. in accordance with the legal regulations oprative in the Commonwealth of Australia. As legal form will be chosen the most useful.

3. The A.B.C. makes it his object:
   1. the building of houses for the use of the members of the A.B.C. and for sale to others;
   2. everything else that may be profitable for the members of the A.B.C.

4. The currency of the community of interests, as expressed in section 1, is unlimited; the currency of the contract meant in section 2 is from 1st January 1951 till 31st December 1953. The company cannot be terminated before 31st December 1951 and will be extented from year to year unless by written termination.

5. The nominal capital of the A.B.C. amounts to hfl.20.000.— divided into 8 shares of hfl.2500.—. Each of the members, named above, acquires one share of hfl.2500.—. Shares must be paid up one month after date of this contract He who retires unless forced by Act of God, looses all rights.

6. All members are obliged to pay into the cash of the A.B.C. as a loan the full amount of the allowance on the fares they receive for themselves and all members of their family as assisted immigrants from the Commonwealth of Australia. The members will be credited for the full amount of the said loans with 4% per annum interest.

7. Every partner is bound also to lend to the A.B.C. any and all capital he has in the Commonwealth of Australia over and above the amounts meant in the sections 5 and 6; he receives 4% per annum; as security for these loans will serve the properties of the company to be acquired. Every partner will receive a claim. The loans are redeemable after three years to an amount of 25% and further every year 25%, besides other regulations made by mutual consent.
8. The houses built by the A.B.C. for the benefit of the partners will be the property of the A.B.C. and may be sold at cost prices to the members. Regulations about payment and redemption are to be made by mutual consent.
9. Every member undertakes to work full time for the A.B.C. for the first three years at a wage to be fixed later. Every partner will use all his time and energies for the benefit of the A.B.C. and he cannot participate in any other firm or work independently unless written permission has been given by the management.

If at any time the cash in hand of the A.B.C. should be insufficient to pay the full wages to the members in cash, they will be paid partly in cash and the other part will be credited to their a/c in A.B.C.'s books and they will receive 4% per annum. The want of the families will be decisive for the proportion of the wages to be paid in cash.

If the company should at any time be unable to employ all members profitably, the management of the company may terminate the employment of one or more members. Such dismissals however will not affect any other rights and duties as members of the company.

10. The death occurring at one of the partners, his heirs will succeed in all his rights. If not provided sufficiently under Australian social services, the A.B.C. is bound in case of death, illness or disablement of one of the members, to take care of his family. The management is bound to insure all health and occupational risks of its members as soon as possible. The A.B.C. will look after the wellbeing of the family of any deceased member to the extent the members of such family should not be able to provide for the wants of such family.
11. All members will form the management of the A.B.C. One from among them is to be chosen as president, as secretary and as bookkeeper. Every year they retire; they are immediately eligible for re-election; interim vacancies are to be filled as soon as possible. The president calls the meetings and is chairman; the secretary keeps the minutes of the meetings and conducts the correspondence; the bookkeeper takes care of the finances and keeps the books. These will be honory functions. Chairman, secretary and bookkeeper will manage all daily business and to them are to be granted the necessary powers and proxies. The signature of two of them is to be binding for the A.B.C.
12. Authorization of the whole managing board is required for:
    a. buying, selling and encumbering with mortgage of real property of the company.
    b. lending and borrowing of moneys, buying or selling or pawning of claims and securities, normal banking transactions of the A.B.C. not included.
    c. pawning and transferring for giving security of all other movables not included sub b.
    d. participating in others concerns.
    e. granting and cancelling power of proxy.
    f. giving securities, agreeing. coming to arrangements, compromising.
    g. opening current accounts and overdrafts with banks.
    h. litigating as well as claiming as defending, recovering of debts in justice not included.
    i. abandoning of claims.
    j. generally all actions exceeding the amount of A£ 250.—

13. Two members are entitled to ask the president to call a meeting; the president is obliged to do so within seven days. Although unanimity is desired for all decesions it will not be necessary and in case of any division a singlem majority decides, not included the stipulations of the sections 17, 19 and 20. Voting about business matters is to be verbal and about persons written.
14. The financial year of the A.B.C. runs from 1st January to 31st December, for the first time the year ending 31st December 1951.
15. Within three months after the end of the financial year the bookkeeper produces to the managing board a balance sheet and a pmfit and loss account for the past year. The balance sheet, the profit and loss account and the profits are to be finally determined by the managing board.
16. The profits are divided in equal shares among all members. If the cash in hand of the A.B.C. should be insufficient to pay the profits in cash, such profits will be placed to the members' credit and they receive 4% per annum.
17. Alteration of the stipulations of this contract and disconinuing of the A.B.C. requires a genarally meeting of all members. For decision is required two third of the full number of votes. The managing board decides the way how the liquidation will be done. If plenary meeting is required and not all members are present, a new meeting will be called within 14 days. Two third of the votes of the members then present will be sufficient for decision.
18. Initial and formation expenses are chargeable to the A.B.C. including the expenses of the persons, chosen to proceed to the Commonwelath of Australia, the expenses of their special equipment and the expenses of their preparations.
19. If one of thepartners should want to retire, the full managing board can discharge him, if this should be useful to the A.B.C. For this decision two third of the votes are equally required. Section 7 governs the redembtion of loans.
20. If a member injures the reputation and the interests of the A.B.C. the managing board can deprive him of his membership. For decision will be required two third of the votes, and the date to be fixed from which such member will be expelled. His share and all amounts loaned by him to the A.B.C. will be repaid to him on such date.
21. Not named and pressing matters will be decided by the full managing board,

DONE AND SIGNED, 16th March 1950.

Directors of ABC, Little Groningen

Eric van der Laan, Ep Pinkster, Jan de Vries, Tom Steen, Bart Folkerts, Geert de Haan and Piet Laning

Kusha Bolt in traditional costume from Groningen, just before her departure from Holland in 1950. She arrived in Tasmania shortly after her father, Eric van der Laan, migrated there.

In 2008, she wrote an account of the events in Dutch, *Brieven uit Tasmanië,* which was published under the name of AMC Bolt. Kusha now lives with her husband in Scotland, where she wrote this book. It incorporates further research and added information on the members of the group from the many readers who responded to the first book.

Printed in Great Britain
by Amazon